FROM TRICKSTER
TO BADMAN

FROM TRICKSTER
TO BADMAN

The Black Folk Hero
in Slavery and Freedom

JOHN W. ROBERTS

upp

University of Pennsylvania Press
Philadelphia

Library of Congress Cataloging-in-Publication Data

Roberts, John W. (John Willie), 1949–
    From trickster to badman : the Black folk hero in slavery and freedom /
John W. Roberts.
        p.   cm.
    Bibliography: p.
    Includes index.
    ISBN 0-8122-8141-1
    1. Afro-Americans—Folklore. 2. Folklore—United States—History and
criticism. 3. Heroes—United States—Folklore. I. Title.
GR111.A47R63 1989
398'.352'0880396—dc19
                                                                88-20804
                                                                    CIP

CONTENTS

ACKNOWLEDGMENTS

Acknowledging all of the individuals who, in some way, contributed to the writing of this book is impossible, but I would like to recognize those who through overt acts of kindness, goodwill, and expressions of confidence supported its completion.

First of all, I would like to thank the University of Pennsylvania and the department of Folklore and Folklife for their generous support in the form of compensated leave time to develop the ideas for this book. I would especially like to express my gratitude to my colleagues in the department of Folklore and Folklife and the Afro-American Studies Program who, in various ways, made it possible for me to complete the project. To professors Kenneth Goldstein and Roger Abrahams who gave me free run of their libraries, I owe a special debt of gratitude. I would also like to acknowledge my graduate research assistants who became partners in this "scholarly adventure," and students in my Afro-American folklore classes who suffered through my efforts to develop and articulate many of the ideas presented in this book. And to the students who lived in the W. E. B. DuBois College House from 1982 through 1986, I owe a particular debt of gratitude for keeping me in touch with who we are.

To Adrienne Lanier Seward, I owe an incredible debt of gratitude for having the courage to expose our scholarly legacy and for making it our responsibility to change it. More importantly, I thank her for being there when I needed a friend, a colleague, and a critic. In more ways than one, she made writing this book not only possible but necessary. I also owe much to Betty Roberts, whose patient and careful reading of my work I have always valued. I especially thank her for her reading of an early draft of this manuscript and, by her silence, sending me in search of our true ancestral voices. I heard you even when you did not say a "mumbling word."

Finally, I want to thank my family, whose patience, love and support have always seen me through the worst of times. Thank you for believing in me even when you did not understand. I want to especially thank Lewis and Darryl, who heroically endured the writing of this book and adjusted their lives to my erratic schedule.

ONE

Introduction

We often use the term "hero" as if it denoted a universally recognized character type, and the concept of "heroism" as if it referred to a generally accepted behavioral category. In reality, figures (both real and mythic) and actions dubbed heroic in one context or by one group of people may be viewed as ordinary or even criminal in another context or by other groups, or even by the same ones at different times. The diverse ways in which people conceptualize the hero and heroic action seem to be precisely what Robert Penn Warren had in mind when he observed that "To create a hero is, indeed, to create a self."[1] To create a hero, however, from Warren's perspective, is not merely to embody in a literary form a mirror image of the self at a given moment in time. Rather, the heroes that we create are figures who, from our vantage point on the world, appear to possess personal traits and/or perform actions that exemplify our conception of our ideal self, the self that our personal or group history, in the best of all possible worlds, has prepared us to become. Or, as Warren notes, "The hero does not merely express a pre-existing soul, is not merely a projection of that soul, the hero belongs primarily to the process whereby the soul emerges."[2] In other words, a hero is the product of a creative process and exists as a symbol of our differential identity. As such, our heroes act within boundaries defined by our perception of immanent social needs and goals which are, in turn, determined by historical and emergent realities of which we, as individuals and groups, may be only dimly aware.

In this regard, heroic creation is a process very much like culture-building—the means by which a group creates and maintains an image of itself to proclaim difference from others by objectifying in its institutions the ideals that it claims for itself. In addition, heroic creation and culture-building share at least one other important feature: in both instances, difference is equated with superiority, which, in turn, serves as the basis of group allegiance and attraction. Heroic creation is not the same thing as culture-building, but it often serves as an important activity for enhancing and facilitating the attainment of cultural goals. A group may employ heroic creation to "cover cracks" in the basic structure of its culture, so that an ideal image of itself can be projected as if it were actual. Inasmuch as all cultures are continually subjected to stresses from both within and without, both culture-building and heroic creation are on-going activities that are both remedial and expansive.

The relationship between differential identity as a function of culture-building and heroic creation as a culture-specific activity has been the element most often missing in discussions of the hero in folklore, where heroic creation has the greatest interface with culture. The absence of a perception of this relationship has been particularly evident in discussions of the African American folk heroic tradition, where figures accepted as heroic by African Americans have seldom been discussed as symbols of black cultural identity. Bill R. Hampton, for instance, notes that in the study of the African American folk hero "the discussion has been a controversy over whether there has been any identification at all" between African Americans and their folk heroes.[3] Fred O. Weldon contends directly that African American folk heroes do not serve as symbols of black differential identity because "group identification has been so weakened that these feelings [those necessary for folk heroic creation] cannot manifest themselves in the form of group heroes."[4] The heroes that do emerge in African American folklore, according to Weldon, "are ineffectual dissembling tricksters who, all too often, get only private revenge."[5] From this perspective, folklorists, with few exceptions, view the actions of black folk heroes as incapable of serving the culture-building needs of African Americans. More often than not, they study African American folk heroic literature as a primary example of how heroic fiction serves the needs of a people in creating a dream-life rather than in maintaining cultural identity and values.

This approach to study of the African American folk heroic tradition reflects a tendency in folkloristics to conceptualize the hero, at least implicitly, as a universal character-type whose actions are defined within a so-called normative model of heroic action. This model of heroism assumes that, at some point in the past, there existed an "heroic age" which established a set of heroic values and actions for all times and all people. Roger Abrahams summarized this view when he noted that "The actions that *we* recognize as heroic are based on contest values and a model of a male-centered family. A hero is a man whose deeds epitomize the masculine attributes most highly valued within a society."[6] The normative function of hero stories, according to Abrahams, is to project values in story form to serve as "a guide for future action in real life" in "a warlike age where heroic values are operative."[7] He also notes, however, that hero stories serve simultaneously as "an expression of dreamlife, of wishfulfillment," a function which comes to the fore when an "heroic age" or, in Abrahams' terms, an "heroic culture" disappears and "the war and resultant contest values" associated with such an age or culture may become embodied in stories about figures identified with other activities in a society. The hero stories which result from the transfer of contest values to activities other than war cannot, however, serve a normative function, because "To encourage such action would be to place the existence of the group in jeopardy."[9] Therefore, hero stories created or performed in such a socio-cultural milieu serve only the vicarious needs of the performers and audiences in defining masculinity; they cannot offer a model of emulative behavior for confronting similiar situations in real life.

The requirement that normative heroic action be conceptualized as the product of an "heroic age" and reflect values guiding action associated with war has been extremely influential in the study of the folklore of heroism. Richard Dorson, in a study of Davy Crockett as an American folk hero, argues "Heroic literature not only portrays an heroic age; it must date from that age."[10] While folklorists generally point to the western mythical and epic traditions which emphasize warlike values and physical confrontation as the prototypical "heroic age," they also agree that conditions have conspired at various time to create an "heroic age" in which the values of this earlier era can once again become operative. Abrahams contends, for example, that "there was much in the early national experience in the United States which was conducive to thinking and acting in such heroic terms."[11] Although folklorists recognize that all heroic literature neither portrays nor dates from an "heroic age," they simply do not view these expressions of heroic values, as in the case of African American heroic literature, as functioning normatively.

The conceptual model for study of folk heroic literature that has emerged from an emphasis on the actions and values associated with western epic and mythic traditions as universal highlights the need for culture-specific models in the study of folk heroic literature. This so-called normative model envisions the types of actions and values that have traditionally influenced folk and popular heroic creation in western cultures as an objective, if not universal, basis for evaluating the heroic literature of diverse groups. It turns out to be extremely narrow and ethnocentric, especially when applied to folk heroic traditions in the American context. At the least, this model leads us to devalue expressions of heroic ideals by groups whose values are not defined either historically or traditionally by the patriarchical norms on which much of western literature is based. Because we study folklore as a reflection of the socio-cultural experiences of those who create it, our adherence to a normative model forces us to view folk heroic literature that does not reflect an idealized American value system as the product of a distorted cultural experience at best and subterfuge at worst. In many ways, this approach to the study of folk heroic literature reveals the intimate relationship that folklorists envision between folklore creation and culture-building and reflects the assumption, implicit in folkloristics, that folklore should support culture-building by serving as a means of transmitting the values on which a group bases its ideal image of itself.

Folk heroic literature, however, is the product of creative cultural processes indulged in by groups for whom the values guiding action are not necessarily the idealized heroic values of the western world. The African American folk heroic tradition is a case in point. African American folk heroic creation is a normative cultural activity linked to black culture-building in America. Black culture-building in America, however, represents an extension of African culture-building and not European as it has so often been conceptualized. To examine the African American folk heroic tradition as a reflection of cultural values grounded in the African cultural experience requires that we reorient our thinking both about the culture-specific nature and function of heroic expression and about black culture-building in America.

Abrahams' observation that "legendary heroes arise because values guiding action exist within a group and individuals appear or are imagined who act in line with these values to a superlative degree" offers a starting point for conceptualizing a culture-specific model for discussing heroic literature.[12] We must recognize, however, that heroes do not "appear or are imagined" simply because values, warlike or otherwise, exist that are inherently heroic, but rather because values guiding action perceived as important to culture-building are threatened. Culture-building is the means by which a group institutionalizes potential solutions to the problem of how to live based on certain stable relationships, the relationships of human beings to God or the supernatural, to nature, and to each other. Heroic creation then can result from conditions which threaten or create obstacles to the maintenance of behaviors that best exemplify a group's values in regard to any of these relationships. War, in and of itself, arises as a response to some real or perceived threat to group values from some outside or, in the case of civil war, inside source. War, however, as a physical confrontation between two groups representing different value orientations, represents only one possible heroic response to a threat to group values, and therefore can produce only one type of hero—an individual whose actions are perceived as the most advantageous for protecting group values during times of war. However, the values guiding action within groups are not universal, nor are the actions necessary to protect group values always those recognized as the most advantageous during times of war.

In reality, the actions that a group recognizes as heroic are those that it perceives as the most advantageous behaviors for dealing with an obstacle or situation that threatens the values that guide action within specific temporal or social, political, and economic contexts. However, because groups do not recognize certain actions as inherently heroic, heroic creation is not a natural consequence of the imposition of conditions threatening group values. Folk heroic creation, or the embodiment of a conception of the heroic in oral traditions surrounding specific figures, must be viewed as opportunistic. "Just as a species does not 'struggle to survive' as a collective entity, but survives or not as a consequence of adaptive changes of individual organisms, so too do socio-cultural systems survive or not as a consequence of the adaptive changes in the thought and activities of individual men and women who respond opportunistically to cost-benefit options."[13] Unlike other organisms, human beings have the ability to communicate thoughts and actions in words and symbols to each other, and thus enhance their potential for taking advantage of adaptive behaviors opportunistically selected for by others. The creation of folk heroic literature represents an effort to capitalize on behaviors which present themselves opportunistically in the actions of certain figures at crucial times in a group's cultural history. In other words, folk heroic creation occurs because groups, at critical moments in time, recognize in the actions of certain figures, which may already be known to them, qualities or behaviors that they have reason to believe would enhance culture-building (that is, their ability to protect the identity and values of the group in the face of a threat to them).

The general conditions which serve as catalysts for heroic creation are those which, by virtue of their severity, jeopardize a group's ability to maintain the behaviors which reflect values accepted as important to survival or prosperity. Since such conditions can arise within the group or be imposed on it by some external force, folk heroic creation, or, more specifically, the type of hero that a group will embrace, depends, first of all, on the nature of the forces responsible for the situation perceived as threatening to culture-building. Eric Hobsbawm, for instance, argues in his study *Bandits* that creation of bandit or outlaw heroes arises when the way of life of one segment of a society is threatened by natural disaster or the law, while another segment of the society seems unaffected or even prospers from the same conditions.[14] Therefore, outlaw folk heroic traditions represent the expressive embodiment of a conception of behavior that members of the affected group might adapt to equalize social, economic, or even political conditions in the society. However, because of the very nature of the conditions which influence creation of the outlaw hero, to function as normative models of heroic action, such traditions cannot serve the expressive needs of the entire society. In most instances, the members of the society against whom outlaw heroes direct their actions envision them as mere criminals whose very existence threatens the well-being of the society as a whole.

Secondly, since folk heroic creation culminates in oral expressive traditions surrounding figures whose actions serve as a model of adaptive behavior for a group, the costs and benefits of a figure's actions, calculated in terms of their consequences for culture-building, must also be considered. In other words, not all figures, real or imagined, who act in a way that could potentially overcome an obstacle to group values will become heroes. The "costs" of certain actions, even though successful in some cases, may be perceived as too "high" to serve as a guide for action in real life situations. The actions that will most likely result in a conception of the heroic—that is, a model of behavior perceived as adaptable—will be those viewed as offering maximum benefits as a way of protecting group identity and values with minimal cost to the group's well-being and survival. Therefore, the actions of a group's folk heroes, regardless of the socio-cultural contexts in which they act, do not, from the group's point of view, place its existence or well-being in jeopardy.

Moreover, the embodiment of the exploits of a particular figure in folk heroic literature is not designed to provide a model of adaptive behavior in a literal sense. Rather, folk heroic literature offers a conception of attributes and actions that a group perceives as the most advantageous for maintaining and protecting its identity in the face of a threat to values guiding action. Folk heroic literature always portrays the exceptional actor whose exploits offer the group a glimpse of its own possibilites in handling similiar situations in everyday life and specific situations. In essence, folk heroic literature facilitates the group's ability to identify its antagonist, the nature of the threat that the antagonist's actions pose for the group, and the types of behavior most advantageous for dealing with the threat.

Finally, how a group conceptualizes the folk hero will be influenced by the way it has handled similar threats to group values in the past. In other words, the expression of heroic values that a group will accept as normative must also be viewed against the backdrop of its cultural heritage and traditions. It is in this regard that the personal traits associated with a heroic figure become important in evaluating heroic literature created by specific groups. While the hero is preeminently an individual who acts, the hero also serves as a symbol of a group's differential identity. For example, a group for which culture-building has proceeded through warlike confrontations would be more likely to conceptualize an individual as heroic who selects warlike actions and displays a warlike personality in the face of any threat to group values. By the same token, an individual in such a culture who responded to a threat to values in another way would likely be perceived as weak and ineffectual.

Within American folk heroic literary traditions, Anglo-American and African American folk heroes have traditionally displayed contrasting styles in dealing with threats to culture-building. But, African American folk heroes, having been consistently evaluated on the basis of criteria more appropriate to an understanding of folk heroic creation among people of European descent, have consistently been conceptualized not only, in Weldon's terms, as "ineffectual dissembling tricksters," but also as subversive actors. The tendency to evaluate all African American folklore as a reflection of Euro-American values is deeply rooted in folkloristic thinking. This approach to African American folklore has served from the earliest times as a denial of the importance of the African cultural heritage of African Americans to an understanding of black folk traditions. Adrienne Lanier Seward, for instance, observes that

> When Afro-American folk culture has been examined in terms of its African antecedents, the results have been predictably, if not inherently, controversial. Resistance to so-called Africanists' views has rested less on the overwhelming weight of scholarly evidence than on a conceptual framework influenced by long and deeply held notions about the aberrant nature of black cultural development under slavery in the United States.[15]

Lanier Seward concludes that "Afro-American folk culture has been seen as self-evident and capable of being understood solely within the context of conventional wisdom about slavery in the antebellum South."[16] The "conventional wisdom" has been based on a view of slavery as an experience which left African people in the United States culturally bankrupt and dependent on European cultural coffers for new capital as they began life in the New World. From this perspective, slavery constitutes the temporal and social environment to which we must turn for an understanding of black culture and folklore in America.

While slavery, in my view, represents a logical starting point for a discussion of black culture-building and folklore creation in America, it is not a logical point of departure for a consideration of black culture-building and, by extension, folklore creation. To use James A. Snead's insurance metaphor for apprehending the nature of culture, it is unrealistic and, ultimately, unproductive to assume that, despite the well-documented brutality and hostility exhibited by Europeans toward Africans enslaved in America, they abandoned, as a form of "'coverage' against both external and internal threats," their African cultural heritage in which they had invested for literally thousands of years and totally reinvested in a European cultural perspective whose actuaries demonstrated little interest in their survival or well-being.[17] In light of recent historiographies of slavery, we realize that the basic social and material conditions with which enslaved Africans had to contend for their survival militated against their aligning either their identity or welfare with that of their enslavers. Therefore, a realistic and considered view of culture and cultural processes, especially when viewed against the backdrop of black history in America, makes a denial of a profound and enduring relationship between African and African American cultures untenable.

While some students of black folk culture have consistently argued that a significant relationship between African and African American cultures and folk traditions must be recognized, they have not developed a systematic approach for conceptualizing the relationship between the two cultures and folk traditions. Abrahams and Szwed have argued that "The difficulty of describing the cultural relationship between African American people and their African progenitors is not due to any lack of data."[18] They suggest instead that the presentation of data relevant to an understanding of the relationship between the two cultures has been distorted by a tendency of scholars to take "a casual, anecdotal approach in which the encounter [between African and European cultures] is seen from the viewpoint of the politically and economically superordinate people as against the subordinate, with the assumption that such subordination leads to cultural as well as political domination."[19] The cogency of this argument cannot be denied when considering the study of African American folk traditions. Folklore scholarship has demonstrated a strong Eurocentric bias—a bias most clearly revealed in a tendency to attribute any African American expressive tradition with an apparent parallel in European tradition to European rather than African cultural provenance.

However, so-called Africanists have done little toward developing a more Afrocentric approach to the study of African American folk traditions—one which envisions black culture-building and folklore creation as activities "whereby African people attempt to understand all phenomena by virtue of their relationship to their survival and prosperity."[20] In most instances, they have approached the issue in ways that have simply provided scholars from a Eurocentric perspective with ammunition for their assaults on the notion of a dynamic continuity between African and African American cultures and folk traditions. The Africanist's mission has traditionally proceeded as a search for "Africanisms," or discrete items, practices, and customs that have somehow survived virtually intact among African Americans. Furthermore, and probably more revealing of the superficiality of the Africanist's view of the relationship between the two cultures, the identification of "Africanisms" has been made an end in itself. For example, folktale scholars have devoted much energy to identifying African analogues to African American folktales, yet they have consistently failed to address how the recognition of these parallel tales aids our understanding of the relationship between the African and African American traditions. While the Africanist's fascination with "Africanisms" and cultural retentions has revealed in rather startling terms that African cultural patterns and traditions have survived in America, for the most part, it has done little to dispel the persistent belief that African American folklore is essentially Euro-American in origin and character.

The absence of an Afrocentric perspective—one which envisions a dynamic relationship between the two cultures and folk traditions—has been one of the primary reasons that scholars have emphasized African retentions or "Africanisms." A Eurocentric perspective all too readily accepts "Africanisms" as the most obvious result of culture-building among Africans in America who came from diverse cultural backgrounds. The issue of African cultural diversity must be a central focus of an Afrocentric approach to the study of African American culture and folklore. That Africans enslaved in America were forcefully uprooted from diverse cultures is a reality which cannot be denied. However, we must also accept the reality that these cultures were far more similar to each other at the deepest levels of organization and in terms of the factors which influenced their structures than they were to the European cultures with which they had to compete in America. Therefore, an Afrocentric approach to the study of black culture must focus on deep structural similarities, rather than superficial differences, between African cultures as the foundation of black culture-building in American.

Mintz and Price argue, for instance, that positing African cultural diversity as a reason for denying the African foundation of black cultures in the New World is based on a surface view of culture. They suggest that Africans enslaved in the New World shared "certain common orientations to reality [which] tended to focus the attention of individuals from West African cultures upon similar kinds of events, even though the ways for handling these events may seem quite diverse in formal terms."[21] While the "common orientations to reality" shared by Africans may not have been sufficient to support the re-creation of African cultural institutions in the New World in their pristine form, they could and did have the ability to serve as the foundation for African culture-building in a new environment. Therefore, in describing the relationship between African and Afro-American cultures, according to Mintz and Price, we should concern ourselves more with "cognitive orientations" shared by Africans of diverse cultures than with simply institutional manifestations of culture. In other words, we discover more about the dynamic relationship between African and African American cultures and traditions by examining their basic assumptions about social relations and how the world functions phenomenologically than we can by insisting that the absence of African cultural institutions in America indicates that African people abandoned their cultural heritage in the New World.

When we accept the existence of deep structural similarities between African cultures, as an important aid to and catalyst for black culture-building in the New World, we can begin to unravel the African response to the New World from an Afrocentric perspective. First of all, European enslavement of Africans involved more than an encounter between African people and European cultures; it involved an encounter between two cultural systems equally capable of providing "coverage" against both external and internal threats to their abilities to perpetuate themselves. Second, the encounter was one characterized by hostility and conflict which enhanced the possibility that Africans, as the more threatened of the two groups, would act tenaciously to protect their cultural identity and values from what they undoubtedly envisioned as an attempt at cultural attachment. Finally, and most important, while European economic and political domination of Africans had profound individual and collective effect on them it did so by creating concrete and specific conditions and situations that Africans could identify as threats to their identity and to the values guiding action that they had traditionally recognized as the most advantageous to their survival and well-being. Although Africans undoubtedly had situations and conditions imposed on them in America for which their cultural heritage did not offer them specific "coverage," they were not novices in acting to protect their cultures from repression, attachment, and annihilation from external threats. Moreover, as cultured beings, Africans also had developed ways of protecting themselves from internal threats of self-dissolution and loss of identity created by external pressures or even by new behaviors selected by Africans in response to new social patterns and environments. In many ways, African enslavement created the need for rewriting the cultural policies that they already possessed, not wholesale reinvestment in the limited "coverage" offered by Europeans.

In the following chapters, I offer an analysis of African American folk heroic creation during the period of black chattel slavery and in the post-emancipation era which emphasizes a profound and enduring relationship between African and African American cultures and oral traditions. In my view, the task of describing the relationship between the two cultures and folk traditions must involve more than the simple identification of surface manifestations of African culture among African Americans. The dynamic continuity between African and African American cultures and folk traditions can only be revealed when we approach both black culture-building and folklore creation as historically continuous Afrocentric activities. An Afrocentric approach to African American culture and folklore requires studying them as the reflection of a process that is not unique but influenced by factors similar to those which shape culture-building and folklore creation in other groups. In other words, we must approach African American culture and folklore as a reflection of the beliefs, concerns and values of African Americans.

In a more general sense, we must recognize that culture-building is a recursive, rather than linear, process of endlessly devising solutions to both old and new problems of how to live under ever-changing social, political, and economic conditions. While culture is dynamic and creative as it adapts to social needs and goals, it is also enduring in that it changes by building upon previous manifestations of itself. Snead notes that "Culture as a reservoir of inexhaustible novelty is unthinkable. Therefore, repetition would inevitably creep into the dimensions of culture just as into that of language and signification because of the finite supply of elementary units and the need for recognizability."[22] Culture-building then proceeds as a process of "transformation" which becomes "culture's response to its own apprehension of repetition."[23] However, unless we understand previous manifestations of cultural phenomena and the factors influencing their form, we cannot recognize their transformation through time or space, for "whenever we encounter repetition in cultural forms, we are indeed not viewing 'the same thing' but its transformation, not just a formal ploy but often the willed grafting onto culture of an essentially philosophical insight about the shape of time and history."[24]

Inasmuch as transformation is a normative cultural process experienced as and indulged in by all groups as an on-going activity, the institutional and expressive forms by which a cultural group communicates and upholds its vision of the ideals by which it lives are equally susceptible to transformation. Cultural change through transformation, however, does not lead to an abandonment of the values guiding action recognized by a group, but rather represents an attempt to maintain group values by facilitating adherence to them under new conditions. Therefore, the expressive forms that emerge as a result of cultural transformation are not the "same thing" but, in Dan Ben-Amos' terms, may be conceptualized as "new wine in old bottles."[25]

Folk heroic creation as an emergent process is one of the ways by which cultural groups attempt to facilitate adherence to group values during periods of intense change. For Africans enslaved in America and for black freedpeople in the late nineteenth century, both cultural transformation and folk heroic creation became almost inevitable as they sought under incredibly adverse conditions to maintain their identity and values through culture-building. At the same time, repetition to maintain and enhance recognizability also became inevitable as African people in America transformed their historically revered cultural patterns and forms to develop a normative cultural response to America and the obstacles that it created to black survival and well-being.

Thanks to the early emphasis of folkloristics on textual studies, and the tireless efforts of folklore collectors to amass texts, we possess a wealth of information on the products of the black folk imagination in the form of tales, songs, and so forth from the slave and post-emancipation eras. However, because of the emphasis on texts and the ethnocentric assumptions and approaches which have informed the study of African American folklore over time, we know little about the

Afrocentric process or the ways in which Africans in America transformed their cultural forms and created a dynamic folk tradition in America. The dynamic character of African American folklore, however, can only be revealed when we demonstrate an equal concern with the factors which shaped both the creative product and the process of creativity. We must envision, from an Afrocentric perspective, the creative center of both the product and the process as African culture and cultural forms.

In the following chapters, I examine the folklore surrounding the trickster, conjurer, biblical figures, and the badman from the vantage point of African cultural values and forms as transformed under the conditions of slavery and in the socio-cultural environment of the late nineteenth century. I approach black folk heroic creation as a continuous process—one intimately related historically to black culture building. The process began in Africa and continues in America as a dynamic creative activity aimed at facilitating and enhancing the adaptability of certain behavioral patterns traditionally accepted by African people as advantageous for maintaining and protecting their identity and values in certain types of situations. I argue that, in transforming African culture and cultural forms in America, African people were influenced not merely by surface differences in their lifestyle in America from that they had known on the continent but equally, if not more so, by their perceptions of the deep structural similarities in the factors—social, economic, and political—influencing its structure. In essence, Africans in America, in creating a lifestyle and expressive forms supportive of culture-building, were influenced less by surface differences in what they experienced in the New World than by the concrete realities they faced on a day-to-day basis which facilitated their clinging tenaciously to a value system both recognizable to them and alternative to that imposed on them. In freedom, African people in America did not abandon this value system as an influence on folk heroic creation, but rather transformed it to reflect new realities and insights about the shape of both time and history as they perceived it from their vantage point on the society.

The study of African American folklore in general and folk heroic literature in particular has suffered too long under the weight of a conceptual framework which envisions the idealized values of western Europe as transformed in America as the basis for evaluating them. While historians have for some time now recognized the value of folklore in recovering the past of African Americans, folklorists have been far more reluctant to use historical insights and realities as aids in the analysis of the performance of African American folklore texts. In this study, I embrace black history as a record of the lived experiences of African people, one which provides insights into those factors which have traditionally influenced black culture-building and, therefore, folk heroic creation over time. In so doing, I attempt to demonstrate that the folklore of heroism created by African Americans reflects the values of a people who do not have their roots in western tradition either historically or culturally, even though behaviors which reflect western values have had a profound and continuous influence on it. In addition, the differential experiences of Africans in America and their creative responses to them, when historically situated, can be shown to have facilitated rather than inhibited the maintenance of a value orientation and esthetic tradition deeply rooted in the African cultural heritage.

In black folk heroic literature, the fact that the actions of African American folk heroes reflect values that would be recognizable neither to Africans on the continent nor to Anglo-Americans as supportive of culture-building should not be surprising, or accepted as an indication of deviance from some accepted standard in either tradition. When we encounter the African American folk hero, we meet a figure whose actions reflect the transformed and, in some ways, transmuted values of African people shaped by situations and conditions in America. To suggest that the African American folk heroic tradition does not reflect values guiding actions generally accepted as the most advantageous by Anglo-American people does not negate or deny the fact that black folk heroes are products of the American historical and cultural experience. On the contrary, the African American folk heroic tradition is very much a creative response to the experiences of African people in America. However, when we examine those factors—cultural, historical, material, physical, and social—which have traditionally influenced values guiding action among African people, we come to realize that the basis on which African Americans evaluate the actions of their folk heroes as normative is deeply rooted in their African cultural heritage.

NOTES

1. Robert Penn Warren, "Introduction" to *The Hero In America*, by Dixon Wecter (New York: Charles Scribners' Sons, 1972) xiv.
2. Warren xv.

3. Bill R. Hampton, "On Identification and the Trickster," *Southern Folklore Quarterly* 31(1967): 55.

4. Fred O. Weldon, "Negro Folktale Heroes," *Publication of the Texas Folklore Society* No. 29(1969):187.

5. Weldon 187.

6. Roger D. Abrahams, "Some Varieties of Heroes in America," *Journal of the Folklore Institute* 3(1967): 341.

7. Abrahams 341.

8. Abrahams 343.

9. Abrahams 342.

10. Richard M. Dorson, "Davy Crockett and the Heroic Age," *Southern Folklore Quarterly* 6(1942):102.

11. Abrahams 353.

12. Abrahams 341.

13. Marvin Harris, *Cultural Materialism* (New York: Vintage Books, 1980) 61.

14. Eric Hobsbawm, *Bandits* (New York: Dell, 1969).

15. Adrienne Lanier Seward, "The Legacy of Early Afro-American Folklore Scholarship," in *Handbook of American Folklore*, ed. Richard M. Dorson (Bloomington: Indiana University Press, 1983) 49.

16. Lanier Seward 49.

17. James A. Snead, "Repetition as a Figure of Black Culture," in *Black Literature and Literary Theory*, ed. Henry Louis Gates, Jr. (New York: Methuen, 1984) 61.

18. Roger D. Abrahams and John Szwed, "After the Myth: Studying Afro-American Cultural Patterns in the Plantation Literature," in *African Folklore in the New World*, ed. Daniel J. Crowley (Austin: University of Texas Press, 1977) 65.

19. Abrahams and Szwed 65.

20. Clovis E. Semmes, "Foundations of an Afrocentric Social Science," *Journal of Black Studies* 12(1981): 3.

21. Sidney W. Mintz and Richard Price, *An Anthropological Approach to the Afro-American Past: A Caribbean Perspective* (Philadelphia: Institute for the Study of Human Issues, 1976) 5.

22. Snead 60.

23. Snead 59.

24. Snead 59-60.

25. Dan Ben-Amos, "Toward a Definition of Folklore in Context," in *Toward New Perspectives in Folklore*, ed. Americo Paredes and Richard Bauman (Austin: University of Texas Press, 1972) 5.

TWO

Br'er Rabbit and John:
Trickster Heroes in Slavery

Trickster tale traditions, especially those in which clever animals acted as humans, were ubiquitous in the cultures from which Africans enslaved in the United States had come. Therefore, it is not surprising that tales of trickery built around the exploits of anthropomorphized animals occupied a central position in the oral narrative performances of Africans enslaved in America. Although the existence of animal trickster tales was seldom noted during slavery, folktale collectors in the late nineteenth and early twentieth century constantly expressed amazement over the sheer number and the wide distribution and coherence of the black trickster tale repertoire. For example, in 1892, Octave Thanet declared "All over the South the stories of Br'er Rabbit are told. Everywhere not only ideas and plots are repeated, but the very words often are the same; one gets a new vision of the power of oral tradition."[1] The trickster tales of enslaved Africans not only appeared to be remarkably similar to each other throughout the South, but they also exhibited a close kinship to trickster tales in African oral traditions. Shortly after the appearance in print of the first animal trickster tales found among African Americans, scholars began publishing parallel tales from African traditions demonstrating that, in some instances, trickster tales of African Americans were developed around the same plots and situations as those found in African tales.[2]

Early students of the African American animal trickster tale tradition accepted not only the African origins of the tales but also the idea that African Americans conceptualized the trickster as a folk hero. William Owens, one of the first to discuss the tales in print, raised the specter of African origins when he noted that animal trickster tales were "as purely African as their faces or their own plantation melodies."[3] Joel Chandler Harris, one the earliest collectors of the tales and the foremost popularizer of them in the late nineteenth century, was a strong advocate of both African origins and the trickster as hero. On the subject of the origins of animal trickster tales, he noted that "One thing is certain, they did not get them from the whites: they are probably of remote African origins."[4] Harris' views on the African origins of the tales, however, were much stronger than this statement implies. In another context, he argued that "if ethnologists should discover that they did not originate with the African, the proof to that effect should be accompanied by a good deal of persuasive eloquence."[5] As to the trickster's heroism, Harris was much more determined from the outset, and asserted that "It takes no scientific investigation to show why he [the African American] selects as his hero the weakest and most harmless of all animals, and brings him out victorious in contests with the bear, the wolf, and the fox. It is not virtue which triumphs but helplessness; it is not malice but mischievousness."[6]

In the late nineteeth century, most folktale scholars would probably have agreed with Harris that the burden of proof was clearly on those who would claim other than African origins for the heroic animal trickster of black folktales. In early discussions of the tradition, the African origins of animal trickster tales and the trickster as hero became interrelated issues. That students of African American animal trickster tales in the late nineteenth century would merge these issues in discussing the tales was virtually inescapable. On one level, their view of the origins and functions of the tales was strongly influenced by the popular conception of folklore as a survival from the savage past of humankind which existed in the present as a kind of mental relic among those closest to this stage of cultural development.[7] Even before the period of slavery, Europeans had begun to propagate the idea that African cultures were arrested in a savage state of development by the innate inferiority of African people. However, white Americans had during the period of slavery defended black subjugation by promulgating the idea that, though innately inferior to whites, black acculturation "under the discipline of slavery" had served to eradicate the more savage aspects of the African character, an effect reflected in their docile and childlike behavior as slaves.[8] Therefore, when folktale scholars were confronted with the animal trickster tale tradition which portrayed a hero in the form of a small animal whose cunning and wit could explode into acts of brutality and violence, their approach was dictated by the duality which governed their own thinking about African people.[9] Most could readily equate the character and actions of the animal trickster with those of Africans on the continent, but could not, however, so easily accept them as a completely accurate reflection of black identity or behavior, actual or potential, in America.

Consequently, early scholars clung tenaciously to the African origins thesis and suggested that animal trickster tales in their more "savage" aspects reflected their creation in Africa. Africans enslaved in America, they argued, continued to perform animal trickster tales because they could identify with the witty and cunning trickster who had been assigned an inferior position in the natural order which, in many ways, was not unlike their own in the human order. Abigail Christensen wrote in the introduction to her collection of animal trickster tales, for example, "It must be remembered that the Rabbit represents the colored man. He is not as large, nor as strong, as swift, as wise nor as handsome as the elephant, the alligator, the bear, the deer, the serpent, the fox, but he is 'de mos' cunnin' man dat go on fo' leg' and by this cunning he gains success."[10] Thanet argued that the trickster's uncanny ability to succeed through cunning and immoral deception reflected not only the African roots of the tales but also the African character of blacks in America. Africans, he observed, are an extremely "vain" and unrealistic people whose vanity inclines them toward uninhibited acts of immorality toward each other. To support his view of African immorality, he noted that the trickster in Africa was a religious figure and his immorality was "a reflection of the African religion, which interferes with morals less than any I know. Br'er Rabbit, indeed, personifies the obscure ideals of his race."[11] Since black "ideals" were ultimately unrealistic in Thanet's view, the animal trickster served as a perfect heroic symbol for both Africans and African Americans since, given his innate limitations, he could not possibly succeed in the wild against his antagonists in folktales. By the same token, African Americans who recounted tales of the animal trickster's exploits in which he virtually always succeeds were indulging in African wishful thinking since they could not succeed in a battle of wits with whites. Therefore, black admiration for the animal trickster, though vicariously pleasing, did not offer African Americans a model of emulative behavior and certainly did not threaten the *status quo*.

Throughout the late nineteenth and early twentieth century, folktale collectors recorded literally hundreds of animal trickster tales from African American storytellers and found little reason to question either the basic thesis of African origins or the trickster as a harmless heroic symbol. However, Richard Dorson collected some thousand African American folktales in the early 1950s, a small number of which were animal trickster tales. In the introduction to his compilation of these tales, *American Negro Folktales*, he challenged the African origins thesis as unsupportable by strict folkloristic standards. He noted in particular that "Many of the fictions, notably the animal tales, are of demonstrably European origin. Others have entered the Negro repertoire from England, from the West Indies, from American white tradition, and from the social and historical experiences of colored people in the South." He concludes that "Only a few plots and incidents can be distinguished as West African."[12] In reaching this conclusion, Dorson utilized tale-type and motif analysis to demonstrate the dominance of European influence on Afro-American folktales.

In the wake of Dorson's contention, folktale scholars who continued to be interested in the question of origins seldom retreated from the African origins thesis but rather followed his lead and turned to motif and tale-type analysis to support their conclusions, often exclaiming at the same time that available indices for such analysis were unreliable in dealing with African derived tales.[13] In addition, these scholars almost invariably based their conclusions on a small corpus of tales and, as Dorson repeatedly stated in defense of his thesis, failed to establish that more than a handful of African American trickster tales could be traced to Africa. Since mid-century, the debate over the origins of African American trickster tales has occupied most students of the traditions. Those interested in the trickster as hero have demonstrated in their approach to the issue at least an indirect influence from the origins controversy. After mid-century, scholars who have discussed the animal trickster as hero have been far more likely to ignore the question of origins altogether or suggest that it is unimporant to an understanding of any aspect of the tradition. Typical of this approach is that of Lawrence W. Levine, who has offered the most extensive recent discussion of the early manifestation of the tradition. In *Black Culture and Black Consciousness*, Levine acknowledges the possibility of African influence on the tradition, but suggests that "regardless of where the tales came from, the essential point is that slaves quickly made them their own and through them revealed much about themselves and their world."[14]

With the shift in emphasis from African origins as an explanation for the trickster as hero, scholars turned to the repressive social climate of slavery to explain the animal trickster as a black folk hero. Folklorists continue to argue that the African American trickster tale tradition is an expressive embodiment of the ambiguous situation of blacks brought about, in this instance, by conditions which forced them to accept an identity as inferior and dependent beings in the slave system. Roger Abrahams succinctly summarized this view of the trickster as folk hero: "in the guise of the small (childlike) animal, the Negro is perhaps fulfilling the role in which he has been cast by his white 'masters' (the childlike Uncle Tom who is convinced of his simple state and thus needs the protection of his masters). At the same time, in this role he is able to show a superiority over those larger and more important than himself through his tricks, thus partially salving his wounded ego."[15] From this perspective, the trickster's character as a small animal reflected the retarded psycho-social development of black identity under white oppression, while the trickster's actions revealed black feelings of rebelliousness against the values of the system which denied opportunities for self-definition. However, the rebellious animal trickster, in adopting behaviors that were not only socially unacceptable by the values of the slave system but also "morally tainted," jeopardized the well-being of enslaved Africans within the slave system that was their only source of values and identity. Therefore, the animal trickster tales, though psychologically fulfilling as compensatory devices, could neither serve enslaved Africans as a symbol of group identity nor offer them a normative model of adaptive behavior.

Obviously, when the African American animal trickster tale tradition is accepted as having its roots solely in the slave South, and the values of the slave system as the basis on which we must evaluate the trickster's actions, the animal trickster emerges as a figure whose actions must be viewed as simply rebellious and ultimately threatening both to the slave system itself and to the well-being of black people within it. The ability of the animal trickster tale tradition to function as a normative model of heroic action cannot, however, be understood within a conceptual framework which envisions slavery as the primary source of the values that enslaved Africans associated with this figure. While slavery influenced both how and why African people in America continued to value actions embodied in animal trickster tales as a source of behaviors for their community, the African roots of the tradition in which the actions of animal tricksters represented behavioral patterns traditionally valued by African people must also be viewed as important. Despite the apparent rebelliousness of animal tricksters or even the brutality of their behavior in some tales, Africans had historically accepted the animal tricksters' characteristic actions as protecting their identity and values under certain types of situations. Therefore, to understand why African Americans transformed the African trickster tale tradition in America to create a model of heroic action, it is essential that we acknowledge the African roots of the tradition as central to an understanding of its meaning to African people in America.

In the past, folklorists, even those who have advocated a strong African influence on African American trickster tales, have demonstrated a primary and most often singular concern with establishing expressive links between African and African American trickster traditions, and practically no concern with deep structural similarities between African and African American cultures which may have influenced the transformation of the African trickster tales tradition in America. The similarities between trickster traditions throughout Africa and those found among people of African descent thoughout the New World, even on a surface level, would seem to suggest that similar concerns at some level very likely played a role in the perpetuation of similarly structured tales among African people, even those geographically and culturally removed from the continent. It also seems highly probable that the common concerns of African people must be viewed as the primary reason for the trickster in black folk heroic creation, concerns that can only be uncovered through an examination of the role and function of trickster tales in the African cultures from which black people in America were forcibly uprooted.

The African Trickster Tale Traditions

In the study of African animal trickster tale traditions, scholars have frequently noted that they are not only ubiquitous on the continent but also exhibit remarkably similar characteristics among diverse groups. Throughout sub-Saharan Africa, trickster tale traditions, though not infrequently associated with specific religions, have been shown to be extremely adaptable in that tales with similar plots but different characters appear in the oral traditions of different cultural groups. Although the principal actors tend to be animals, they characteristically act as humans and sometimes appear in human and divine forms. In many African cultural traditions, the animal trickster is believed to have once been either a man or a god. Moreover, the characteristic attitude and behaviors displayed by African animal tricksters exhibit enough similarities to allow for a general assessment of them as a type. Susan Feldmann, for instance, suggests that African tricksters, like those in other cultures, have as their principal character trait "superior cleverness;" she further observes, however, that in contrast to tricksters in the folk traditions of Native Americans, for example, African tricksters exhibit some unique characteristics.

Unlike the New World trickster he [the African trickster] is represented by the underdog rather than the chief. His amorality is not that of the anomic, presocialized individual, who has not yet matured to a sense of responsibility. Suave, urbane and calculating, the African trickster acts with premeditation, always in control of the situation; though self-seeking, his social sense is sufficiently developed to enable him to manipulate others to his advantage. He is mercenary rather than promiscuous. On the whole, he shows a singular indifference to sex in favor of food or the sheer enjoyment of making a dupe of others.[16]

Feldmann also offers a similar composite sketch of the African trickster's dupe:

Though in a given cycle trickster will victimize any of his fellow creatures, he usually concentrates on a particular prey. Trickster's favorite foils and dupes are Lion, Elephant and Hyena. The victim is always larger and therefore stronger; inevitably slow and dull-witted, often hard-working and honest.[17]

As to be expected in an attempt to generalize about African folk traditions, Feldmann's assessment of the general characters, behaviors, and relationships of African tricksters and their dupes should be viewed as only a basic characterization of the African trickster tale tradition. However, it does capture the essential characteristics of the tradition as it appears in numerous African cultures.

Despite numerous surface differences, especially in the identity of the tricksters and dupes that populate tales of the animal trickster in Africa, diverse cultural groups throughout sub-Saharan Africa can be shown to have created animal trickster tales based on the exploits of very similar character types and placed them in remarkably similar types of situations. For example, Jay D. Edwards, on the basis of a deep structural analysis of African animal trickster tales, notes, for instance, that "a distinctly African emphasis" in trickster tales is the "focus on the seeming inevitability of making and then terminating social ties in order to gain material (or other) goals. An assumption underlying the tales seems to be that material (or other) rewards are strictly limited, and that actors tend to be greedy."[18] In African animal trickster tales, the material reward which most frequently motivates the trickster is food, a not so curious concern on the African continent. The emphasis on material acquisition, especially food, through the breaking of social ties suggests that the wide distribution and coherence of trickster traditions across sub-Saharan Africa was probably related to material and social conditions widely shared by Africans of diverse cultural backgrounds.

In the most general sense, Africans have historically contended with subsistence-level existence as well as chronic shortages of basic material necessities occasioned by various factors peculiar to life on the African continent. In the efforts of African peoples to cope with material shortages, the acquisition and maintenance of an adequate food supply has traditionally confronted them with an incredible obstacle. Dependent historically on agriculture and hunting, Africans have faced numerous hazards in attempting through these activities to maintain a stable food supply. Although agriculture has been essential to survival in Africa, its success has hinged to a large extent on favorable environmental conditions and a stable labor force, both of which can be difficult to maintain. Among many groups, especially in West Africa, agriculture has traditionally been the province of women while hunting has fallen to the men. The technology of agriculture and the environment throughout much of black Africa has not allowed for the production of large crops or the accumulation and storage of large reserves. On the one hand, climatic and soil conditions have favored the growing of tubers and shoot plants such as plantain and yams which can be stored for only short periods of time. On the other hand, fluctuations in environmental conditions from excessive rain to prolonged drought have been common, easily producing scarcities of agricultural products. The results have all too often been famines and other human misfortunes associated with food shortages.

For Africans, many of the same factors which have impacted negatively on agricultural production have also influenced the success of hunting. Although most African groups raise domestic animals for food, hunting has traditionally served as the primary source of meat among many groups. For these Africans, hunting has constituted a full-time activity, a risky enterprise at best. Its success has depended not only on the skill of the hunters but also on favorable environmental conditions which determined the availability of game. In addition, because of the indistinguishability of the techniques and weapons of hunting from those of war, hunters have had to be concerned with territorial violations, since encroachment could easily culminate in armed conflict with other groups. Furthermore, when environmental conditions have produced shortfalls in the wild game supply, the domestic animal population has dwindled quickly as Africans have sought to supplement their diets with the only meat available.

The material conditions created by existence in the African environment and the African trickster's constant quest for food cannot be accepted as accidental or unimportant to an understanding of the meaning that African people derived from trickster tale narration. For example, the African conception of the trickster as a figure particularly adept at securing the material means of survival, especially food, under famine-like conditions and through deception and false friendship is aptly captured in the following tale from the Azande in which Ture, the sacred spider trickster, emerges as a culture hero who is credited with having brought food to earth:

How Ture Got Food from the Sky God

Once there was no food on the earth. There was only one man who had food, and he had come down from the sky. When people began to die of hunger they went to that man so that he might give them food, but he chased them away. So, many people died of hunger. They told this affair to Ture, saying, "There is a man here with food, besides which he gets very angry." Ture said "You be silent, I am certainly going after that man."

Ture went to that man's house and deceived him, saying "Let us make blood-brotherhood, master." It pleased this man very much. He and Ture made blood-brotherhood. Shortly afterwards Ture went to this man and said "O my blood-brother, please give me some food, my children are dying of hunger." Ture's blood-brother bent and said "My blood brother Ture, put your head between my legs." Then this man flew with Ture to the sky. When they arrived there this man spoke to Ture thus: "My blood-brother, collect some eleusine and some manioc and dig up twelve rats, and then come and we will leave." Ture did this completely. So once again this man bent and Ture put his head between his legs and he descended with Ture to this world here.

Ture returned to his home and gave the food to his wives. As they were eating this food Ture began to abuse this man, saying "The man to whose home I went is bad. He told me to put my head between his legs before he would fly me to get food." This man heard what Ture said about him and he was very annoyed by it.

Afterwards, when the food Ture had brought was finished, hunger tightened on Ture and his wives. So he went to his blood-brother again and he flew with Ture to the sky. Ture collected every kind of food there is in the world and put them into his big bag. But Ture's blood-brother went away from him and descended to earth here. Rain caught Ture in the sky and rained upon him till he was soaked. Ture then began to look for the way by which they had come. Ture found a very narrow path descending to the earth. Ture walked for some distance and when he arrived at a bare stone-flat he tapped on a drum, and people came from all over the world. Ture distributed every kind of food to them and he returned home with his. Because of Ture people eat today.

In African trickster tales, the trickster's need to compensate for shortages in the food supply, often under famine-like conditions, is mentioned often enough to almost be considered a formulaic opening sequence for African trickster tales. In tale after tale and among various groups, African raconteurs introduced their audiences to the adventures of tricksters whose actions were motivated by conditions such as the following:

> There was great lack of meat in the country and people's mouths were sour from eating leaves of manioc and of sweet potatoes . . .
> . . . .
> They say that once upon a time a great famine came, and that Father Ananse the spider, and his wife Aso, and his children . . . built a little settlement and lived in it . . .
> . . . .
> There was once a famine in the country, a terrible famine. Nobody had enough to eat. People and animals and plants were all dying, so the animals of the forest called a meeting. . . .

The African environment could be a hostile one in which chronic shortages of basic material necessities constantly threatened survival and individual and group autonomy. When faced with food or other material shortages, whether caused by natural disasters or by human induced ones such as war, members of a group have had to compete both with each other and with neighboring groups, often equally affected by the conditions, for the same scarce resources. In such situations, which have tended to reoccur frequently in Sub-Saharan Africa, both intra- and intergroup alliances and friendships have become tenuous as individuals have been forced by conditions to secure the means of physical survival as best they could—often at each other's expense.

Therefore, African animal trickster tales which characteristically portray situations in which the principal actors create alliances, which they inevitably break, or break longstanding ones in pursuit of their own apparent egocentric goals, are undoubtedly related to a perception that these types of behavior are advantageous in certain well-defined situations. When faced with social and natural conditions in which individuals find themselves literally in a struggle for their physical survival, harmony, friendship, and trust are ideals difficult to sustain, while deception, greed, and cleverness can easily emerge as valuable adaptive behavioral traits if pursued in ways that do not threaten the well-being of the group. In this regard, the African conception of the trickster as a sacred being, usually a god, undoubtedly influenced African attitudes toward the adaptability of behaviors embodied in trickster tales in certain kinds of situations. As gods or god-like figures, the actions of sacred tricksters conveyed the idea that material shortage was an aspect of the natural order of things, and that behavior which involved trickery to compensate for it was appropriate under certain conditions.

The African attitude toward tricksters and the actions associated with them, however, was related to their religious beliefs in a more profound way than is indicated by the mere appearance of the trickster in divine form. Feldmann observes, for instance, that "what is striking is that unlike the fairy tale hero, trickster accomplishes the seemingly impossible by trickery rather than by supernatural aid. Trickster operates in a real world where the hero cannot count on supernatural helpers and clever cheating replaces magic."[19] From the perspective of African religious beliefs, the absence of magic in African animal trickster tales must be seen as an important clue to an understanding of the value that Africans placed on wit and trickery as normative behaviors in certain types of situations. Certainly, in African religious worldviews and cultures, magic played an important role in everyday life, especially in facilitating the ability of individuals to achieve personal ends at the expense of others. However, in traditional African religious worldviews, the manipulation of the mystical force in nature, or magic, created one of the greatest threats to their values and the integrity of social life.[20]

The attitude toward magic in African cultures derives from their socio-religious view of human beings as intricately linked to each other by a mystical force in the universe which also connects them to nature and the supernatural in a hierarchical and interdependent relationship. The mystical force in nature determined not only "being" in an ontological sense but also what a being could do. In the universal order, those at the top of the hierarchy, especially those in the supernatural realm, possessed both power (a share of the mystical force in nature) and the right to directly influence those at a lower level for good or ill. The natural state of the universal order, however, was harmony, with each being acting cooperatively with all others. At the level of community, African social structure existed as a microcosm of the larger universal order in which an individual's share of the mystical force in nature was determined by position in the social hierarchy. Therefore, those at the top of the social hierarchy, whether defined by age, status, rank, or spiritual role, possessed a kind of divine right to use their superior power to directly influence those at the bottom. At the same time, those of inferior rank or status possessed neither the power nor the right to directly influence those above them. However, they could, through indirect means or acts of magic, which involved surreptitiously acquiring additional power from another being, influence those above them—an act which, in African socio-religious worldview, threatened the harmony of the entire universal order. As a result, African social values emphasized strong communal bonds, respect for a hierarchy of social and religious powers, and harmony in social relationships. The individual in African societies was expected to value behaviors which promoted communal welfare and preserved communal harmony above those which provided individualistic gain. However, because African's social values were directly and continually influenced by their religious beliefs, the behaviors that constituted violations of them were defined in religious terms. Consequently, to act in disharmony with one's own community by seeking individual gain through magic was considered one of the worst moral evils that individuals could commit, and exposed them to even greater acts of magic by those empowered in the community to punish evil.

The hierarchy of being and the structure that it imposed on social life in African cultures was extremely important in determining the ability of African people to accept the trickster's actions as beneficial adaptive behaviors under certain types of conditions. During times of material shortage as at other times, those who lacked power, as defined by African socio-religious law and custom, were not only more likely to experience the greatest share of the misery but also more likely to resort to magic to compensate for it. To prevent the use of magic as a way of dealing with social repression and material shortage, Africans placed a high value on native intelligence as a way of dealing with situations that disadvantaged the individual. Feldmann argues, for instance, that African trickster tales "Illustrate the traditional right of the individual to contest irrational authority."[21] Whether Africans viewed their authority system as irrational is doubtful. However, their recognition of it as potentially repressive of and destructive to the well-being of the individual under certain types of conditions appears evident in the prominent position that they gave animal trickster tales in their oral performances.

Additionally, in a harsh natural environment and a rigid hierarchical social structure, the trickster's actions offered Africans a model of behavior which allowed for the development and maintenance of behavioral patterns that facilitated both individual and communal well-being without violating or threatening communal identity and values. While those at the top of the hierarchy could rely on their inherent power—defined in both religious and social terms—those at the bottom demonstrated worth and ability to survive through native intelligence. This natural state of affairs was constantly reinforced through the trickster's interactions with antagonists in the natural world as well as in the supernatural. For example, in numerous West African trickster tales, the trickster wages an on-going battle of wits with the Sky God. Through sheer cunning and wit, the spider trickster, sometimes conceptualized as a demi-god, manages to obtain from the all-powerful Sky God his food, thoughts, and stories. In these tales, the trickster's actions not only win the Sky God's respect but also benefit the community.[22] Such tales obviously offered more than a behavioral strategy; they infused the trickster's actions with a kind of moral integrity not readily apparent on the surface.

In essence, Africans enslaved in America had their cultural roots in societies which had historically faced chronic shortages of the basic material necessities and existence in a rigid, hierarchical social structure. The rigidity of African social structure, however, was designed to facilitate individual well-being in a harsh natural environment which allowed only a subsistence level of existence. In this environment, those behaviors which reflected and facilitated harmonious relationships with nature, the supernatural, and other human beings gained a level of social acceptability denied those which disrupted the harmony of the natural order through magic. In African trickster tales, the relationship most often portrayed as existing between trickster and dupe offered both a conception of behaviors and a type of relationship in which the trickster's characteristic actions represented the most advantageous behaviors for securing individual interests without disrupting the order and harmony of society. Therefore, the actions of the African trickster whose relationship to his dupe was one familiar to Africans in both religious and social terms could serve as an important model of behavior for individuals in certain well-

defined and recognizable situations. Furthermore, the frequent association of the African trickster with religion infused the trickster's
behavior with a sense of moral and cultural significance even when
their actions involved the most outrageous behaviors.

THE AFRO-AMERICAN
TRICKSTER TALE TRADITION

I have been so pinched with hunger that I have fought with the
dog for the smallest crumbs that fell from the kitchen table.
Many times have I followed, with eager step, the waiting girl when
she went out to shake the table cloth, to get the crumbs and small
bones flung out for the cats.
Frederick Douglass, *My Bondage and My Freedom* [23]

The lifestyles of Africans on the continent and those enslaved in
America, though different in many ways, both revolved around patterns of behavior designed to solve the problem of how to live with
chronic shortages of basic material necessities and within a rigid social hierarchy. The physical plight of Africans enslaved in America,
however, was obscured by the fact that they were incorporated into a
materially productive system in which they produced the basic necessities of life, often in abundance. They, nevertheless, realized minimal material benefits from the enormous amount of energy that they
expended. The fruits of their labor benefited the slave system, which
the enslavers controlled through their physical power over the enslaved, while denying them free access to the material rewards that
they produced. While the slavemasters did make an effort to provide
for the basic material needs of Africans, they determined what they
needed to survive. Moreover, as William D. Postell concludes from
his examination of slaveowner records on the physical care of enslaved Africans, slavemasters, in providing for material needs of their
slaves, placed their emphasis "on quantity and not quality," an emphasis which created conditions for enslaved Africans which posed
constant threats to their survival and well-being as a people.[24]
Throughout the slave South, the slaveholders' attention to the material and physical needs of enslaved Africans was indifferent at best,
dehumanizing in almost every respect, and ultimately devastating to
their physical well-being. Of the complications created for them by
the masters' practices and control over their lives, none were more
serious than those to their health, especially the illness and disease

created by the inadequacy of their food supply.[25] Blassingame notes, for instance, that most slavemasters based their food allotments to enslaved Africans on their perception of an "average" amount. As he further notes, an amount that proved "sufficient for one man was not necessarily enough for another."[26] From the point of view of enslaved Africans, the food supplied them by the slavemasters was seldom adequate. For example, William Brooks, who spent his days in bondage in Virginia, in describing the slaves' weekly food allotment, noted that "Dey use to gib de slaves bout 6 pounds meat an' 5 pounds o' flour a week effen you ain' got chillun. If you got chillun, you git a little mo'. Well dat ain' 'nough lasten a dog a day."[27] While the quantities may have varied according to the miserliness or generosity of the particular master, they were never of a quality or reached such proportions that an enslaved African was "ever likely to suffer from gout superinduced by excessive high living," to quote Solomon Northup in his slave narrative.[28]

The physical conditions imposed on enslaved Africans were made all the more difficult to negotiate by the rigidity of the socio-economic system into which they were forcibly inserted. As property, they were expected to allow their behavior to be governed by rigid rules devised and enforced by the masters. They were subjected to floggings for the least infraction of the requirements of work, real or supposed transgressions against the rules of the system, and at the masters' discretion. Both at work and during moments of leisure, their movements were carefully regulated and controlled by individual masters and overseers as well as patrols constituted for the purpose of restricting their movements. In addition, they were expected to be deferential when in the presence of whites and were punished with verbal and physcial attacks when they were not. They were, in essence, treated and cared for like the other domestic animals the masters owned.

Despite their complete control over the ownership and distribution of the rewards produced under the slave system as well as the lives of the enslaved, slavemasters constantly attempted to foist on enslaved Africans an illusion of the system as a cooperative enterprise in whose success both master and slave had a significant stake. Enslaved Africans, however, recognized that such a claim was illusory and its propagation ultimately in the interest only of slavemasters, who expended little if any energy in directly affecting the productivity of the system. From their vantage point on the system, enslaved Africans saw that they were forced to work endlessly to make it productive while the masters went to great length to limit their autonomy and access to its material rewards. As the producers within the system, enslaved Africans were the ones forced to begin work at sunup and often not complete their workday until well into the night, leaving little time for family and leisure time activities. Although the nature of work varied from plantation to plantation and from season to season, it nevertheless required long hours under the watchful eye of master, mistress, or overseer, a reality which made the illusion all the more transparent.

While the enslavers undoubtedly viewed their treatment of enslaved Africans as expedient and necessary to insure the productivity of the system and the cooperation of the enslaved, their actions repeatedly created for the enslaved conditions which threatened their individual and collective sense of well-being. However, the socio-cultural environment created by the masters' actions also facilitated the ability of enslaved Africans to maintain behaviors reflecting their traditional values. Though influenced by factors peculiar to life in the slave system, the continuation of a subsistence level of existence in a rigid hierarchically ordered social system had a profound influence on the creative response of enslaved Africans to the material and physical conditions imposed on them by the masters. Confronted daily with chronic material shortages and dehumanizing physical conditions, and inhibited by the masters' power in the options available to compensate for them, enslaved Africans came to view their situation as one in which behaviors that circumvented the masters' power rather directly challenging it, offered the greatest advantages in securing their interests.

Therefore, in their everyday lives, enslaved Africans turned to behaviors which allowed them to subvert the masters' authority and control in ways that did not disrupt the system. Subversive behaviors became both a part of the everyday strategies of the enslaved and a primary focus of many personal experience stories told by former enslaved Africans. "I tell you, honey," recalled Alice Marshall of her experiences as slave, "mistiss Sally had a plenty, but we ain' fared de bes' by no means. She ain' never give us 'nough to eat; so my mother had to git food de bes' way she could." She continued:

> I 'member one way special. When de preacher come to mistiss' for Sunday morning breakfast, de white folks all git together an' have prayers. Den 'tis my mother tek basket, go in de smoke house, git all de meat she want. When de preacher dere, mistiss ain' bother 'bout nothin'. 'Minds you, we ain' 'lowed to ever put our foot inside de meat house. Ole mistress kept de floor cov-

ered wid sawdus' an' dat smoothed off hit even. An' she better not find nary track in dat sawdus'. Anyhow my mother gwan in dere, but she ain' never fergit to rub out her tracks. We got meat an' my mother ain' got caught neither.[29]

Given the desperate and oppressive circumstances under which they lived, enslaved Africans could not be overly concerned with the masters' definition of the "morality" of behaviors that enhanced their prospects for physical survival and material well-being. The task that they confronted, however, was how to make such individually devised solutions to a collective problem function as a behavioral strategy for the group without endangering their adaptability or the physical well-being of members of their community.

Opportunistically, however, as enslaved Africans pooled their individual memories and contested their abilities as raconteurs in the telling of animal trickster tales in the course of evening entertainments, they soon realized that the basic behaviors of their African animal tricksters and the situations in which their actions unfolded objectified types of situations with which they had not only been all too familiar in Africa but also continued to experience in America. As such, the animal tricksters' actions could continue to serve as a focus for creating an expressive tradition to transmit a conception of behaviors appropriate and beneficial for protecting their values and well-being under the conditions faced in slavery. Therefore, they turned to the African animal trickster whose egocentric and solitary approach to material acquisition and physical survival continued to represent an ideal model of behavior for enhancing the quality of life for African people in America.

The viability of the animal trickster as a model of behavior for enslaved Africans was greatly influenced by the fact that animal trickster tale traditions, though widely distributed and developed around various animals in Africa, reflected, in the most general sense, a view of the world in which individuals who behaved in accordance with the first law of the jungle—survival of the fittest—gain an advantage over forces in the social world inhibitive to material and social well-being. In this regard, the dehumanization of Africans in America was an important catalyst for their transforming and transmitting in oral traditions a conception of the animal trickster as a folk hero. The animal trickster, whose actions were conceptualized as occurring in a context free of the moral and social restraints governing human behavior in the social world, offered an ideal model of adaptive behaviors for those forced to contend with social and material conditions which forced upon the consciousness such a view of their situation. In fact, Africans enslaved in America freely and repeatedly testified to the fact that they envisioned the physical control of the slavemasters over them as placing them in a situation where the demands of physical survival took precedence over the morality of behavior in the peculiar social environment of slavery: "Those whites made us lie," declared one former enslaved African. "We had to lie to live." "They learned us to steal," declared Robert Falls, an African enslaved in Tennessee, of white treatment during slavery. "They didn't half feed us. They fed the animals better. They give the mules the roughages and such, to chaw on all night. But they give us nothing to chaw on. Why we would steal anything we could lay our hands on, when we was hungry. Then they'd whip us for lying when we say we don't know nothing about it. But it was easier to stand when the stomach was full."[30]

In creating animal trickster tales, however, the cultural and practical differences in the situation of Africans in America from those they had known in Africa led to a transformation in the conception of the animal trickster. For example, on the continent, Africans had conceptualized the animal trickster's characteristic actions as advantageous adaptive behaviors in the struggle to protect their socio-religious values and the well-being of their community from behaviors and situations influenced by existence in a harsh natural environment and a rigidly hierarchical social structure. In America, Africans created and re-created tales of the animal trickster to serve as a model of behavior under artificially created conditions of destructive material shortages imposed on them by the power and control of the slavemasters within a socio-political system that they did not accept as legitimate. Of equal importance, Africans on the continent had justified the actions of the trickster as culturally and socially acceptable by opposing them to the practice of magic, a form of subversive behavior that they envisioned as a threat to the values guiding action that they accepted as advantageous to their well-being. In America the enslavers' efforts at control by suppressing African religious expression had a profound influence on how the enslaved were to conceptualize and justify the animal trickster's characteristic behaviors as those facilitating and protecting their values.

The most pronounced effect of the slaveholders' suppression of African religious practices in America was the loss of sacred tricksters and the ability to justify the tricksters' actions in specifically religious terms. Enslaved Africans, however, found in their social relationship to and material and physical treatment by the slavemasters sufficient justification for transmitting in trickster tales a conception of the animal trickster as a folk hero. In reality, the conspicuous disparity between their social status and that of the masters and the differences in their respective material and physical situations did not offer them reasons to envision their situation as resulting from the natural order of things, a worldview implied by the African animal trickster's divine association. They found in these situations sufficient justification for transforming the African animal trickster tale tradition as a model of behavior that helped them maintain the value traditionally placed on native intelligence as a source of behaviors for protecting physical and social well-being. Moreover, they could continue to view their situation as having a clear analogue in nature in which those possessing physical power and those not possessing it were equally endowed with mechanisms for protecting their well-being and survival. In many ways theirs was a world not unlike that inhabited by the animal trickster, in which those who could rely on physical power constantly attempted to create an illusion of harmony to secure their interests at the expense of those who lacked physical power and, therefore, had to rely on their survival instincts.

In essence, the perpetuation of the animal trickster tale tradition in America was greatly influenced by the perception of both similarities and differences in the conditions faced by the enslaved to those they had known in Africa. These conditions, which threatened their ability to maintain the behaviors on which they had traditionally based their identity and values, served as the basis for the conception of the trickster as a folk hero during slavery. Although their African ancestors had turned to the world of nature for a model of trickster-like behavior based on their view of both the natural and social worlds as microcosms of a larger universal order, enslaved Africans were influenced to a greater extent by their view of enslavement as a dehumanizing experience and animalistic behavior as a justifiable response to it. Nevertheless, like their ancestors on the African continent, enslaved Africans embodied their conception of the trickster in tales of animals, primarily Br'er Rabbit and other animals who, in the wild, would have been considered prey for those animals most often acting as dupes. They also continued to portray the animal trickster as possessing a physical stature smaller than that of his dupes against whose physical power the trickster had to match wits for his survival. This physical relationship portrayed in the animal trickster tales of the enslaved, though not the only possible one between trickster and dupe, predominated and allowed enslaved Africans to transmit a conception not only of the behaviors but also of the relationship within which they envisioned behaviors adapted from the animal trickster as morally and socially justifiable. Although the relationship between trickster and dupe consistently allowed them to be placed in situations which served as perfect metaphors for those faced by enslaved Africans as the dehumanized, exploited, and preyed-upon victims of the slavemasters, it also allowed them an opportunity to infuse the trickster tale tradition with a moral and social ethos important for protecting their identity and values from the actions that they associated with the trickster.

Not surprisingly, in the animal trickster tales performed by enslaved Africans, the African animal trickster's superior abilities in acquiring food through wit, guile, and deception became primary topics. In numerous tales, animal tricksters not only acquired the material rewards that they sought but they also routinely violated social contracts in the process:

> Once upon a time Brother Rabbit and Brother Wolf decided to by a cow together. And they bought the cow. So Ber Rabbit tell Ber Wolf that he must go and fetch a knife to butcher the cow with. After Ber Wolf was gone, Ber Rabbit kill the cow, and stuck the tail and horns and feet up in the mud. And begin to cry, "O Ber Wolf! the cow gone down in de mud!" And Ber Wolf run in. And he begin to pull on the cow's horn, and the horn fling him yonder. He pull on the tail, but the tail fling him yonder. And poor Ber Wolf look so pitiful! And Brother Rabbit said the cow gone down in the mud fast as he pull.[31]

In the quest to obtain food and other material rewards, however, the animal tricksters of enslaved Africans interacted and based their actions on the demands of living in a world not unlike that inhabited by the enslaved. Famine or material scarcity is seldom mentioned as a motivation for Br'er Rabbit's actions.

In this regard, the trickster tale tradition of enslaved Africans reflected both the reality of their world and their perception of their situation within it. From their point of view, they were surrounded by an effusion of material plenty yet denied free access to it by the slaveholders' physical control over their lives and the material rewards that they desperately needed. Moreover, as the producers within the slave system, they viewed access to its material rewards as both their right and as essential to their physical well-being. However, enslaved Africans, like the animal trickster, whose world represented a thinly disguised version of their own, did not possess the physical power to openly and directly challenge the masters for their fair share. Consequently, "Of course they'd steal. Had to steal. That the best way to git what they wanted." However, "cose when dey steal dey git caught, an' when you git caught you git beat. I seen 'em take 'em in-a-de barn an' jes tie 'em over lak dis an' den beat 'em 'twell de blood run down."[32] Although enslaved Africans recognized the risks involved in adopting behaviors which attempted to subvert and/or circumvent the masters' physical power and control over their lives, they also accepted the animal trickster's action as a model of behavior for minimizing the risks.

Therefore, in their portrayal of the animal trickster's world, enslaved Africans justified the trickster's actions on the basis of his constant need to protect his well-being in situations in which his physical survival was always in jeopardy. No matter how many times the trickster secured the makings of a meal from his dupes or how clever the ruse he used to escape annihilation in a particular tale, he still emerged in his next adventure as the prey of his dupes, a situation which justified his repeatedly acting in any way that protected his survival. Not uncommonly, the trickster simply emerged as a thief and malicious liar who manipulated others to achieve his goals. For example, one of the most popular animal trickster tales finds Br'er Rabbit in a food sharing scheme with other animals. Although they all presumably have equal access to the food, Br'er Rabbit invariably concocts a ruse which allows him to slip away from his partners to steal the food. When the theft is uncovered, Br'er Rabbit boldly lies and then devises a plan to uncover the culprit, which allows him to place blame on another animal. The wisdom of the trickster's approach to material acquisition and physical survival was not lost on enslaved Africans nor unrelated to recurrent situations faced by them. When viewed within the reality faced by the creators of the tales, the moral and social justification for Br'er Rabbit's duplicity in the literal situation pictured in many of the tales becomes clear. From the viewpoint of enslaved Africans who found themselves consistently short-portioned at the communal dinner table on the plantation, the actions of the trickster in tales in which he victimizes others to cover his deeds can be revealed as a reflection of the kind of situational moral code that they had to embrace to secure their interests and well-being within the slave system.

Despite their importance as models of behavior, the animal trickster tales of enslaved Africans were not intended to provide a literal guide for actions in everyday life, but rather served as an expressive mechanism for transmitting a perception of cleverness, guile, and wit as the most advantageous behavioral options for dealing with the power of the slavemasters in certain generic situations. Therefore, in many tales, the trickster's characteristic and skillful use of wit to achieve a goal was simply played off against the stupidity and ineptness of the dupe in dealing with the same situation:

> Oncet Ber Rabbit know where some heagle-eggs is. An' he wen' back an' tol' Ber Wolf. An' he wen' back de nex' day an' get some mo' eggs. An' tol' Ber Wolf when go dere he mus' say "Veel," an' when he wan' to come out mus' say "Val," and de do' open. An' instead he say "Ber Val," he say "Ber Veel," an' de do' close dat much tighter. An' when Ber Eagle come in, he tol' his daughter to get some flour to bakin' some bread. An' de girl tol' her fader some one in de flour An' when Ber Eagle wen' dere, dere was Ber Wolf in de flour. An' he kill him. An' dat was de las' of Ber Wolf.[33]

Not uncommonly in such tales, the dupe's fate is a severe beating and, sometimes, death, a consequence of ineptness not unknown to enslaved Africans: "I never whip a nigger for stealing, but I'll lick him half to death for being found out," declared a nineteenth-century slaveholder. "They will steal; all nigs will, but if they aren't smart enough to hide it, they deserve to be thrashed, and I tell my niggers so."[34] In essence, animal trickster tales served to remind enslaved Africans not only of the value of behaviors that they associated with the trickster but also of the consequences of acting like the dupe.

In many ways, the sheer number of animal trickster tales that enslaved Africans created and the variety of situations in which they placed the trickster reveal that they recognized that, like their animal trickster, they were in a contest of an indeterminate duration for both physical and cultural survival, with a limited number of ways of protecting themselves without jeopardizing their own well-being within the system. Therefore, both creatively and in their own lives, they had to rely to a great extent on their own ingenuity to develop endless variations on a single theme: the transcendent power of wit. Consequently, in creating animal trickster tales, they repeatedly portrayed the trickster as an actor in types of situations that they were very likely to encounter in the slave system. They also portrayed the trickster as an actor whose characteristic behavior enhanced the possibility of success in dealing with situations peculiar to the slave-master relationship. At the same time, they incorporated, in a number of tales, the idea that, though susceptible to subversive behaviors that undermined their control and power, the antagonists in the battle of wits between trickster and dupe were not stupid. In these tales, the trickster preys on the gullibility of his dupe to reveal that behaviors which proved successful in a particular situation, no matter how clever, were unlikely to work again.

> Man comin' along de road with a kyartload o' fish. Ber Rabbit lay down alongside de road like he dead. De man saw him lay down. De man jump out his kyar' an' pick him up an' t'row him right on de kyartload o' fish. While Ber Rabbit layin' on de kyartload o' fish, he t'rowed enough for 'e to tote. After he t'row enough, den 'e jump off de kyart. An' de man didn' know. After he jump off, den he picked up dose fish. So while he pick up de fish now, he have a chance now to meet Ber Fox. After meet Ber Fox, Ber Fox say, "Ber Rabbit, where you get all dem fish?" He said, "O man! you kyan do like me." Say, "Man, I lay 'longside de road, an' a man comin' wid' kyartload fish. Man pick me up, 'e t'row me on de kyart. An' I t'row as much as I want. Man, I took dem fish, I gone home." He said, "Man, you do jus' like you see me do. Yo go 'longside de road an' lay down, an' dey pick you up an' t'row you on de kyart. Den, man, you will get de fish how I do it." So Ber Wolf [Fox] done de same trick. After he done de trick so, de man come along an' see Ber Wolf lay down 'longside de road. Jump off de kyart, ketch him by de two hin' foot, raise him up. An' lick him on de two hin' wheel, knock him on de wheel-tire. Man said, "You wouldn' done me like Ber Rabbit." He kill Ber Wolf.[35]

Although enslaved Africans, like their trickster, depended to a great extent on their own ingenuity to succeed against their antagonists, the slavemasters, they also relied on the masters' perception of them as inferior beings and blindness to their humanity as important aids to success in their on-going struggle. Like the trickster's dupes who repeatedly fell victim to their own predatory needs and underestimation of the trickster's ingenuity, the slavemasters often blinded themselves to the potential of enslaved Africans to act in their own best interests by a view of them as grateful partners in the system.

> I cannot bear the thought that I have among my servants a wretch so depraved of every sense of gratitude to his mistress and myself as to break open the garden fence in order to rob my small patch

of ten or fifteen small watermelons for to eat or sell in town, when the price it would bring could not be more than perhaps a dollar or a dollar and a half.[36]

While the slavemasters' paternalism supported their own illusion of the slave system as a cooperative enterprise accepted as legitimate by enslaved Africans, it also left them open to trickster-like manipulations which allowed enslaved Africans to gain an advantage in negotiating some of its harsher realities. "I knew that the best way to get around master was to be very humble," wrote Israel Campbell in his autobiography. "I set my wits to work to find out something that would please him."[37] Enslaved Africans permeated the animal trickster tales with their conception of cajoling and flattering behaviors which made the dupes in the battle of wits in the animal world susceptible to manipulation.

> The Fox was after the Rabbit to kill him. So Ber Fox was about to catch Brother Rabbit. There was a well down in the flat between two hills. It had two water buckets, one on each end of the rope. When you let one down, you'd be pulling one bucket up. Brother Rabbit jumped in the bucket was up. Down he went, the other bucket come up. The moon was shining right in the well. It looked like a round hoop of cheese. Ber Rabbit didn't know how he was goin' git back up after he was down there. He commenced hollering for Mr. Fox to come here quick.
> Mr. Fox goes up to the well and looked down in there, says, "What you want, Brother Rabbit?"
> "See this big old hoop of cheese I got down in here?" Says, "Man, it sure is good."
> Ber Fox says, "How did you get down in there?"
> Says, "Git in that bucket up there," says "That's the way I come down." Mr. Fox jumped in that bucket was up, Brother Rabbit jumped in the one was down. Down goes Mr. Fox, up come Brother Rabbit. Brother Rabbit passed Brother Fox. "Hey Brother Fox, this the the way the world goes, some going and some coming."[38]

In the world of the animal trickster, this illusion of a cooperative relationship between trickster and dupe was nowhere better revealed than in the social etiquette that the animals observed in their interactions with each other. Decorously, the animals in the tales addressed each other as "Br'er" and "Sis'" as they victimized and plotted against each other.

Obviously, the worldview which influenced enslaved Africans' finding in the values that they had traditionally associated with the African animal trickster a focus for folk heroic creation under the conditions of slavery is one which derives meaning from an understanding of the workings of the slave system from their point of view. Without taking their perspective into account, their appreciation of and ability to incorporate into their lifestyle behaviors similar to those of animal tricksters appear problematic indeed. For example, collecting animal trickster tales in the late nineteenth century, A. H. M. Christensen noted of her informant that "he regards the rabbit stories with much respect, evidently considering them types of human experience, his own in particular. He praises the Rabbit when successful in spite of his treachery."[39] Ms. Christensen was repulsed by the enthusiasm and delight expressed by her informant for what she viewed as the immoral antics of the wily trickster and warned her readers that "We of the New South cannot wish our children to pause long over these pages."[40] From the point of view of enslaved Africans who created and derived pleasure and meaning from the tales, treachery was not a behavior from which they could protect their children. Slavery itself was a treacherous system in which illusions paraded as reality; it was for its victims the ultimate trick—a trick with words that turned a human being into a piece of property. In the world of enslaved Africans, however, the ways of the treacherous had to be learned, mastered, and dealt with on a daily basis:

Now I tell yer a riddle 'bout Ber Rabbit. In dat part of country he used to dig well. So man wen' aroun' to all de animals, 'cause de animal couldn' get no water, an' ax dem to he'p an' dig de well. So all 'gree, all but Ber Rabbit. Ber Rabbit he refuse. Say he could get water, jew [dew], off de grass an t'ings. So, after de well done dig, all de animals get water dere, an' de man fo'bid Ber Rabbit to get no water to his well. Ev'y mornin' de man go, see Ber Rabbit track roun' de well. So de man wen' after him, an' tell him to keep away from his well. Rabbit say he don' go dere. So de man wen' home an' make a tar baby, an' set him to de well. So 'fo' day he wen' to get his water. He see dis tar baby standin' up right side de well. So he went wid his jug to de well, an' say, "Who you? Who you? You bes' talk. Ef you don' talk, I'll slap you." An' slap him wid one hand', an' dat one fasten on him. "Le' me loose! I'll slap you wid de oder one." Slap him wid de oder one, an' dat one fasten. Said, "Min', I got two mo' laig." Slap him, dat one fasten. Ain't had power to raise de oder one at all.

Day clean. So de fahmer walk down to his well, an' saw Ber Rabbit hangin' on to de tar baby. "Hellow, Ber Rabbit! what you doin'?" — "I come down, suh, an' I see dis t'ing, an' I try to run him f'om yer well, an' he fasten me dere." De man say, "Dis day, Ber Rabbit, I'll t'row you dat brair, cockspu', t'ick' [thicket], together." Rabbit say, "Do, for Gwad's sake, t'row me in de riber! Don' t'trow me in de brair-patch!" De man loosen f'om de tar baby an' star' to t'row him in de riber. "Do, fo' Gawd's sake, t'row me in de riber! Don' t'row me in de briar patch!" De man pick 'em up an' t'row him in de briar-patch. Rabbit say, "Keeng! Keeng! Man, I was born in de briar patch."

Slavery was not a simple system; nor was the socio-cultural environment that it created for enslaved Africans as its preyed-upon victims one that they found easy to negotiate. As the story of the trickster and the tar baby reveals, one of the easiest traps that an enslaved African could get caught up in was that of accepting illusion for reality, especially the illusion of shared identity that the masters were all too capable of creating. However, as the actions of the trickster revealed, the solution to the dilemmas created by existence in an a socio-cultural environment in which trickster and dupe could suddenly reverse their roles was to always remember one's cultural roots. By embracing their roots, enslaved Africans found in their cultural heritage and their tradition of animal trickster tale creation, if not a solution to slavery as an institution, a system of values guiding action which greatly minimized its impact on their lives.

In the animal trickster's status as preyed-upon victim and in his cleverness, guile, and wit, enslaved Africans discovered heroic attributes and behaviors which served as important models of heroic action within their situations. They adapted behaviors associated with the animal trickster, however, within a situation where displaying the ability to think and act on one's own was an attribute which could carry dire physical consequences, especially if the results were perceived as serving their interests rather than those of the masters. It is certainly not accidental that the denouement in many animal trickster tales revolved as much around how the trickster was going to get the makings of his next meal from his dupes as how he was going to escape being their meal. While the physical well-being of enslaved Africans, in a literal sense, was protected up to a point by the masters' interests in protecting their value as negotiable properties, they nevertheless constantly faced the ever-present danger of an even worse form of death—the total surrender of their humanity and identity to the interests of the slave system. Although enslaved Africans undoubtedly recognized the value of their physical well-being to the masters, they also recognized that, by clinging to their own values, they could enhance both their physical and material well-being in ways important to them. They also realized that despite their worth and value in the overall scheme of things in the slave system, and no matter how much they contributed to its productivity, they remained its preyed-upon victims. Consequently, from their point of view, no behavior against those who assumed the right to determine the quality, character, or even cessation of one's existence was too outrageous.

One day the wolf said, "Brother Rabbit, I am going to eat you up." —"No," said Brother Rabbit, "don't eat me! I know where some fine geese is. If you let me tie you here, I will go and get them for you."— "All right," said the wolf. So the rabbit tied the wolf. Then the rabbit went on his way until he came to a farmyard. Then he said, "Farmer, give me trouble." So the farmer went into the yard and get a hound-dog and two hound-puppies and put them in a bag, and said, "When you get out in the field, you must open the bag, and you will have all the trouble you want." —"All right," said the rabbit. So the rabbit went back to the wolf. He waited until he came near the wolf, then he loose the bag and ran the dogs behind him. He ran right straight for the wolf. Wolf said, "Bear off, Rabbit, bear off!" So he saw the rabbit was close upon him, he called out harder, "Bear off, Rabbit, bear off!" The rabbit said, "Not a bit. I am running in straight deal this morning." So the dogs killed the wolf and eat him up. The story is end.[41]

Had enslaved Africans been able to take a straight path in dealing with the power and control of the slavemasters over their lives and literally, rather than metaphorically, feed them to the dogs, the story of black oppression under slavery would have, indeed, ended. However, the reality was that they could not. Nevertheless, they revealed in their animal trickster tales that through wit and trickery they could bring "trouble" to the masters in ways that constantly undermined their efforts to impose on them a value system that they had no reason to accept as a guide for action or as a reflection of their identity. The trickster tales may not have offered patterns of behavior capable of annihilating their real-life antagonists, but they did provide a conception of behaviors which prevented physical and cultural annihilation.

THE RISE OF THE JOHN AND OLD MASTER TRICKSTER TALE CYCLE

The precise point in time that Africans enslaved in America began to perform tales in which John, a human trickster, played a prominent role is impossible to determine. However, the John and Old Master cycle of tales undoubtedly had their origins during the period of black chattel slavery and reflected realities and situations peculiar to the black experience during this era, especially the slave-master relationship. Bruce Dickson, who examined the John and Old Master tales from an historical point of view, concluded that, on the basis of their realistic content, they could easily be conceptualized as anecdotes of slavery.[42] While most enslaved Africans probably accepted the tales as fictional accounts reflective of real-life stituations, some undoubtedly viewed them as "true" accounts of actual experiences, as evidenced by the frequency with which versions of them appear in slave narratives and reminiscences of slave life.[43] Although the tales in which John engages Old Master in an on-going battle of wits involve human actors in social settings recognizable to participants in the slave system, they also reveal that enslaved Africans continued, throughout the period of slavery, to accept trickster-like behaviors as the most advantageous for securing their interests within the slave system. At the same time, the tales in which John serves as a folk hero reveal that, at some point, enslaved Africans discovered the need to redefine (and, therefore, transform their conception of) the trickster figure to maintain the behaviors associated with this character as a symbol of their differential identity and a model of behavior within their community. Specifically, the black conception of John, as a human actor. interacting repeatedly with Old Master, another human actor, indicates that folk heroic creation in the John and Old Master tales was influenced by changes in the perceptions of enslaved Africans concerning their group identity, their situation as the dehumanized victims of the system, and their relationship to the master class.

In the most general sense, the John and Old Master trickster tale cycle suggests that the factors which had led enslaved Africans to find in the animal trickster a model of heroic action changed over time and created a need for transformation. Although enslaved Africans placed a great deal of emphasis on trickster-like behavior as a reflection of their values, their animal trickster tale tradition was precarious from the beginning as an expressive model of heroic action in the socio-cultural environment of the slave system. The differences in socio-cultural characteristics of the slave system from those on the African continent were the primary source of the problematic inherent in the trickster tale tradition of the enslaved. In Africa, the strong communal ethos which had pervaded cultures and the frequent association of the trickster with the gods of particular religions had infused tales of his exploits with allegorical and ritual significance which had, in turn, made them important expressive vehicles embodying a view of moral cause and effect in the African world. In addition, the all-encompassing religious and communal ethos that characterized African community life on the continent minimized the possibility that individuals would misinterpret the actions of tricksters or the values they protected. In America, however, the morality that enslaved Africans associated with the animal trickster was based on the acceptance and recognition of the exploitive socio-economic relationship between slave and master in an illusory communal environment. In essence, enslaved Africans envisioned the trickster's actions as protecting communal values not so much from behavior that threatened them from within as from physical and cultural annihilation from an external force. Consequently, in the slave system, the trickster's actions could be easily misinterpreted, as the trickster's world often appeared to be governed by an individual, secular ethos which envisioned all encounters in terms of a "me" and "them." In the view of the world inherent in the vast majority of slave animal trickster tales, everyone outside of self was ripe for manipulation and exploitation because the distinction between "us" and "them" or between goal-oriented trickery and trickery as a behavior integral to existence was often not explicit in many of the tales.

Nevertheless, in creating their tales, enslaved Africans did attempt to infuse them with a moral and ethical code which would prevent the behaviors associated with the trickster from invading and destroying their own ranks. Through the telling of tales which involved animal tricksters whose characteristic status in the wild was that of prey for those animals acting as dupes, enslaved Africans attempted to inculcate an appropriate attitude toward trickster-like actions, by portraying the relationship between the trickster and dupe as the only type which justified trickster-like actions against another. In addition, they recounted a number of tales in which the animal trickster loses the battle of wits when he attempts to deceive other animals who by virtue of their natural relationship to each other should be allies:

> 'Bout Ber Rabbit an' Ber Pahtridge. Day bof went to kill a cow. An' after done killin' de cow, Ber Rabbit goin' call his brother, mother, sister, an' all, to sha' de meat. Firs' one come was an ol' lady. Say, "Ber Pahtridge, see dat ol' lady? Give him a piece o' meat." Ber Pahtridge take an' gi' him a piece. Ber Pahtridge didn' know it was Ber Rabbit mother. Nex' one comin' along was an ol' man. Jus' de same form. "Ber Pahtridge, give de ol' man a piece o' meat." After what came, bother an' sister come now. "Give de poor boy an' girl a piece o' meat." Pahtridge put a piece o' meat on de fire roastin' it. By that time de boy get out of de way, an' de girl, de meat was done enough fer ter eat. Den de pahtridge commence to eat de meat, and commence ter flutter an' stumble all about an' kick, kick. Then Ber Rabbit cry out, "Mamma! Papa! Brother! Sister! bring dat meat back hyere! It kill Ber Pahtridge." So day all come back. Ber Pahtridge lie like he die. Den Ber pahtridge get up, say, "Now deal jus', suh, sha' just'!"[44]

However, in the majority of the animal trickster tales of enslaved Africans, the idea of just dealings ran counter to the basic message of this tale. More often than not, the animal trickster was portrayed as victorious regardless of whom he victimized.

> In de winter-time some time it be col'. Ber Pa'tridge would light down an' take he head an' put um under-neat' he wing. So Ber Rabbit come along, an' he meet Ber Pa'tridge wid he head underneat' he wing. He ax him, say, "Ber Pa'tridge, whey your head?" Ber Pa'tridge tell him, say, "Man, I leave ma head home." Say, "'Mos' eve'y time I comin' from home, I leave ma head company wid ma wife." Ber Rabbit say, "Den I goin' to do de same t'in'." Ber Rabbit ax Ber Pa'tridge, say, "Well, how you getshyer head off?" He say, "Man, when I ready to go, I jus' go to ma wife an' let ma wife just' knock ma head right off." He said, "But een knockin' you mus' tell yer wife don' knockin' too hard, knock yer head off easy." So Ber Rabbit goin' home an' tell his wife he wan' his head off, but musn' hit um too hard. Den his wife knock off his head. An' he [she] goin' to Ber pa'tridge, an' tell him dat Ber

Rabbit ain't wake up. Den Ber Pa'tridge gone dere, an' tell um, say, "Oh what a pity you knock um too hard!" Pa'tridge still had his head on, an' Rabbit was dead.[45]

That such a trick should be perpetrated on one who, by virtue of physical size and customary status as prey, should be an ally was abominable. Nevertheless, it reflected a situation of intragroup victimization not unknown to enslaved Africans: "They taught us to be against one another," recalled a former enslaved African, "and no matter where you would go you would find one that would be tattling and would have the white folks pecking on us."[46] Within the immoral atmosphere of the slave system, individuals, whether motivated by overwhelming need, a desire for self-advancement, revenge, or even a confused sense of identity, could easily be taken in by the illusion of gain at the expense of their fellow sufferers. Therefore, the loss of one's "head" was an ever-present danger within the slave system.

In many ways, the material and physical conditions under which enslaved Africans lived fostered an attitude toward life in which self-interest could easily take precedence over community allegiance, an attitude that animal trickster tales in the illusory communal environment of the slave system could easily support. In other words, portraying the trickster as an animal interacting repeatedly with other animals could not to any great extent make explicit the precise nature of the relationship between trickster and dupe that made the trickster's actions a reflection of black communal values as opposed to values guiding action in all encounters. In addition, one of the primary catalysts for trickster tale creation by the slave community had been a perception of its situation as one in which its relationship to and dehumanization by the masters, rather than a strong sense of communal values, justified trickster-like behaviors to secure individual interests at the expense of others. Being based initially on a perception of this relationship between the enslaved and the enslavers, the trickster tale tradition as an expressive model of behavior could easily become problematic with changes in either the enslaved's relationship to each other or to the masters. Moreover, as the conception of the trickster was transmitted to new generations of enslaved Africans, this figure could easily become a problematic symbol of group identity and the actions associated with it a threat to the values they were designed to protect. In essence, much as they may have valued the behaviors that they associated with the animal trickster, enslaved Africans did not have in the animal trickster tale tradition a moral or ethical code capable of preventing these behaviors from invading their community or a way of avoiding the consequences such behaviors could have for their well-being with the masters.

From the point of view of enslaved Africans, the need to promote trickster-like behaviors as a reflection of their values was greatly influenced by their view of such actions both as essential to their material and physical well-being and as retaliatory actions against the masters. "We stole so many chickens," declared a former enslaved African, "that if a chicken would see a darky he'd run straight to the house."[47] In any way they could "they schemed to get revenge on their masters without incurring the risk of death," concludes Blassingame. "The offensive weapons included the slowdown, riding their master's horses to death, stealing from him, and breaking his plows and hoes."[48] As long as such behaviors proved beneficial in allowing enslaved Africans to compensate for some of the harsher realities of their existence, they were unlikely to abandon them as a model of behavior. Their view of such actions as both essential and beneficial infused efforts to maintain them with a kind of moral imperative which made it difficult for the enslaved to abandon them. In addition, their acceptance of these behaviors as morally justifiable made it even more difficult for the masters to control them.

From the slavemasters' point of view, the occasional loss of a pig or chicken or being taken in by a particularly clever ruse to escape work or punishment could be ignored. However, they could not allow such actions to go unchecked when they began occurring frequently or on a large scale. While the masters could and did use the trickster-like behavior to support their view of enslaved Africans as amoral children at best and immoral animals at worst, they could not and did not ignore the consequences of trickster-like behavior in the slave quarters or directed against themselves when it threatened their property. Successful trickster-like behavior on a large scale threatened both the masters' control of the slave population and the profitability of the system. As Thomas Affleck noted from the point of view of a slaveholder, "Many planters raise an ample supply of hogs for their families, both black and white. Many more find it a thing impossible, from the destruction of their young stock by the negroes, who have all a particular penchant for roast pig, and especially when stolen."[49] From the masters' point of view, however, control of the slave populations demanded that, for both their economic and personal well-being, they take actions in cases where the violation of their authority and property was evident. As many discovered, however, consistent harsh punishment "made shiftless, careless, and indolent slaves, who being used to the lash as a remedy for every offense, had no fears of it."[50]

The slavemasters' attempts to resolve the dilemma created for them by their recognition of the destructive potential of uncontrolled trickster-like behavior and the limitations of physical punishment in controlling the behavior of their slaves proved opportunistic for black folk heroic creation. Although their actions were undoubtedly motivated primarily by their interests in maintaining and securing their own advantage over the enslaved, the slavemasters, over time, were forced to make concessions to the cleverness of enslaved Africans, who became adept at finding ways to minimize their control and power. One of the most important concessions was to appear to give enslaved Africans increased responsibility for regulating their own behavior on the plantation. A key figure in the masters' plan was the black slave driver who served under the master or overseer. "The term 'driver' itself," according to Genovese, "expresses the primary function of keeping the field hands moving."[51] However, the driver's role was perceived by the slavemasters in much broader terms, as indicated by one slaveowner's description of the position:

> To see that no negro idles or does bad work in the field, and to punish with discretion on the spot. The driver is not to be flogged except by the master but in emergencies that will not admit of delay. He is expected to communicate freely whatever attracts his attention or he thinks information to the owner.[52]

The masters' perception of the social control function of the black driver's role was further illustrated by the fact that "formally designated drivers did not constitute the whole of the foreman category, for the farms and plantations that had no such designated personage normally did have, with or without some title, slave leaders on whom the masters relied."[53] These leaders may have been older slaves, cooks, house servants, coachmen, or any slave who by virtue of intimate contact and a position of trust with the master had his ear, so to speak. In most cases, drivers were given responsibility not only for regulating the pace of work, but also for enforcing the masters' rules in the slave quarters, punishing under the supervision of the master, doling out rations and supplies, and keeping the master informed on issues relating to his property, both human and nonhuman.

From the masters' point of view, the creation of a black foreman class must have appeared to be an ideal solution to the problem of controlling the behavior of their slaves from within. "To moralize and induce the slave to assimilate with the master and his interest has been the great desideration to be aimed at," wrote Charles Pettigrew to his son as he passed the mastership of the plantation to him, "but I am sorry to say I have long since desponded in the completion of this task."[54] As the sense of community among enslaved Africans increased and the masters despaired of ever gaining their allegiance, the black slave driver was latched onto as both a weapon and a shield. By assigning specific enslaved Africans the responsibility of regulating and controlling the behavior of their fellow bondsmen, the masters sought to circumvent their hostility and penetrate the protective shell enveloping the quarters. In the black slave driver, the masters, from their point of view, had an individual who could be held responsible when enslaved Africans violated the rules of the system and whose loyalty could be counted on.

In the case of black slave drivers, however, the masters' plan had a serious flaw: they did not, in most instances, provide the drivers with enough incentives to place the masters' interests above their own or that of their fellow sufferers. Although the masters usually provided black slave drivers with certain benefits denied the majority of enslaved Africans, they, on the whole, subjected them to the same basic conditions and treatment as any other black person in the system. While most drivers could look foward to an extra allotment of food and clothing, better living conditions than their fellow sufferers, their pick of women on the plantation, and less rigorous and demanding work, they remained "slaves" and, in some instances, because of their increased responsibilities and visibility to the master, became more subject to the lash, public and private humiliation by the master, and being sold away.[55] Therefore, while some drivers were unfailingly loyal, and others loyal up to a point, most clearly placed their own interests first.

As human beings who craved status, most black drivers and others privileged by the masters as leaders undoubtedly saw their positions as an important recognition of their potential as human beings. However, as members of an oppressed and degraded black community, these individuals realized that "they were black and knew that no accomplishment would change their station—the constraints of being black inexorably prevailed."[56] Although some black slave drivers in particular garnered reputations for being extremely cruel, their reputations and the harsh evaluation of their actions by enslaved Africans were undoubtedly influenced, in most instances, by the very fact that they were black. Therefore, regardless of their level of commitment to the masters and their duties, blacks in the foreman class had to be sensitive to the fact that they were in a precarious situation. On the one hand, they had to perform at a level of efficiency and produce results that satisfied the masters. On the other hand, to maintain their positions required the cooperation of their fellow sufferers. In their interaction with other blacks, they acted with the knowledge that they not only had to live among them but were also often related by blood to many. Consequently, despite the privileges that being a favorite of the master could offer an individual personally, individuals in positions of favor with the masters frequently exploited their roles for the benefit of their own community. The duplicity with which such individuals acted was most clearly exemplified in the actions of black slave drivers. In slave narratives and reminiscences, enslaved Africans often recalled how certain black slave drivers exploited situations and the masters' trust in them for the benefit of their fellow sufferers:

Anytime old Marsa get a slave dat been cuttin' up or sumepin' he tell Gabe [the black driver] to give dat slave a lashin'. Sometimes he come down to de barn to watch it, but most times he jus' set on de porch an' listen to de blows. Ole Gabe didn't like dat whippin' bus'ness, but he couldn't he'p hisself. When Marsa was dere, he would lay it on 'cause he had to. But when ole Marsa warn't lookin', he never would beat dem slaves. Would tie de slave up to one post an' lash another one. 'Cose de slave would scream an' yell to satisfy Marsa, but he wasn't gettin' no lashin'. After while Gabe would come out de barn an' ast Marsa if dat was enough. "Sho, dat's plenty," say Marsa. Once ole Gabe was beatin' de post so hard an' de slave was yellin' so dat Marsa call out to Gabe, "Quit beatin' dat nigger, Gabe. What you tryin' to do, kill him?" Slave come runnin' out screamin' wid berry wine rubbed all over his back an' Marsa tole Gabe if he didn't stop beatin' his slaves so hard, he gonna git a lashin' hisself.[57]

In addition to deceptive practices such as the one described above, many black slave drivers, to maintain their social well-being in the slave community, took advantage of their position of trust in the absence of the masters. They allowed the slaves to work at a more leisurely pace, hold unsupervised religious meetings, or attend parties on neighboring plantations; slipped them extra food and clothing when they could get away with it; and they turned their heads to petty thefts and feigned illnesses to avoid work.[58] On the other hand, to maintain their credibility with the masters, black slave drivers "asserted their authority and resolutely crushed, when they could, all challenges from below."[59]

The rise of a black foreman class during the period of black chattel slavery had a profound influence on the black perception of both self and the relationship between the enslaved and the enslavers. As the most representative and visible member of this class, the black slave drivers' position of authority and responsibility, which paralleled that of the masters in many respects, represented not only an important change in the social structure of the slave system but also the most important concession to black humanity granted an enslaved African. However, their continued dehumanization, reflected most clearly in their being kept in bondage, revealed the intransigency of the masters' view of all blacks as beings whose humanity would never be completely conceded. Consequently, black drivers, like all enslaved Africans, found that in dealing with the masters the most advantageous behaviors were ultimately those which exploited the masters' view of them as little more than trained animals.

Nevertheless, by altering the slave system's hierarchy to include a black foreman class, the masters made an inadvertent concession to black humanity. This concession proved opportunistic for enslaved Africans who found in it a means of perpetuating their tradition of heroic creation in which the trickster's actions served as model of behavior. More importantly, from the point of view of the enslaved, the relationship with the masters which had formed the basis on which the slaves conceptualized and justified the animal trickster as a folk hero had been altered. In the absence of blacks in supervisory positions, enslaved Africans related to the masters or their surrogates, the white overseers, in face-to-face encounters on a daily basis. Moreover, the most frequent contact occurred in a context in which the masters' power and control over their lives and the rewards of the system were very much in evidence—in rationing out supplies, doling out orders, regulating their work both in the house and field, and exacting punishment. On the basis of these types of encounters, enslaved Africans were confronted daily with certain proof that the masters viewed them as beasts of burden, incapable of defining their own human and physical needs. Therefore, they experienced little difficulty in transmitting through the telling of animal trickster tales a conception of the relationship which made the animal trickster's actions an ideal model of behavior for securing the means of physical survival at the expense of the masters. However, the relationship of enslaved Africans to the masters changed with the imposition of the black slave driver into the system's power structure in that the majority of slaves no longer on a regular basis related face-to-face to the masters but rather with a member of their own community. This situation, which could influence individuals' perceptions of their identity and situation vis-à-vis the masters, also affected their ability to use the animal trickster's actions as a model of behavior justifiable in terms of their relationship to the slave system's power structure.

As enslaved Africans became familiar with the the presence of black slave drivers, they found in the black slave driver an ideal focus for folk heroic creation to protect the values associated with the trickster in their community and their identity as human beings. The black slave driver's precarious situation which forced him to display wit, guile, and deception in dealings with the master, and, in some instances, members of his own community, proved opportunistic for black folk heroic creation in terms of the trickster.[60] The conception of the driver as a trickster hero was embodied in tales revolving primarily around the exploits of John and his constant antagonist, Old Master. In the tales of John and Old Master, enslaved Africans made John a human trickster whose status within the slave system and relationship to the master closely resembled that of slave drivers. In the tales they portrayed John as a talented and skillful exploiter of his exploitation by Old Master, his dupe or foil in most of the tales. Although John emerged victorious in many of his exploits, the John and Old Master tales exhibited a far more complex view of trickster-like behavior than did the animal trickster tales.

Although John almost invariably attempts to take advantage of his position of intimacy and trust with Old Master for his own personal gain, his humanity, or, more precisely, his potential as a human being, is often an implicit issue in the tales of his exploits:

Coon in the Box

Durin' slavery time dere was an' ole slave who usta steal an' hide ev'ything he git his hands on. One day his mastah los' his ridin' coat and he called John an' tole im'

"All right," said John, "I'll git it fo' you."

Then after that ev'ything Mastah los' he call John to git it. He thought John knowed ev'ything an' could find ev'ything. So one day de mastah made a bet on John. He betted de next plantation owner dat he had a smart nigger dat knowed ev'ything an' that's whar de bet come in.

"What you be?" ax the next plantation owner.

"I bet my farm 'gainst yours dat John kin tell you anything you want to know!"

"Well, dat's a bet," said de plantation owner. "I'll git a coon, put 'im inna box an' give John three guesses. Ef he guess right, my farm is yourn."

John come out looking wise, wonderin' what dey was gonna do wid 'im. He went on de stage, looked all 'round an' his mastah say: "What's in dat box, John?"

"It's a cat."

De mastah looked worried but de otter mastah was glad John couldn't answer.

"Another guess," he yelled. "What's in dat box?"

"Taint no cat; it's a rabbit I reckon."

John's Mastah got nervous, 'cause he thought he gonna lose his farm.

"One more guess," said John Mastah. "What's in dat box?"

"Well," said John, "de ole black coon bin caught at las'!"

So John's mastah win de other mastah's farm.[61]

Not uncommonly, as in "Coon in the Box," John finds himself confronted with a dilemma created by his claim to some superhuman ability on which Old Master attempts to make "capital". The resolution of the tales, however, reveals that John's real advantage in dealing with situations peculiar to the slave-master relationship lay in his talent, hidden from the master by an animalistic view of him, to think and act in his own best interest.

If we can draw conclusions from the number of times that tales in which John must guess the identity of an invisible animal have been collected or culled from slave reminisences (as is the case with the one just cited), the "Coon in the Box," as a general title for the tale, was by far the most popular in the John and Old Master cycle. In many ways, the dilemma John faced in this situation revealed that enslaved Africans were aware of what Mintz and Price characterize as the "central contradiction" inherent in the slave-master relationship:

Slaves were defined legally as property; but being human, they were called upon to act in sentient, articulate and human ways: the slaves were not animals, even if the barbarities visited upon them were inhuman. The often unquestioning acceptance of their right to treat the slaves as if they were not human rationalized the system of control. In practice, however, it is abundantly clear that the masters did recognize that they were dealing with fellow humans, even if they did not want to concede as much.[62]

Through John's characteristic actions in this tale, enslaved Africans were able to reinforce and transmit their perception of wit as the most advantageous behavior in dealing with the masters' exploitation and treatment of them as animals. In most versions of this tale, John, in a symbolically significant action, scratches his head prior to correctly guessing the identity of the varmint. Of equal symbolic significance in such tales is Old Master's readiness to exploit John's bogus claim to exceptional skill or talent and his complete blindness to John's final admission of human failure.

Even if this contradiction inherent in the treatment of enslaved Africans, especially those elevated to positions of intimacy and trust, was lost on the masters, it did not escape the slave population's notice. Instead, they incorporated their perception of it again and again in the John and Old Master tales. In tales such as "Coon in the Box," Old Master attempts to exploit John's humanity for his own economic gain while John escapes physical annihilation by exploiting the master's view of him as an animal by appropriating the master's terminology for members of his community, a term which, in itself, denies black humanity. Enslaved Africans, however, could envision Old Master's exploitation and blindness to John's claim of mere human abilities as a clear parallel to their own situation, one which allowed them to envision John's actions in various tales as justifiable regardless of how outrageous and, in some instances, self-effacing they may have appeared.

The Swimming Contest

The master and his wife were leaving on a ship—probably for the Old Country, since they were going away from this country. So the slave stowed away, and when they got nearly to land he began to call out, "Oh, Massie George, oh, Missie George." At first it sounded faint, and then it kept getting louder. They said, "That must be John," but they couldn't believe it. He slipped out and began swimming toward the boat. So they pulled him aboard, all dripping, and asked him how he got there. "Well, I swim all the way here; I wasn't going to let you leave me."

So he went along with them, and his master was bragging about how he had the best swimmer in the world. There was a white swimmer parading around, and they made a date with him to have a contest. The day of the contest he was waiting on the beach, until finally the colored man came, puffing and making a lot of noise, with a cookstove and provisions on his back. He said,

"Where's that white fellow who's goin' to swim with me?" (in a big voice). The white man said, "Here I am" (in a little voice). John said, "Man, ain't you carrying nothing to eat with you?" He answered "No." "Well, you'd better, for I'm a-fixing to stay." The white man ran away.[63]

If enslaved Africans could not live up to or, more likely, down to the masters' erroneous view of their humanity, they discovered that they could exploit and manipulate it to achieve their own ends.

In contrast to the animal trickster tales in which enslaved Africans used the portrayal of the trickster as natural prey for his dupes to attempt to transmit a conception of the nature of the relationship which justified trickster-like actions against another, they left little room for doubt in the John and Old Master tales. John, though a trusted and constant companion of Old Master, was a "slave," subject to the whims and passions of his owner. In addition, enslaved Africans demonstrated little concern with defining the nature of trickster-like behaviors by endlessly devising plots to portray the actions of John as a trickster. Since they did not abandon the animal trickster tale tradition, they possessed a storehouse of trickster-like actions. The problem they faced was how to protect the values guiding action that they associated with the trickster in the face of an illusion of dramatic changes in their relationship with the masters. Therefore, in the John and Old Master tales, enslaved Africans made one of their emphases, as revealed in the divergence of outcomes, the appropriate use of trickster-like behavior in dealing with situations peculiar to existence in the slave system. To this end, tales in which John schemes to advance his interests in one-on-one contests of wits with Old Master consistently end in a victory for John.[64] In some, he both gained the material reward resulting from his behavior and succeeded in making Old Master look foolish in the process.

Old Marster Eats Crow

John was hunting on Old Marster's place, shooting squirrels, and Old Marster caught him, and told him not to shoot there any more. "You can keep the two squirrels you got but don't be caught down here no more." John goes out the next morning and shoots a crow. Old Marster went down that morning and caught him, and asked John to let him see the gun. John gave him the gun, an Marster put the shell in the gun. Then he backed off from John, pointing the gun, and told John to pick the feathers off the crow, halfway down. "Now start at his head, John, and eat the crow up to where you stopped picking the feathers at." When John finished eating, Marster gave him the gun back and throwed him the crow. Then he told John to go on and not let him be caught there no more.

John turned around and started off, and got a little piece away. Then he stopped and turned and called Old Marster. Old Marster says, "What you want, John?" John pointed the gun and says, "Lookee here, Old Marster," and throwed Old Marster half the crow. "I want you to start at his ass and eat all the way, and don't let a feather fly from your mouth."[65]

On the other hand, tales in which John attempts to exploit Old Master by involving other enslaved Africans usually end in disaster for him.

Master Disguised

Ev'y winter dat de mawsah go to Philamadelphia, always go to New York. Him hab all de key. An' he look after de whole house 'til his mawsah come back. So when his mawsah go, he go all 'roun' an' inwite all de neighbors, an' have big dance. Dress up in his mawsah suit. Dat time dere never use to be no fiddle, beat wid a stick on de flo'. Goin' all 'roun'. so his mawsah t'ink he ketch him now, see waht him doin'. "John, goin' off to-morro to Philamadelphia."—"All right, mawsah, tak kyare of everyt'in'." Mawsah gone. Mawsah go in de wood, stay in de wood dat night 'til de dance start. So de mawsah muddy up hisse'f. Come whey he hear de beat. He all de time have a man at de do' to watch to tu'n people in. Man say, "Raf' man out dere." So he come to de do'. "What you doin' here?"—"I jus' kyarryin' de raf' here, such!"—"Come in here, suh!" Sit right down, poor buckra! Mawsah gone to Philmadelphia. Po'-Buckra! kan you read?"— "Yes, suh! I can read a little bit, suh."—Come hyeah!" Kyarry to mawsah pantry. "Read dat!"—"Dat brandy." Po' pint o' dat. "Wat dis yere?"—"Dat rum."—"Give me a gallon o' dat. What are dey?"—"Dat wine."—"All right, two quart o' dat. Come back now, po'-buckra!" So de driver wife look at de man so. Say, "Dat man look like mawsah."—"Mawsah gone to Philmadelphia. Poor buckra! Gi' him somet'in to eat." Mawsah in de dark wipe off mud from his face. An' den he saw it was mawsah. He flew in de wood, an' be in de wood two year.[66]

As in "Master Disguised," Old Master's actions in some tales revealed the awareness of enslaved Africans that, in the world of tricks, none could be more tricky than the master himself. The master's skillful manipulation of individuals, such as black slave drivers, to exploit and control their fellow sufferers demonstrated that he was a force to be reckoned with in the world of tricks. As enslaved Africans developed a sense of themselves as a community united against the interests of the masters, the behavior of individuals who were willing to advance themselves with the masters at the expense of their own community became problematic. Within the situation that they confronted, individuals whose actions, whether intentional or inadvertent, supported the interests of the masters threatened the entire slave community's ability to maintain behaviors valued as ways of securing material and physical well-being. John, in not foreseeing the potential of Old Master to act deceptively in "Master Disguised," placed himself as well as members of his community in a position to be further exploited and abused through physical punishment.

In a number of tales, John acts in a more deliberate manner to involve other enslaved Africans in his schemes and, in the process, makes them dupes. In these tales, John's success depends on his fellow sufferers accepting his actions as models of behavior. In one tale, for example, John displays a generous gift which he claims is a reward for having cursed Old Master:

> Thereupon two or three of the men went to the house and began cursing the master to his face, and he in turn gave each a handsome flogging. As soon as they could, they, of course, went for John to find out what he meant by telling them such a tale. His reply was, "Yes, I did curse him, but I cursed him at the big gate."[67]

In other versions of this trick, John claims that he placed his hand under the mistress's dress without incurring any punishment. Only after his fellow sufferers have emulated what they believed to be John's example and received the inevitable flogging does he tell them that the mistress was not wearing the dress at the time. In these tales, John's apparent act of intragroup victimization seems less salient as the point of the tales than his dupe's literal-mindedness which causes them to be punished. The dupes in these narratives are revealed less as victims of John's trickery than as numskulls whose ineptness in dealing with the ambiguities and subtleties of the slave system jeopardizes their well-being. Their jeopardy results from their failure to recognize that John, despite the appearance of intimacy with Old Master and the mistress, is a member of their community whose actions reflect their values when it comes to interaction with masters and mistresses. In his admission of trickery as the key to his success in these situations, John reminds the audience for the tales of the values guiding action accepted within their community.

The consequences of acting on the illusion created by the appearance of intimacy with the masters were not confined to those who viewed it from a distance. In a real sense, those who became intimates of the masters could more easily be taken in by a literal acceptance of their responsibilities and duties as a legitimate recognition of their humanity than those who had a marginal relationship to the masters. Therefore, it is not surprising that as a "trusty" of Old Master, John emerges as a numskull or flunky over whom Old Master triumphs in a number of tales. In these tales, John's blind allegiance to Old Master threatens both his well-being and, as often, other members of the community.

Dividing Souls

During the period of slavery time Old Marster always kept one slave that would keep him posted on the others, so that he would know how to deal with them when they got unruly. So this slave was walking around in the moonlight one night. And he heard a noise coming from the cemetery. And it was two slaves counting apples, which they had stole from Old Marster's orchard. They couldn't count, so they were exchanging 'em. "You take dis un and I'll take dat un. Dis un's yours and dat un's mine."

So this slave hear them, and he listened, and he ran back to Old Marster. And running he fell over a skeleton head, and he spoke to the skeleton head. "What you doing here?"

And the skeleton head said, "Same thing got me here will get you here."

So he told Old Marster when he got to the house that the Devil and the Good Lord was in the cemetery counting out souls. "Dis un's yours and dat un's mine, dis un's yours and dat un's mine."

Old Marster didn't believe him, but he went with him to the cemetery. And Old Marster told him, said, "Now if the Devil and the Good Lord ain't counting out souls I'm goin to cut your head off."

Sure enough the slaves had gone and Old Marster didn't hear anything, and he cut John's head off. Then John's head fell beside the skeleton head. Then the head turned over and said, "I

told you something that got me here would get you here. You
talk too much."[68]

John's punishment in this tale reveals the value that the slave community placed on discretion in dealing with the masters, a value clearly
threatened by the actions of those members of the community who
accepted the responsibility for protecting the masters' interests in the
system. Enslaved Africans viewed the violations of this norm as important enough to reiterate the norm in a number of tales. In another
group of tales, John is warned by a talking animal about his penchant
for indiscreet talk. However, John ignores the warning and immediately reports to Old Master his discovery of the animal's ability to
speak:

Talking Turtle

Every day John had to tote water from the bayou, and every time
he'd go to the bayou he would start fussin'. "I'm tired of toting
water every day." The next day he went to the bayou and he repeated the same thing (you know just like you repeat the same
thing). So last one day John went to the bayou, the turtle sittin
on a log.

Turtle raised up and looked at him, and told John, "Black man,
you talk too much."

So John didn't want to think the turtle was talking. He went
back to the bayou, got another bucketful of water. The turtle told
him the same thing. John throwed the buckets down, took and
run to the house, and called Old Marster, and told him the turtle
was down there talking. As so Old Marster didn't want to go because he didn't believe it. But John kept telling him the turtle
was talking. So finally Old Boss 'cided he could go. But he told
John if the turtle didn't talk he was going to give him a good beating. So they all went on down to the bayou, and when they got
down to the bayou the turtle was sitting on a log with his head
back halfway in his shell.

And so John told the turtle, "Tell Old Marster what you told
me." So John begged the turtle to talk. So the turtle still didn't
say anything. So Old Marster taken him back to the house, and
give him a good beating, and made him git his buckets, and keep
totin' water.

When John got back down to the bayou, the turtle had his head
sticking up. John dipped up his water, and the turtle raised up

and told him, says, "Black man, didn't I tell you you talked too much?"[69]

Even if we ignore the symbolism of a talking animal offering John advice, we can nevertheless appreciate the tale as a revelation of black communal values in the slave system. Invariably, John is punished for his failure to heed the advice of the animal or, more precisely, his blind trust in Old Master's willingness to accept his reality.

The conception of John as a transformation of the animal trickster allowed the tales of his exploits to reflect enslaved Africans' changing insights about the "shape of time and history." In turning to a human actor to create heroic tales revolving around trickster-like actions, enslaved Africans clearly enhanced their ability to transmit their conception of the trickster as a reflection of their identity and the trickster's actions as a model of behavior for their community. In the John and Old Master tales, John's characteristic actions served constantly to remind enslaved Africans of their identity as the exploited human victims of a system which made animalistic behaviors the most advantageous for securing their interests. Whether John emerged victorious over Old Master or appeared as a numskull over whom Old Master triumphed was less important in their evaluation of John's actions than the fact that the tales revealed the master-slave relationship as one which justified trickster-like behavior. In addition, regardless of the outcome in a particular tale, enslaved Africans were able constantly to remind members of their community that their relationship to the masters was one characterized by conflict, in which victory on either side would most likely be only temporary. However, the tales also reminded the enslaved that they had in the trickster a source of behaviors guiding actions that gave them an advantage in negotiating the slave system.

NOTES

1. Octave Thanet, "Folklore in Arkansas," *Journal of American Folklore* 5(1892):121.

2. T. F. Crane, "Plantation Folklore," *Popular Science Monthly* (1880): 824–33; A. E. Ellis, "Evolution in Folklore: Some West African Prototypes of the Uncle Remus Stories," *Popular Science Monthly* (1895): 93–104; A. Gerber, "Uncle Remus Traced to the Old World," *Journal of American Folklore* (1893): 243–57.

3. William Owens, "Folklore of the Southern Negroes," *Lippincott's Magazine* 20(1877): 748.

4. Joel Chandler Harris, *Uncle Remus: His Songs and Sayings* (New York: Penguin Books, 1982 reprint) 57.

5. Harris 45.

6. Harris 44.

7. Alan Dundes offers a brief summary of the theories of folklore origins in the nineteenth century in *The Study of Folklore* (Englewood Cliffs, N.J.: Prentice-Hall, 1976) 53–56.

8. For an informative summary of theories of the effects of slavery on Africans and African culture in America, see Adrienne Lanier Seward, "The Legacy of Early Afro-American Folklore Scholarship," in *Handbook of American Folklore*, ed. Richard M. Dorson (Bloomington: University of Indiana Press, 1983) 48–56.

9. George M. Frederickson, *The Black Image in the White Mind* (New York: Harper Torchbooks, 1971). Frederickson offers extended analysis of the dualism which characterized white thinking about blacks with particular emphasis on the late nineteenth century. He also offers informative analysis of Joel Chandler Harris who he claims attempted to use Afro-American animal trickster tales in combination with the character of Uncle Remus to integrate these incongruous perspectives.

10. A. H. M. Christensen, *Afro-American Folk Lore* (New York: Negro University Press, 1892).

11. Thanet 122.

12. Richard M. Dorson, *American Negro Folktales* (Greenwich, Conn: Fawcett Publications, Inc., 1967) 15–16.

13. See, for example, the essays on the African origins of Afro-American folktales in Daniel J. Crowley, *African Folklore in the New World* (Austin: University of Texas Press, 1977).

14. Lawrence W. Levine, *Black Culture and Black Consciousness:Afro-American Folk Thought from Slavery to Freedom* (New York: Oxford University Press, 1977) 82.

15. Roger D. Abrahams, *Deep Down In the Jungle: Negro Narrative Folklore from the Streets of Philadelphia* (Chicago: Aldine, 1970) 64. Similar conclusions concerning black folk heroic creation in terms of the animal trickster can also be found in Bruce Jackson, *Get Your Ass in the Water and Swim Like Me: Narrative Poetry from Black Oral Tradition* (Cambridge, Mass.: Harvard University Press, 1974); Fred O. Weldon, "Negro Folktale Heroes:" 170–89.

16. Susan Feldmann, *African Myths and Tales* (New York: Dell Publishing, 1963) 15.

17. Feldmann 15–16.

18. Jay D. Edwards, *The Afro-American Trickster Tale: A Structural Analysis* (Bloomington, Ind.: Folklore Pulication Group, 1978) 57.

19. Feldmann 17.

20. I will discuss in depth in the next chapter the role of magic in defining social behavior. Numerous writers have offered analysis of African religious and society with particular emphasis on the role of magic. See, for example,

John S. Mbiti, *African Religions and Philosophy* (Garden City, N.Y.: Doubleday, 1970); E. A. Ruch and K. C. Anyanwu, *African Philosophy* (Rome: Catholic Book Agency, 1984): E. J. Marias, *African Thought* (Cape Province: Fort Hare University Press, 1972).

21. Feldmann 17.

22. Feldmann 17.

23. Frederick Douglass, *My Bondage and My Freedom* (New York: Miller, Orton, and Mulligen, 1855) 87.

24. William D. Postell, *The Health of Slaves on Southern Plantations* (Baton Rouge: Louisiana State University Press, 1951) 26.

25. Postell devotes considerable attention to the relationship between diet and illness among enslaved Africans. In addition, this topic will be explored more fully in Chapter 3.

26. John W. Blassingame, *The Slave Community* (New York: Oxford University Press, 1972) 158. Also, see, Eugene Genovese, *Roll, Jordan, Roll: The World the Slaves Made* (New York: Vintage Books, 1976) 603–04 and 638–39.

27. From an interview with William Brooks in Charles L. Perdue, Jr., Thomas E. Burden, and Robert K. Phillips, eds., *Weevils in the Wheat* (Bloomington: Indiana University Press, 1976) 57.

28. Solomon Northup, *Twelve Years A Slave* (New York: Dover Publications, 1970) 169.

29. Perdue, et al. 201–02.

30. From an interview with Robert Falls in Norman R. Yetman, ed., *Voices of Slavery* (New York: Holt, Rinehart and Winston, 1970) 116.

31. Elsie Clews Parsons, *Folklore of the Sea Islands, South Carolina* (New York: American Folklore Society, 1923) 31.

32. Perdue, et al. 57.

33. Parsons 36.

34. Elizabeth Batume, *First Days Amongst the Contraband* (Boston, 1893) 279.

35. Parsons 89.

36. From an 1834 entry in the plantation records in the Jackson-Prince papers in the Southern Historical Collection at the University of North Carolina, excerpted in Genovese 601.

37. Israel Campbell, *An Autobiography* (Philadelphia, 1861) 62.

38. Dorson, *American Negro Folktales* 97–98.

39. Christensen 2.

40. Christensen xii.

41. Parsons 67.

42. Bruce Dickson, Jr., "The 'John and Old Master' Stories and the World of Slavery: A Study in Folktales and History," *Phylon* 35 (1974): 422.

43. Dickson 422.

44. Parsons 30–31.

45. Parsons 34.

46. Unidentified source quoted in Genovese 622.

47. Fisk University, *Unwritten Record of Slavery: Autobiographical Accounts of Negro Ex-Slaves* comp. and ed. Ophelia Settle Egypt, J. Musuoka, and Charles S. Johnson (Washington, D. C., 1968 [1945]).

48. Blassingame 211.

49. From Thomas Affleck, communication to U. S. commission of patents, *Report On Agriculture*, 1849, 62, excerpted in Genovese 600.

50. Blassingame 211.

51. Genovese 366. Also see Blassingame 161–62. Both authors discuss the role of the black slave drivers in some detail.

52. From Plantation Manual in the Hammond Papers, excerpted in Genovese 382.

53. Genovese 366.

54. B. McBride, "Directions for Cultivating Various Crops Grown at Hickory Hill," *American Agriculturalists* 3(May 1830): 238.

55. Genovese 370; Blassingame 161–62.

56. Genovese 378.

57. Perdue, et al. 290–91.

58. Genovese 380–84; Blassingame 210.

59. Genovese 378.

60. In African folklore, trickster tales developed around the exploits of humans who acted in the role of trickster were not uncommon.

61. From an interview with Tessie White in Perdue, et al. 312.

62. Mintz and Price 13.

63. Dorson, *American Negro Folktales* 131–32.

64. Dickson 424–425.

65. Dorson, *American Negro Folktales* 164–65.

66. Parsons 76–77.

67. *Southern Workman*, XXV (September, 1895) 185.

68. Dorson, *American Negro Folktales* 146–47.

69. Dorson, *American Negro Folktales* 148–49.

The Power Within:
The Conjurer as Folk Hero

He [the African priest or medicine-man] appeared early on the
plantation and found his function as the healer of the sick, the
interpreter of the unknown, the comforter of the sorrowing, the
supernatural avenger of wrong, and the one who rudely but pic-
turesquely expressed the longing and disappointment of a stolen
and oppressed people.[1]

W.E.B. Du Bois

Throughout the period of black chattel slavery in the United States,
slaveholders and observers of slavery noted the existence of individuals whom enslaved Africans regarded with a kind of religious awe.
Referred to by enslaved Africans variously as conjurers, hoodooers,
rootworkers, and two-heads, these individuals commanded a great
deal of respect from fellow Africans who enshrined them as folk heroes and recalled their deeds in oral narratives generally referred to
as conjure tales. Unlike the fictive animal trickster whose existence as
a folk hero in folktales went virtually unrecorded in the written records of whites during slavery, conjurers were frequently mentioned by
whites who regarded their influence over enslaved Africans as a challenge to their own authority and designs:

On every large plantation of Negroes there is one among them
who holds great sway over the minds and opinions of the rest; to
him they look as the oracle—and this same oracle is, in ninety-
nine cases the most consummate villain and hypocrite on the
premise. It is more likely that he has seen sundry miraculous visions, equal to those of John on the Isle of Patmos; angels have
talked with him, etc., etc. The influence of such a negro is incal-
culable. He steals his master's pigs, and is still an object com-

manding the peculiar regard of Heaven, and why may not his disciples?[2]

While few whites professed belief in the "alleged" magical or supernatural powers that enslaved Africans attributed to conjurers, they nevertheless acknowledged conjurers' real ability to influence slave behavior and frequently expressed concern over its implications for their own well-being:

> On certain occasions they have been made to believe that while they carried about their persons some charm with which they had been furnished, they were invulnerable. They have, on certain other occasions, been made to believe that they were under a protection that rendered them invincible. That they might go any where and do any thing they pleased, and it would be impossible for them to be discovered or known; in fine, to will was to do—safely, successfully. They have been known to be so perfectly and fearfully under the influence of some leader or conjurer that they have not dared disobey him in the least particular; nor to disclose their own intended or perpetrated crimes, in view of inevitable death itself; notwithstanding all other influences brought to bear upon them.[3]

Whites often viewed the respect that enslaved Africans accorded the conjurer not only as a threat to their authority and physical well-being but also as a clear affront to the enlightened Christian values that they attempted to instill in their chattel. The threat in the latter instance issued primarily from the white view of conjuration as a retention of African values among their slaves—a system of values that whites viewed as dangerous because of associations with "Pagan darkness, idolatry and superstition" emanating from a savage African past.[4] While many slaveholders undoubtedly accepted the practice of conjuration among enslaved Africans as innocent superstitious behavior and used it to confirm their view of them as naive children, Eugene Genovese argues that "most [whites] feared the effects of strange beliefs on their slaves and tried to suppress them. Plantation papers usually mention voodoo, conjure, and superstition as something to be abhorred and punished, and the blacks similarly reported their masters' hostility."[5]

Despite the efforts of slaveholders to eradicate the practice of conjuration, students of African American folklore and culture in the years following emancipation documented the persistence of beliefs in the powers of conjurers. For instance, Julien A. Hall, an early collector of black folklore, asserted that

> Beliefs of the negro race in regard to 'conjuring' and 'tricking' were brought from Africa by the first comers and continue in full force to this day, notwithstanding the negro is a freedman and living amongst the white people of the United States, who are probably as practical as any human beings on earth. They firmly believe that certain ones amongst them are able to conjure or trick those they have a grudge against, and when one is supposed to be possessed of this ability he is called a "conjure doctor," and is looked up to by the others with the profoundest awe and dread. The conjure doctor's word is law, and he can generally live without working, as he frightens his companions into contributing freely to his support.[6]

Most early students and collectors agreed with Hall's assessment that black belief in conjuration was widespread and that conjuration as practiced in the black community was purely an African derived tradition. Leonora Herron, who, along with Alice Bacon, offered one of the earliest systematic examinations of the tradition, characterized the belief in conjuration as a "relic of African days" which existed in the present as a "gruesome conglomeration of fetishism, divination, quackery, incantation and demology" practiced by conjurers both "disliked and feared" by blacks.[7] Louis Pendleton, critiquing Phillip A. Bruce's *The Plantation Negro as Freedman* in the *Journal of American Folklore*, noted that the blacks described by Bruce "have as firm a belief in witchcraft as those savages of the African bush who file their teeth and perforate the cartilage of their noses. Mr. Bruce proceeds to describe communities in rural Virginia, which so far resemble an African tribe as to have a professional 'trick doctor,' who is far more important than a preacher and who indeed follows a more lucrative pursuit."[8]

In the late nineteenth century, the collection and documentation of beliefs in conjuration established the existence in the black community of a coherent system of beliefs revolving around the actions of conjurers. Most students of the tradition attributed the coherence and wide distribution of conjure beliefs to a generalized African heritage in which magic, superstition, and witchcraft were commonplace. To explain the perpetuation of occult practices among blacks in America, they consistently pointed to the fact that, as slaves, African Americans had continued like their African ancestors to live in igno-

rance and isolation from whites, at least in some respects.[9] For instance, Pendleton suggested that the blacks studied by Bruce retained
their African beliefs and lifestyle because they lived "at a convenient
distance from churches, schools and railroads."[10] Newbell N. Puckett,
writing in the 1920s, explained in a more systematic fashion that
blacks retained African beliefs only in areas of life in which they consistently lacked contact with whites—specifically "in matters relating
to self-gratification and the supernatural."[11] Other folk beliefs found
among blacks, according to Puckett, were essentially European in
character and reflected the truism that "to the Negro, the white man
stood as a model to be emulated in all things, from superstition to
straight hair."[12] Therefore, for Puckett as well as other early scholars,
the retention of the African tradition of conjuration and belief in the
power of conjurers reflected a lack of black acculturation to Euro-
American values.

Most studies of the African American conjure tradition, however,
have focused on the beliefs and behaviors associated with the practice
of conjuration, while the role and function of conjurers has received
very little attention. Bacon's and Herron's contention that conjurers
were "both disliked and feared" in the black community has come to
represent an accepted view of these figures in the literature. The
conception of conjurers as individuals who used their power to induce fear was undoubtedly influenced by the view of many that the
prototype for the conjurer in black culture was the African witch-doctor and conjuration merely a form of witchcraft. Therefore, in their
discussions, scholars imposed many of their western biases concerning witches and witchcraft onto the conjure tradition. The most obvious effect of the view of conjurers as witch-doctors and conjuration as
witchcraft has been a tendency to ignore or misrepresent the importance of the religious roots of the tradition. When conjuration has
been discussed from the viewpoint of African religions, the conclusions have been colored by an ethnocentric view of these religions as
little more than superstitions. Puckett, for instance, suggests that the
witch-doctor who served as the prototype for the conjurer in southern
black communities was a religious figure. However, he also argues
with equal intensity that, though a religious figure in Africa, the
witch-doctor had a role that was basically evil and immoral. As a ser-
vant of African gods, he claims, the witch-doctor's immorality was
understandable since "we must remember that the African gods are
not concerned with moral practices."[13]

Although the religious roots of conjuration have been either ignored or misrepresented in discussions of the tradition, Africans en-

slaved in America had come from societies in which "Religion permeate[d] all departments of life so fully that it [was] not easy or always possible to isolate it."[14] Although significant religious differences existed among the African people who made up the slave population in the United States, Albert J. Raboteau, for instance, argues convincingly that "similar modes of religious perception, shared basic principles, and common patterns of ritual were widespread among different West African religions. Beneath the diversity enough fundamental similarities did exist to allow for a general description of the slaves' religious heritage."[15] He further observes that an important similarity among African religions was "priests and others expert in practical knowledge of the gods and spirits."[16] During the period of the trans-Atlantic slave trade, African priests and other religious leaders were captured and, along with their devotees, transported to America. Vincent Harding argues, for instance, that the presence of African religious leaders among enslaved Africans served as an early catalyst for slave unrest in some instances:

> None was more essential to the life of the people than the priest and musicians who illuminated, intensified and celebrated the integument and ritual center of African life. They too were in those terrible temporary settlements by the water, and their prayers and songs for freedom must have filled the air like bittersweet dust. Often, they were among the natural leaders in planning the struggle to break free.[17]

Undoubtedly influenced by the presence of religious experts, from all available evidence, Africans enslaved in America attempted to reconstitute their religious institutions in America.[18] However, the conditions imposed on them by enslavement prevented them from reconstituting their religions in pristine forms. Africans confronted conditions in America which so altered the patterns of social organization that had made their religions meaningful in the African world, that transformation rather than reconstitution became inevitable. For example, the process of enslavement itself was designed to de-individualize Africans by stripping them of any previous social identity that they may have possessed (and, as we will see, social identity was extremely important in African religious worldview). In addition, slaveholders routinely separated Africans from the same ethnic/religious backgrounds, placed restrictions on communal gatherings, and banned the use of ritual instruments—most notably the drums.[19] In the process, they severely circumscribed the ability of African religious leaders to command a following of individuals whose faith in them represented an extension of their belief in a higher order to the universe as defined within a particular African religion. The enslavers' behavior toward Africans, however, did not prevent the transformation of the common elements in the ritual and oral expressive traditions surrounding African religious specialists to create the conjure tradition in America.

While the conception of conjurers in black folk tradition is deeply rooted in religious roles recognized by Africans on the continent, the role and function that conjurers served in the efforts of enslaved Africans to build a culture (and continued to play in black communities well after emancipation) cannot be understood in terms of an ethnocentric equation between conjuration and witchcraft. In addition, the transformation of African ritual and expressive traditions surrounding African religious specialists to create the role of conjurer in black culture cannot be understood merely in terms of conditions which kept enslaved Africans ignorant, isolated, and fearful. To appreciate the function and meaning of the lore of conjuration to enslaved Africans and, more precisely, the conjurer as a folk hero in black culture, we must recognize that the role of religious specialists in African religious practice and worldview was not peripheral but central, especially as it related to the practice of magic. Moreover, the factors which influenced how Africans, both on the continent and those enslaved in America, conceptualized the role of these religious figures can only be appreciated by delving into the African religious universe and the role that African people assigned them for maintaining its equilibrium.

AFRICAN RELIGIOUS ROLES

Religious leaders, as we have suggested, played an important role in the cultures from which Africans enslaved in America had come.[20] Acting in the primary roles of priest and medicine-man, they were "the concrete symbols of man's participation in and experience of the religious universe. Without them," concludes Mbiti, "African societies would lose sight of and contact with this religious phenomenon."[21] Although the role of priest and medicine-man may have been vested in one individual in some African religions, Mbiti suggests that in some instances the roles would have been performed by different individuals. In either case, the priestly role would have been functionally different from that of medicine-man. "Strictly speaking," notes Mbiti, "priests are religious servants associated with temples." In other words, the priest's role was basically that of "spiritual pastor of the community and nation" in that priests served as intermediaries between man and God or other dieties.[22] Therefore, the priestly role was reserved for occasions when the community came together to celebrate and/or propitiate the gods. To perform as a priest, especially among groups that recognized this as a separate religious office, individuals underwent training often under institutional supervision. Parrinder observes that "the tradition of priest is strongest in West Africa than in other parts of the continent."[23] He further notes:

> There are different methods of training, from very simple to highly elaborate, but the priesthood as a class is distinct and developed. Their training may comprise seclusion from the world, instruction in the laws, and sometimes possession by the divinity.[24]

The medicine-man role, on the other hand, was less directly institutional in that it dealt with individual concerns, "with illness, disease, and misfortune." Since these were "generally believed to be caused by ill-will or ill-action of one individual against another, normally through the agency of witchcraft or magic," the medicine-man worked primarily as an intermediary between human beings to ferret out the causes of misfortune, identify its human agents, provide counteractants, and prevent future occurrences.[25] In addition, "There is no fixed rule governing the 'calling' of someone to become a medicine-man. This may come when he is still young and unmarried, or in his middle or later life. In other cases, a medicine-man passes on the profession to his son or other younger relatives. On the whole," concludes Mbiti, "they are influential, though in some societies, they have no official position outside of their professional duties."[26] Their role, nevertheless, was perceived in religious terms because "In African villages, disease and misfortune are religious experiences, and it requires a religious approach to deal with them."[27] Medicine men, though religious specialists in the African sense of the term, were also expert herbalists and generally proficient in the art of healing with the aid of various natural substances. Their spiritual power was combined with their knowledge of healing to make their role in the life of the community an indispensable one.

Although the religious leader's role was established by religious convention and sanctioned in the mythic performances of the group, his or her actions and duties were often conceptualized and validated in various expressive traditions. Evans-Pritchard, for instance, claims that among the Zande, "The corporation of medicine-men possess powerful magic known only to the members of the corporation. That their magic is genuine is proved by legends which show how in the past great medicine-men performed remarkable feats through its medium."[28] He argues that belief in magic "demands a background of belief in its tradition" which in turn generates legends which sanction its use and establish its traditionality. Bascom, in a study of Ifa divination verse among the Yoruba, describes the structure of divination verse as formulaically developed around the appearance of a diviner whose presence affirms the recurrent nature of the problem and the traditionality of the solution offered in the verse:

> The first portion of the verse names the diviner or diviners and the mythological character who came to consult them. It states his problem or the prediction made for him, and it usually names the items that he did or did not sacrifice. The case of the mythological character serves as a precedent for the client, if his problem is similar. The second part explains what happened to the mythological character as a result of having made, or failed to make, the prescribed sacrifice. This may be stated briefly, or expanded at considerable length by introducing Yoruba myth. Its purpose is to explain the first portion, which is often obscure. The third portion is a statement made directly to the client, giving the prediction and in some cases stating the sacrifice that is required.[29]

The verses recited by diviners, according to Bascom, are virtually infinite in number and many will usually be known by devotees of Ifa who do not act as practitioners.[30] In addition, Melville and Frances Herskovitz, in their study of Dahomean narratives, discuss narratives developed around the actions of diviners. In such narratives, the story traditionally commences with a consultation with the diviner to prescribe proper sacrifice to ensure the success of an enterprise such as hunting. These narratives among the Dahomeans are used both in the divining process and, when told in other contexts, as stories to illustrate the importance of divination as a practical and culturally approved way of conceptualizing the relationship between cause and effect.[31]

While there existed differences in the specific duties, ritual processes, and conceptions of powers associated with religious specialists in various African religions, the ritual practices of African religious leaders revolved around remarkably similar types of activities. African religious specialists were invariably associated with what Evans-Pritchard describes as "important magic," by which he means "all magic associated with those pursuits on which the life of the community depends."[32] Irving, for instance, observes that the *bablawo* [the diviner who served in a dual role as priest and medicine-man among the Yoruba] "is consulted on every undertaking—on going on a journey, entering into a speculation, going to war, or on a kidnapping expedition, in sickness and, in short, wherever there is doubt of the future."[33] In his study of divination among the Nyoro of Uganda, John Beattie notes that

> Nyoro consult diviners when they are in trouble, and want to know the cause of the trouble, and what they should do about it. The commonest kind of trouble is illness, and most consultations relate to a client's health, or that of his child or other close relatives. In rural Bunyoro, miscarriage during pregnacy is frequent, and many women consult diviners to find out why they have miscarried. People also consult diviners to discover why they are impotent or barren, why spouses no longer love them, and to ascertain the identity of a sorcerer or a thief.[34]

In studies of traditional African religious practices, it is clear that religious specialists, especially in the medicine-man role, were frequently consulted to intercede, explain, prevent, and provide counteractants in various situations which threatened the functioning of the community. Mbiti argues that in times of national misfortune such as war, famine, drought, or other natural disasters the religious leader in the role of priest was invariably called upon to offer proper sacrifice or ritual to propitiate the gods on behalf of the community.[35] Regardless of the capacity in which the religious leaders acted, sacrifice to the offended god or spirit, or, in some instances, to the religious figure himself was required as part of the ritual process.

The association of the African religious specialist with illness, disease, injustice, natural disaster, and, in short, situations vital to material productivity and physical survival of the group, suggests that the coherence of the tradition of religious leadership was related to recurrent conditions confronted by Africans that made these situations particularly problematic. Therefore, to understand the role of the African religous leader, we must attempt to discover those factors that influenced the African view of these situations as not only problematic but also religious. E. J. Marais observes, for instance, that in the

African religious worldview "Every sickness, affliction, or adversity, each injustice, every frustration, are all regarded as a diminution of ontological being." He further observes that "The highest form of happiness that man can attain is the fullest ontological being. The worst adversity, and the only real form of misfortune, is a diminution of ontological being."[36] If Africans viewed those situations most often identified with religious specialists as diminutions of ontological being, then we must consider the African concept of ontological being to appreciate the role of religious specialists.

The African concept of ontological being derived from a traditional religious view of "life-force" as a vital principle for apprehending the nature of existence.[37] In diverse African societies, this life-force was believed to have existed from the beginning of time; it manifested itself in all things, although every entity did not possess it to an equal degree. Life-force was the source of all being and determined not only what a being was but also what a being could do. The ultimate source of all life-force in the universe was God, who existed as pure Force or Being. At the moment of creation, God manifested His force in all things and thereby became transcendent. Therefore, all entities in the universe were ontologically connected to each other at the deepest level of being through their connection to the Creator. The natural order existed as a kind of complex machine powered by a common source of energy. Just as the individual parts of a machine contribute to its overall operation and efficiency at different levels of imput, so too did the various forces in the natural order.

As in any complex mechanism, there was constant interaction between forces in the natural order which occurred according to certain well-defined laws of causality. The natural order was governed by an ontological hierarchy which facilitated a downward flow of life-force from the Source. "In the hierarchy the stronger force can paralyze, diminish or even cause the operating of the inferior to cease, but it can never annihilate or destroy another force. On the other hand a living or deceased force can reinforce another force directly provided the law of subordination is maintained."[38] Hierarchically, God was both the source of being or force and its increase. Therefore, all worship in African religions was ultimately directed to God. However, because God was transcendent and effectively present in all things to varying degrees, He could not be approached directly, only through a network of hierarchical forces or intermediaries. Below Him, but seldom worshipped, though always revered, were the founders of clans, the first to whom God communicated His force. Then followed a pantheon of divinities or lesser gods—the children of God or beings allowed to exist by Him. In many instances, they were associated with nature and often manifested their force in such natural occurrences as thunder, rain, trees, etc. Moreover, in a natural order in which force could never be destroyed but only transformed, a powerful class of forces were deceased ancestors—the living dead and those who had become spirits. The ancestors, who served as guardians of social law and customs, exerted a profound and continuous influence on living human beings.

As forces superior to humans, beings on any level of the supernatural hierarchy could directly influence the quality of life in the social world for good or ill. Human beings, as inferior forces, could only have an indirect influence on the actions of supernatural beings through faithful worship, sacrifice, and obedience in observing the social and natural laws governing interaction between forces. The African view of the power of those in the supernatural world to affect the quality of human existence dramatically influenced how they conceptualized their relationship to the ancestors, spirits, and gods of their religions. Raboteau argues, for instance, that African religions incorporated a view of life in which "The welfare of the entire community and of each individual within it derived from the close relationship of man to the gods, ancestors, and unseen spirits. The harmony of this relationship was the ground of all good; its disruption the source of all evil."[39]

The phenomenology of existence in the African religious worldview resulted from the constant interaction and exchange of life-force between beings. While the life-force of any being—spiritual, animate, or inanimate—could be transformed, transmuted, enhanced or diminished, it did not occur through some form of physical causality. The exchange of life-force could only be accomplished through indirect actions—ritual or symbolic forms of causality. As forces interacted, the effect could be either good or evil; however, the effect that an act could have depended on which beings performed it and not on the nature of the act itself. However, human beings, though envisioned as existing in ontological equilibrium with all other forces in the universe, were seen as the only beings capable of creating the kind of disruption to the natural order that produced evil effects. While nature and the supernatural could and did act capriciously, their behavior was accepted as being under the direct or indirect control of human beings. In African religious cosmology, human beings were at the center of African ontology and "everything else acquires meaning in its relation" to them.[40] This view of the place of human beings in the natural order was influenced by the belief that God "created the harmony in nature for man's benefit." Therefore, "It is ultimately man's duty to maintain this harmony of and with nature by humbly and obediently submitting to his role and place in nature."[41] A consequence of this belief was that in the traditional African religious worldview there could be no occurrence that was accidental, since accident implies an absence of a perception of cause. All good or evil had its cause in a human agent whose actions either enhanced or diminished the flow of life-force. The ideal state of the natural order was harmony which allowed for the continuous flow and exchange of force between beings.

Ruch and Anyanwu contend that "the most immediately felt aspect of the order of nature and the one which most intimately and continuously affects man's life is the social order as lived in the family and the clan. It is therefore essential that man should do nothing that would destroy the harmony of his group, but, on the contrary, all his actions should positively contribute to this harmony. There is no purely personal morality."[42] In social life, Africans emphasized the communal or corporate nature of their existence, and African culture-building sought above all to promote the values of solidarity, togetherness, and a family spirit. For Africans, society existed as a microcosm of the universal order in that individuals functioned with different levels of input. Communal or social harmony depended on individuals accepting and acting in accordance with their position in the socio-religious hierarchy and respecting that of others. As a microcosm of the universal order, society ideally functioned as a complex living organism; if one individual became ill or experienced misfortune, the entire body social was infected. A bad act, ontologically speaking, did not merely place the individual in disharmony with the community but disrupted the entire universal order.

Therefore, Africans made maintaining harmony the most important goal of culture-building and, as a result, valued behaviors which reflected communal participation and allegiance above all others. Or, as Ruch and Anyanwu argue, "The 'good' is never seen as an individualistic advantage but always contains the perspective of participation in the communal life."[43] For Africans, the cultural emphasis on harmony, cooperation, and solidarity was influenced directly and continuously by their religious worldview. From the viewpoint of religious beliefs, Africans envisioned harmony in communal life as constituting the most advantageous means of maintaining and strengthening their relationship to the supernatural. To do otherwise threatened their well-being with respect to the supernatural on whose benevolence they depended for the quality of their existence. Consequently, Africans defined ideal individual behavior as that which facilitated communal welfare above individual need, and the "good person" as one who acted within the limits of his or her life-force while respecting that of all other beings.

According to African religious belief, every individual was born with a life-force which determined the action that that individual could perform and be protected from the evil force unleashed by the act. For example, in some African societies, blacksmiths were believed to be born with a life-force which allowed them to transform metal and be protected from the evil unleashed in the process of transforming it. Others who attempted to act as blacksmiths, however, had no protection against the evil force contained in metal and, therefore, could be destroyed by it. However, individuals possessed the ability to enhance their life-force to gain protection to perform acts for which they were not naturally immune. For instance, every "good act" in life enhanced the life-force of the individual, a process which should occur naturally throughout one's life. This view of the "good person" and a "good act" accounted for the revered position that elders held in African societies. In addition, individuals could enhance their life-force by acquiring additional force from those possessed of a greater force by sacrificing to the gods, spirits, or religious specialists to gain protection both for their actions and against those of others.

However, Africans also believed that individuals could enhance their life-force by diminishing that of another being through surreptitious ritual or symbolic acts, an action that Africans viewed as a moral evil. The primary means by which an individual diminished the ontological being of another was through magic in the form of witchcraft and sorcery. On one level, what was magical in the African world was the power of words to transform and transmute forces, a power possessed by every human being. Africans viewed the spoken word as the embodiment of an individual's life-force in that it represented not only the means by which human beings communicated with each other but also the means by which they interacted with all other forces. The ability to use words was what made human beings a superior force to animals, plants, and other inanimate objects. In a physical sense, these inferior forces could have an indirect influence on human beings, i.e., as food or tools to be used. However, because they lacked the power of "word," they could neither transform nor transmute their life-force on their own to affect the quality of human existence. Human beings, on the other hand, could temporarily or permanently endow these inferior forces with their force through symbolic and ritual actions and thereby make them vehicles of their force to do good or evil, an ability possessed to a high degree by witches and medicine-men.

Therefore, words, as the embodiment of an individual's life force, took on an inordinate degree of importance in the context of human relationships. Senghor, for instance, notes that "The black word uttered under the shock of emotion surpasses the emotion. Coinciding with the real, it is not only an expression of knowledge, but knowledge itself, ready for action, already action. The 'word' is thought, speech, action."[44] Consequently, "A man who curses another man is doing him genuine harm; his words are not just sound waves on the air, nor do they have merely a psychological effect of angering the victim of the curse. A curse has a real instrumental causality and effectively achieves what it states or threatens, unless its effect is blocked by stronger magic."[45] Since words once spoken always achieve their effect, their use had always to be guarded.

Ruch and Anyanwu summarize the distinctiveness of the African view of the word in the following way

> The Christian is proclaiming and testifying to the word of God. The African does more than that. He possesses the power of word and this power unceasingly transforms, transmutes, creates, recreates and procreates things and even God. Word alters the world. The African knows about the consequences of word. Word creates images too, and transforms the self—because the self is a force among forces who must be transformed by words. So, the same magical effects of words on things (forces) are found in the realm of self, spirit, living dead, ancestors and Great divinity.[46]

The "word" in African religious worldview constituted the primary means by which African people maintained and strengthened the relationship between forces in the universe. Through the proper use of "word," especially in prayer, ritual, and the offering of sacrifice to those in the supernatural realm, Africans believed that they could insure the flow of vital-force from God. On the other hand, they believed that the improper use of "word" disrupted the flow of vital-force and, therefore, was the source of much misfortune in their lives.

In the use of words and/or the practice of magic, the power of the individual's life-force determined the kind of effect that one's words or actions could have, i.e., whether they enhanced or diminished ontological being. In social interaction, the effect depended on who performed the action on whom, the intent of the actor, and, in an important sense, the perception of advantage that the act could achieve. Since life-force flowed downward, the actions or words of a being with great force (determined by social rank or status) carried an inherent power that could directly influence those with less force for good or ill. For example, the words or actions of a parent to a child or an elder to a younger had a direct effect and could only be blocked by one of equal or greater force. On the other hand, those of lower rank or status did not possess either the life-force or the moral or natural right to directly affect those above them through actions or words; however, they could by acquiring additional force from a being possessed of equal or greater force affect them indirectly. In fact, the efforts of individuals with less force to achieve personal ends against or at the expense of those with greater force constituted one of the primary sources of evil in the African world. [47]

In many ways, the rigid social structure that Africans created based on their perception of a hierarchy of being, though designed to maintain natural harmony, entailed both benefits and costs. On the one hand, the emphasis on harmony in social life caused the community in Africa to be pervaded by a strong communal ethos. On the other hand, the law of subordination allowed for the creation of an atmosphere in which the response to individual perceptions of injustice and frustration as well as creativity and originality often had to be stifled to maintain a perception of social harmony. Therefore, as individuals sought to discover outlets through which they could express their individuality and frustrations without appearing to disrupt the harmony of social life, the force in nature which could be manipulated through indirect actions served as an incredible temptation. Furthermore, the possibility that endless accusations of magic, witchcraft, and sorcery would surface in African societies was enhanced, on the one hand, by the belief that any individual could literally buy into the force in nature by offering sacrifice to beings with great force, and, on the other hand, by the belief that all manifestations of misfortune were caused by a human agent. Therefore, physical causality, though recognized, was not accepted as a complete explanation for misfortune, nor were merely statutory or legal remedies applied in situations that Africans perceived as effectively diminishing ontological being.

Inasmuch as African religions served as the primary source of both religious and social values, religious institutions took on an enormous role in African societies for controlling and punishing acts of magic which disrupted social harmony. Among diverse African groups, the people vested responsibility for handling manifestations of misfortune which led to a diminution of ontological being in the religious specialist, "particularly the medicine-man, diviner, rainmaker who use their knowledge and manipulation of this mystical power [life-force] for the welfare of their community."[48] The African view of religious specialists derived from a view of them as individuals whose life-force was communicated directly from the gods or even God Himself. Therefore, they not only possessed a greater share of the life-force but also communicated it with divine inspiration. As individuals possessed of a superior life-force in their community, their power was relied upon to reinforce and restore harmony to the natural order as well as to block the effects of evil. Their knowledge of the life-force rendered them capable of detecting the points at which ruptures to the natural order had occured. In communal terms, they had a religious duty to ferret out the human agents of evil and punish according to socio-religious law and custom.

The worst offenders of natural order and the greatest threat to the harmony of social life were witches and sorcerers, individuals who possessed a superior life-force and used their power surreptitiously to sow discord in the community. Theirs, in most instances, was seen as an influence so evil that death was often the only remedy that would restore the spiritual health of the community. Although religious specialists carried out their duties by endowing objects in nature with "vicarious force" through their words as well as ritual and symbolic actions in much the same way as witches and sorcerers, and often caused misfortune and even death, their actions were viewed as neither immoral nor destructive to the harmony of social life. Instead, the religious specialist was seen as a kind of generator of life-force and his or her presence in the community as essential to the maintenance of the quality of life that allowed individuals to attain the fullest ontological being. The value of their role in African society was enhanced by the absence in African religious worldview of a belief that individuals were punished in death for what they did in life.

While the African view of the human role in causing evil created endless opportunities for accusations of witchcraft, sorcery, and magic, African culture-building in a hostile natural environment allowed if not made inevitable the frequent occurrence of situations that, in African religious worldview, diminished ontological being. The lifestyle of Africans characterized by subsistence level existence in a precarious and often hostile natural environment has historically made them extremely vulnerable and susceptible to illness and disease—the manifestations of misfortune most often identified with religious specialists. In addition, almost total dependence on the environment for the means of physical survival has made the quality of African life subject to the whims of nature. Furthermore, Africans have historically lacked the technological processes, in a western sense, to control or explain the impact of the environment on their lives to any appreciable degree. The result has been not only subsistence level existence but also chronic material shortage, human suffering, especially in the form of illness and disease, and social and political upheaval and instability.

Though apparently divorced from their lifestyle, African religious beliefs and practices have served a vital role in providing Africans with a means of transmitting a conception of behavior and a cognitive orientation that, from their point of view, offered them advantages in negotiating life in a harsh and unpredictable environment. Anyanwu and Ruch contend that the physical demands of living under the conditions produced by the African environment played a crucial role in determining the values that Africans perceived as most advantageous to survival: "Precisely because of the awareness of the harshness of nature, men are more companionable and take the trouble to live harmoniously together, because they know that only by acting together can they reap the benefits and attempt to overcome nature."[49] Mbiti concurs and argues that the similarities in African religions were intimately related to the lifestyle that developed among Africans in their peculiar circumstances. He insists that African religious beliefs have been "coloured and influenced by the historical, geographical, social and cultural background or environment of each people. This explains the similarities which we find when we consider the beliefs about God all over the continent. It is this which partly accounts also for the beliefs parallel to those held by peoples of other continents and lands, when the background may be similar to that of African people."[50]

Athough African religious specialists have often been referred to as "witch-doctors" in the literature, Mbiti and other modern Africanists suggest that this term "should be buried and forgotten forever."[51] The primary duty of the African religious specialist was to combat "witchcraft and magic by preventing their action and sometimes by sending them back to their authors."[52] Theirs was a power not to be feared but rather to be respected, revered, and even sought after. Mbiti argues that some Africans spent their lives and fortunes attempting to acquire a share of the life-force equal to that possessed by African religious specialists. According to Benjamin C. Ray, the value of religious specialists to the community derived from a view of them as individuals who "contained the life-force which [they rule] to mediate to [their] people."[53] This role was not viewed as temporal or peripheral to the life of the African community. Rather "In them [African religious leaders] are the continuity and essence of African religious thought and life."[54] Their presence in African societies provided "the traditional African with the absolute and intuitive certitude that man is necessarily tied up with and dependent on his fellow-man and on nature."[55]

The Rise of the Conjurer

"Duh root doctuh kin hep yoh too," added Uncle Robert. "Dey is powful smaht. I use tuh heah tell ub a root man name Smaht McCall. Ef yoh git in any trouble, yuh jis go see um an he git yuh out ub it."[56]

Although Africans enslaved in America witnessed various changes in their lifestyle, they continued to live under conditions which made "those pursuits on which the life of the community depends" subject to caprice.[57] The unpredictability of existence in America, however, was influenced less by a precarious and often hostile natural environment or capricious gods and spirits than by enslavement. In slavery, the quality of their lives became subject to the whims of their enslavers who attempted to use their physical power to define the behaviors both toward them and among enslaved Africans that made life propitious in their new environment. Blassingame observes, for instance, that

A master started early trying to impress upon the slave the awesome power of whiteness: he made the slave bow upon meeting him, stand in his presence, and accept floggings from his young children; he flogged the slave for fighting with young whites. The ritual of deference was required at every turn; the slave was flogged for disputing a white man's word, kicked for walking between two whites on the street, and not allowed to call his wife or mother "Mrs."

Many masters tried first to demonstrate their own authority over the slaves and then the superiority of all whites over blacks. They continually told the slave that he was unfit for freedom, that every slave who attempted to escape was captured and sold further South, and that the black man must conform to the white man's every wish.[58]

In their interactions with them, "Planters insisted that their slaves show no signs of dissatisfaction. Instead, they were to demonstrate their humility by cheerful performance of their tasks."[59]

Though isolated physically from whites in the slave quarters, enslaved Africans were also expected to allow their domestic and social lives to be governed by the masters' rules. For example, the masters often took an active role in the pairing of slaves and reserved the right to sever unions by selling away one of the partners or even as a form of punishment. At the least, they reserved the right to decide on what constituted an appropriate or acceptable "marriage" between enslaved Africans by forcing them to seek their permission before they could unite.[60] In addition, marriage for enslaved Africans entailed few of the traditional rights and privileges that they had enjoyed in their homelands:

> After marriage, the slave faced almost insurmountable odds in his efforts to build a strong stable family. First, and most important of all, his authority was restricted by the master. Any decision of his regarding his family could be countermanded by his master. The master determined when both he and his wife would go to work, when or whether his wife cooked his meals, and was often the final arbiter in family disputes. In enforcing discipline, some masters whipped both man and wife when they had loud arguments or fights.[61]

Enslaved Africans were equally restricted in their power to protect, discipline, or make decisions concerning the rearing of their children. In many ways, the family life of enslaved Africans served as a microcosm of the slave community in which the interactions between individuals and the activities that made life propitious were defined and enforced by the masters.

To maintain their vision of what constituted appropriate black behavior both toward themselves and among the enslaved, the masters frequently resorted to physical punishment. Punishment, from the masters' point of view, served not merely as retribution from those who violated their view of ideal behavior in the system but also as a deterrent. Their attitude toward physical punishment as a deterrent was nowhere more evident than in their treatment of those who openly violated the rules. An African enslaved in Virginia recalled the following incident as an example of how masters made the punishment of those who openly violated the rules a means of educating their slave populations:

This woman would work, but if you drove her too hard, she'd git stubborn like a mule and quit. Her name was Julian Walker. Julian worked in the field. When they got rough with her, she got rough on them and ran away in the woods. One day she ran away and hid a long time. They found her by means of bloodhounds. She was sitting in the top of a tree. They took her back and chain her by her leg just as though she were a dog. The band was very tight, too tight, and the chain cut around her ankle. No one paid any attention to her and the sore got worse. Vermin got in the wound and ate the flesh from the bone. Her back was a mass of scars the result of the terrible lashing she received [for] running away. They gave her especially cruel treatment in that they made an example of her for the other slaves.[62]

While the masters most often reserved their harshest punishment for those who ran away—the ultimate violation of the rules—their treatment of runaways and others whose actions they defined as those of a "bad nigger" served to constantly remind enslaved Africans of their awesome power over all Africans. Although the masters' actions in these instances were obviously dramatic and extreme, they more often than not exacted punishment in the form of floggings for the least offense against their authority or property, both human and nonhuman, to remind enslaved Africans of their position and role in the social order:

The slaves were flogged most frequently for running away and for failure to complete tasks assigned them. Slaveholders often punished them for visiting their mates, learning to read, arguing or fighting with whites, working too slowly, stealing, or for trying to prevent the sale of their relatives. They were occasionally punished for impudence, asking the master to sell them, claiming they were free men, breaking household articles, or for giving sexual favors to persons other than their masters.[63]

Given the wide range of behaviors that the masters defined as violations of the rules, enslaved Africans could hardly ignore them or their consequences if they were to survive.

Ironically, the enslavers' efforts to assume a god-like role in the lives of enslaved Africans proved more opportunistic for black culture-building in America than influential in reshaping the African socio-religious worldview. Genovese argues, for example, that the masters' frequent insinuations of themselves into the internal affairs of the slave community resulted from their desire to maintain harmony. The masters' emphasis on harmony among the enslaved, according to Genovese, was a reflection of their view of the values that they believed necessary to maintain order within the institution of slavery:

> Many masters were determined to preserve order in the quarters, for the sense of "family" hung in the balance. But in addition, all quarrels threatened morale, decorum, discipline, and productivity. From the masters' point of view, the defense of the family and the preservation of order and productivity complemented each other and merged into one image of what life should be. Thus they arrogated to themselves, when they could, the role of arbiter in this and other respects.[64]

However, to maintain their "image of what life should be," the masters made physical punishment the consequence of behaviors which violated their rules governing interaction between enslaved Africans as readily as they did for rules in other areas. In addition, they made it virtually impossible for enslaved Africans to hide from them incidents which erupted into physical confrontations or verbal explosions in the quarters, since practically all of their movements were carefully watched and guarded not only by the masters but also by overseers, drivers, and, in some instances, slave spies who were rewarded by the masters for their treachery.

In the end, the enslavers created a social structure which, though defined politically and maintained through physical coercion, in its rigidity, was not unlike that known in Africa. Africans from diverse cultural backgrounds had historically contended with a hierarchically ordered social structure in which the behaviors that made life propitious were defined both horizontally and vertically. There were crucial differences in the situation that they encountered in America, however. First of all, during the process of enslavement, they were systematically stripped of the social distinctions that they had recognized among each other in their homelands. Second, their role and place in the social hierarchy was universally defined as inferior to that of Europeans. Finally, they were expected to value actions which promoted the masters' economic interests and the harmony of their relationship to them above those that facilitated their own individual and collective interests.

However, in evaluating their situation in America, enslaved Africans, though unable to reconstitute their religious institutions, initially had their religious beliefs as the only frame of reference for in-

terpreting and explaining the world phenomenologically. That enslaved Africans would turn to their African religious heritage for an
interpretive framework in slavery was enhanced by the fact that, despite the enslavers' efforts to create a relationship between themselves
and Africans that would force dependency on them in almost every
respect, they demonstrated an almost total disregard for their spiritual needs. The enslavers' indifference to the spiritual needs and
outlooks of enslaved Africans was greatly influenced by their view of
them as little more than animals and their religious beliefs as simply
naive superstitions. This disregard, in many instances, created situations which merely reinforced the value of these beliefs in the minds
of Africans. Such situations occurred most often in instances where
the enslavers' attitude made Africans vulnerable to the supernatural
forces for which their religions and ritual practices had offered them
psychic protection. For example, Raboteau observes that, in Africa,
"Because of the powerful position of the ancestors, burial rites became very important. Improper or incomplete funeral rites can interfere with or delay the entrance of the soul into the spirit world and
may cause his soul to linger about as a restless and malevolen ghost."[65]
Blassingame points out that, in America, "Because of labour requirements on the plantation, a deceased slave was often buried at night
with the rites being held weeks later" if at all.[66] Not surprisingly, enslaved Africans transformed many of their traditional African religious beliefs concerning the actions, behaviors, and motivations of
spirits of the dead, especially those which related to the consequences
of improper burial.

   In other ways as well, the enslavers' attitude toward Africans and
their beliefs created various situations which both facilitated and necessitated the transformation of important aspects of their African
religious heritage to meet their spiritual needs in America. Although
Europeans justified the enslavement of Africans as a way of converting them to Christianity, the predominantly English slaveholding
class demonstrated a great deal of reluctance in providing Christian
religious instruction for their slaves. During the early years of slavery,
many slaveholders refused to allow their slaves to be converted because they believed that they would not be allowed by the state to
keep Christians of any hue in permanent bondage. Even after they
were assured that conversion would have no impact on the legal
status of an African, many still resisted on the grounds that the equali-
tarianism inherent in Christianity would make Africans unruly. Of
equal importance to slaveholders were the economic considerations
involved in converting large numbers of Africans to Christianity as

prescribed by the Anglican church. "For a slave to be catechized properly took time," and time for religious instruction was time away from work.[67] The slaveholders' view of slavery as an economic system meant that most were unwilling to leave time in their slaves' work schedules for religious instruction, especially for a people whose humanity and ability to benefit from religion they questioned. The result of slaveholder obstinacy was that by the end of the eighteenth century only a small number of Africans in America professed Christianity as their religion.[68]

While the absence of a competing religious worldview facilitated the transformation of African religious beliefs, it did not allow for a natural continuation of the religions on which they were based. In many instances, during the early years of slavery, slaveholders both denied their slaves access to Christianity and, at the same time, (acting out of fear, ignorance, and pressure from Christian religious leaders) denied them opportunities to participate in or carry out ritual practices associated with their African religious heritage.[69] For example, slaveholders not only placed restrictions on slave gatherings where they might have performed communal religious rituals but also forbade them to indulge in individual acts based on African religious beliefs such as the wearing of protective amulets. Dena Epstein observes that the "opposition and indifference" of some slaveholders to Christian religious instruction for their slaves caused them to develop a tolerant attitude toward African religious practices.[70] However, these slaveholders permitted ritual singing and dancing in particular because they viewed them as "morally beneficial amusements" rather than religious rites. Therefore, in many instances, they attempted to secularize them by introducing European musical instruments such as the fiddle to enhance the lively atmosphere of the gatherings.[71] While the actions of slaveholders were only partially successful in suppressing African religious practices, their interference in the religious life of Africans was sufficiently disruptive as to create conditions in which Africans were forced to transform their religious beliefs and traditions in America to continue to derive meaning from them.

While the indifferent attention of the enslavers to the spiritual needs of Africans could and did influence the transformation of African religious beliefs, the continuation of a lifestyle characterized by caprice, subsistence level existence, and material and physical conditions which threatened their physical and social well-being served as the most important catalysts for transforming the ritual and expressive traditions surrounding African religious specialists in America.

Of the factors that influenced the transformation of the African conception of religious leaders, none was more important than the behaviors of the enslavers which allowed for the development of conditions for which "medicine" had served as the most efficient and expeditious solution in African cultures. For example, the enslavers' indifferent and often capricious attention to the material and physical needs of enslaved Africans created a situation in which health problems became widespread among them. In many instances, the health problems exhibited by Africans could be attributed to the enslavers' emphasis on "quantity" rather than "quality" in the food provided for them. Pica (dirt and clay eating), for instance, has been frequently cited as a common practice among enslaved Africans. Postell concludes from his examination of slaveholder records that the practice was commonly noted and was considered "the dread of every planter."[72] Although dirt eating could cause dysentery, digestive disturbances, and, in large enough quantities, death, it was merely a symptom of a mineral deficiency associated with a lack of certain essential nutrients in the diet.[73] Numerous other major and minor illnesses resulted from the nutritionally deficient diet of enslaved Africans. Postell concludes, for example, that "The great number of dental caries, sore eyes, sore mouths, sore feet and legs, and skin lesions is suggested of pellagra and other dietary deficiencies."[74]

While the qualitatively and sometimes quantitatively inadequate diet of enslaved Africans was an important reason for health problems' becoming widespread among them, other factors associated with the lifestyle of Africans in America also contributed to the sometimes epidemic proportions of disease in their ranks. For example, living arrangements characterized by overcrowding, squalor, and a lack of sanitation contributed to the spread of diseases, especially those of an infectious nature such as influenza.[75] In addition, enslaved Africans, in some instances, became susceptible to illnesses with which they had not had to deal in their homelands—sickle cell anemia and lactose intolerance being two example often noted. In some areas of the rural South—the Gullah Islands for example—Africans were forced to live under climatic and environmental conditions perceived as so hostile to human existence during certain times of the year that most whites refused to live in them on a year around basis. Furthermore, the health of enslaved Africans was constantly compromised by brutal physical punishment which left them with open wounds, ripe for infection.

The material and, more specifically, physical conditions under which enslaved Africans were forced to live in America often led to interpersonal conflicts among them becoming an intragroup problem. Raboteau argues, for instance, that "the very closeness of the quarters necessitated a degree of tolerance while at the same time exacerbating personal tensions."[76] Africans lumped indiscriminately together in the quarters did not always find social integration and harmony easy to achieve or maintain. In some cases, newly imported Africans undoubtedly found themselves forced to live and work with individuals who, in Africa, would have been their political enemies. In addition, overcrowded communal living arrangements in some areas contributed to the development of conflict and animosities, especially in situations where individuals were forced to live together without regard for kinship ties. Furthermore, they were confronted with new social patterns in which sex ratios were sometimes uneven and competition for the affection of women in particular was often fierce both between African men and from the masters. Moreover, the material and physical conditions faced by Africans as a community which made the animal trickster tale tradition an important model of behavior for securing individual interests at the expense of others facilitated the development of behavioral patterns that could easily lead to chronic intra- and intergroup conflict.

Regardless of their source, the physical and social conditions that developed among enslaved Africans created obstacles to their efforts to maintain and enforce their traditional religious beliefs and values, especially those aspects of their religions in which religious specialists had played an important role.

On the one hand, the slaveholders, despite their sometimes awesome displays of physical power, did not offer viable spiritual or practical alternatives to African religious traditions for conceptualizing or dealing with the situations created by their power and control. For example, although, from available evidence, most slaveholders in America generally acted to preserve the health of their slaves, they could not offer them a quality of health care that would have radically altered the African view of the cause or means of dealing with illness. Most slaveholders apparently not only kept a store of home remedies and popular medicines on hand to minister to slave health complaints but also retained doctors to care for their more serious illnesses.[77] Even so, the state of scientific medicine was so undeveloped during the period of black chattel slavery in the United States that the cures and remedies prescribed by medical doctors were often no more effective than folk remedies. Most doctors in the United States well into the nineteenth century were trained under the apprenticeship system by practitioners who followed the ancient practices of bleeding, blistering, and purging.[78] Some further complicated the health of their black patients by using them as guinea pigs for their pet theories and treatments.[79] Therefore, despite the masters' demonstrated and vested interest in maintaining a healthy slave population, they could offer enslaved Africans a poor quality of health care at best.

On the other hand, the enslavers' solution to social strife and domestic discord among enslaved Africans, though expedient and effective from their point of view, violated the African sense of the interrelatedness of the social, spiritual, and physical health of the individual and the community. In dealing with social conflict among enslaved Africans and toward themselves, slaveholders were strongly motivated by their view of social strife and its physical consequences as disruptions to the social harmony and cooperative spirit viewed as essential to the economic productivity of the slave system. Therefore, to protect their economic interests, they simply utilized their physical advantage over Africans to control any expression of conflict by making its consequences physically costly. "Master didn't whip the niggers much," declared a former enslaved Texan, "'cept for fighting 'mongst themselves."[80] Because the enslavers' view of the cause and remedy for social conflict differed from that of the enslaved, they simply ignored and, in many instances, punished the efforts of enslaved Africans to protect themselves spiritually against the consequences of actions which resulted in misfortune, especially in the form of illness, and that they believed were motivated by ill-will or social strife.

The slavemasters' efforts to define what constituted expressions of social conflict and their efforts to inhibit practices that Africans viewed as the most beneficial in dealing with it continuously threatened their ability to maintain and protect their traditional religious values. At the same time, their repressive practices created an atmosphere conducive to the practice of magic in the slave community as well as the transformation of the ritual and expressive traditions surrounding African religious specialists. Although enslaved Africans neither shared a single conception of religious specialists nor viewed the role and duties of these individuals in the same way, they did share a view of the religious specialist as an individual who embodied the spiritual knowledge that protected the community against forces that threatened its socio-religious values. In addition, their traditions of religious leadership had been influenced by material, physical, and social conditions remarkably similar to those they encountered as slaves. Specifically, in Africa, religious specialists, in addition to their roles as spiritual leaders, had been closely identified with and functioned within a worldview in which there was "no formal distinction between the sacred and the secular, the religious and non-religious, the material and spiritual areas of life."[81] The tradition of African religious leadership, though manifested in various figures, had reflected the existence of values guiding action under harsh material and physical conditions and within a rigid hierarchical social structure. The result was a view of life in which acting harmoniously together offered the greatest advantages in overcoming forces inhibitive to survival and well-being. Under these conditions, the religious specialists, whose mystical knowledge and powers encompassed and made accessible to the community the wisdom of the ages, served as the interpreters and enforcers of the behaviors by which the community dealt with problems in the social world that disrupted the harmony of the natural and social orders. As mediators between the supernatural and human beings, their knowledge had been relied upon as a kind of insurance against the disintegration of social ties and communal processes upon which Africans depended for the survival and continuity of their community.

In essence, the transformation of the expressive and ritual traditions that enslaved Africans had associated with African religious specialists resulted from the recognition that, despite surface changes in their lifestyle, there existed deep structural similarities which justified the perpetuation of their traditional religious practices and worldview. In this regard, the relationship that the masters attempted to create between themselves and enslaved Africans, in which the masters assumed responsibility for determining the quality of life in the slave community, obviously had an important influence. On the one hand, it affected how the enslaved Africans transformed the traditions that had been associated with African religious specialists. Specifically, the god-like role assumed by the masters in the lives of enslaved Africans influenced the way that they defined the power of these figures in America. Although there is no evidence to suggest that the enslaved envisioned their relationship to the masters in specifically religious terms, i.e., as one capable of replacing the pantheon of supernatural beings in African religious worldview, there is evidence to suggest that they viewed their relationship to the masters in terms of the African concept of the hierarchy of life-force, at least on a social level. For example, enslaved Africans frequently expressed the view that their conjurers were ineffective in directly affecting whites: "The niggers could conjure each other," declared a former enslaved African, "but they couldn't do nothing to the white folks." "In those days," noted another, "they had a hoodoo nigger who could hoodoo niggers, but they couldn't hoodoo the masters."[82] Although most enslaved Africans attributed the failure of their efforts to conjure whites to the lack of belief among the master class, a view equally consistent with their African religious heritage would have been that, given the masters' place in the social order and their effect on the quality of their lives, the masters could be conceptualized as witches and sorcerers—individuals who possessed a superior life-force and used it constantly to destroy the harmony of the natural order. This view of their relationship to the masters would have been not only consistent with the African view of the hierarchy of life-forces but would also account for the frequency with which enslaved Africans reported the intervention of conjurers in their interactions with the masters, especially to secure supernatural protection rather than ritual cleansing. In numerous instances, they reported that they consulted conjurers to avoid "punishment, to enable them to escape the 'patrolers' or, in the case of the runaway, to enable him to return home without suffering from the master's anger."[83]

On the other hand, the relationship that the masters attempted to create between themselves and the enslaved influenced how they justified the actions that they associated with the religious specialists in America. Through repeated interaction with the masters, enslaved Africans came to realize that the behaviors that the masters defined as the most advantageous in maintaining a proper relationship to them and with each other could not be ignored. Furthermore, regardless of how they may have viewed the masters' rules, enslaved Africans recognized that violating them threatened not only the well-being of the individual in violation but also that of the entire community by bringing the masters' wrath down on them all. While they did not possess the power to change or influence the masters' rules governing their behavior to any appreciable degree, they could, by transforming their own tradition of religious leadership, create an intragroup mechanism for defining and controlling the actions of members of their own community to maintain a communal atmosphere supportive of their interests.

In transforming the tradition of religious leadership, enslaved Africans probably accepted the masters' power as both god-like and the embodiment of evil, at least in evaluating its effects on their ability to maintain values reflecting behaviors that they accepted as the most advantageous to their well-being. In either case, the power exercised by the masters was capable of reinforcing their African view of the hierarchy of life-force which not only determined what a being was but also what a being could do. In addition, they recognized that it was a power that they had to guard against both offensively and defensively if they were to survive in America. This view of their relationship to the masters undoubtedly influenced the development of the strong communal bonds that enslaved Africans, observers of slavery, and even slavemasters often noted as characteristic of the slave community. "People in my day," reported Susan Davis, who had been enslaved in Missouri, "didn't know book learning but dy studied how to protect each other, and save 'em from such misery as they could."[84] The Reverend C. C. Jones, a chronicler of slave life, noted that

> The Negroes are scrupulous on one point, they make common cause, as servants, in concealing their faults from their owner. Inquiry elicits no information; no one feels at liberty to declare the transgressions; all are profoundly ignorant; the matter assumes the sacredness of a "professional secret."[85]

In many ways, intragroup solidarity in the slave community took on a sacred aura in a peculiarly African sense. Under the conditions that they lived, enslaved Africans came to realize that, as individuals acting alone, they were defenseless and vulnerable to the whims of the masters. However, as a community unified and acting in harmony, they enhanced the opportunities that they could overcome the harshness of their conditions and enhance the quality of their existence through cooperation. Not only was this view of their situation strikingly similar to that which had influenced African religious worldview and social organization but it also became influential in facilitating the transformation of the ritual and expressive traditions surrounding African religious specialists.

In transforming their tradition of African religious leadership, however, the differences in the lifestyle of Africans on the continent from those enslaved in America influenced how they conceptualized the conjurer. For example, the religious persecution of enslaved Africans and the socio-cultural situation which prevented reconstituting religious institutions had a uniform effect on the conception of religious specialists in America—they lost their association with the gods of specific religions. Thus, the priestly role, one of the two most important religious leadership roles in Africa, did not become associated with conjurers in the United States. The priestly role was too dependent on the existence of religious institutions and the ability of devotees to participate in public and communal rites. Therefore, with the exception of voodoo priests, who continued to act as both priests and medicine-men in isolated instances, primarily, in urban areas, the transformation of the traditions surrounding African religious specialists culminated in a figure without priestly duties. However, the medicine-man role, which had been less tied to the institutional or communal practice of religion in Africa, but rather had revolved around individual need and consultation, was more adaptable to the conditions of physical and social isolation of the majority of Africans in America. Therefore, individuals who possessed knowledge of "medicine" could continue to serve a vital function under appropriate circumstances even in the absence of an organized religion or coherent following.

The viability of the medicine-man role was also enhanced by the widespread belief among diverse African groups that knowledge of "medicine" was inherent in the individual. In America, this belief facilitated the transformation of the traditions surrounding the medicine-man in several important ways. First of all, it allowed for the development of diverse belief concerning the source of the conjurer's power and knowledge. "Being born the seventh son of a seventh son or being born with the caul were sources of power. In addition, it was believed that the lore of conjuration could be passed from teacher to pupil."[86] In the absence of a perception of ties between conjurers and an institutionalized religion, a view of their powers and knowledge as either inherent or acquired from one possessed of it best served the needs of a community composed of individuals from diverse religious backgrounds. Secondly, belief in either the inherent or acquired powers of conjurers did not create a serious conflict with the Christian views of enslaved Africans as Christianity became widespread among them. Many Christian slaves expressed the view that God could and did endow individuals on earth with the power to conjure. Finally, an ambiguous view of the source of the powers of conjurers helped enslaved Africans to enshrine them as folk heroes who characteristically performed actions that reflected the spiritual values that Africans had traditionally accepted as the most advantageous in their efforts to order social life. As individuals whose knowledge and power emanated from a source outside the slave system, conjurers were sources of power and knowledge that could be neither controlled nor usurped by the masters. Therefore, conjurers offered enslaved Africans a focus for creating oral expressive traditions to transmit a conception of behaviors alternative to those fostered by existence under European domination.

Interestingly, in the folklore of enslaved Africans, conjurers were sometimes portrayed as individuals who acted in ways that revealed the superiority of their spiritual powers over the masters' physical powers. For example, William Wells Brown described Dinkie, the conjurer on the plantation where he was enslaved, as an individual who acted in perfect defiance of the master's rules. "No one interfered with him," recalled Brown. "Dinkie hunted, slept, was at the table at meal times, roamed through the woods, went to the city, and returned when he pleased. Everybody treated him with respect."[87] According to Brown, Dinkie never worked, never received a flogging, and was revered by both blacks and whites for his powers. Conjurers who garnered such reputations naturally acquired the respect of enslaved Africans, who viewed their actions as a model of behavior in the slave system.

Nevertheless, conjurers such as Dinkie who used their spiritual knowledge openly to challenge the masters' power to define and enforce black behavior were probably rare. Moreover, enslaved Africans enshrined conjurers as folk heroes not because they viewed their actions as a direct threat to the masters' physical power but because their spiritual attributes and behaviors reflected values that they accepted as the most advantageous to their survival and well-being in a rigid hierarchical social structure in which communal welfare had precedence over individual need. The conjurers' antagonist, in the minds of enslaved Africans, was not the masters, but rather the evil effects that could occur from the interaction and exchange of life-forces in everyday life. Although conjurers have often been cast as the arch-villains in the practice of conjuration in the slave community, they did not act capriciously, nor was their power viewed as inherently evil by enslaved Africans. Conjurers, like their African prototypes, served as intermediaries and acted on the basis of consultation and within a socio-cultural environment in which individuals viewed the harmony of their relationship with each other as essential in determining the quality of their existence in a hierarchically ordered social structure.

To understand the conjurer as a folk hero in the slave community, we must consider the role of the conjurer separately from the practice of conjuration. Enslaved Africans, like their African ancestors, continued to believe that any individual possessed the power to transform and transmute the force in nature through ritual and symbolic actions which had the effect of either enhancing or diminishing ontological being. They also continued to believe that individuals could literally buy into the mystical force by making sacrifice to those possessed of a greater share of it. In America, the sacrifice was almost invariably material in the form of food or money, and the conjurer figure was most often the being to whom sacrifice was made. Though apparently with less conviction than in Africa, enslaved Africans also continued to believe in the existence of witches, who in America and under the influence of Christianity were conceptualized as "jis living people wut bin sole to the debil."[88] Investing objects in nature with "vicarious force" through the use of words embued with negative emotion remained the primary way in which one cast a conjure spell. To endow some manifestation of an individual's being such as finger-nails or hair, or some object that had been in bodily contact with the intended victim was believed to be particularly effective in bringing about desired results. "Duh haiah is one of duh mos powful tings yuh enemies kin git hold of," explained a Georgia conjurer, "cuz it grow neah duh brain and a han made out uh haiah kin sho affec duh brain."[89] A "hand," "mojo," "trick," or "gopher," were all names given to the amulet used in a deliberate act of conjuration. The spoken word as the embodiment of an individual's life-force also could be used to conjure both directly and indirectly, especially in the form of the "bad mouth." Although enslaved Africans believed that any indi-vidual possessed the power to manipulate the force in nature to cause harm, they also believed that only the conjurer possessed the knowl-edge and power over this force to enhance ontological being or block the intended effects of a situation which had been caused by its ill-use.

To transmit a conception of conjurers as folk heroes, enslaved Afri-cans recounted the actions of individual conjurers in oral narratives, usually referred to as conjure tales. While we know little about the occasions for the telling of "conjure tales," we can surmise that they probably came up frequently in the context of tale-telling sessions in the community as well as in situations in which consultation with a conjurer appeared to be necessary. In the latter instance, because of the absence of institutional sanction or affiliation for conjurers or the practice of conjuration, they most likely served a persuasive function to overcome skepticism or the fear of reprisal, a not uncommon con-sequence of delving into the world of conjuration. These brief, often first person accounts served as an ideal expressive vehicle for trans-mitting a conception of conjurers as folk heroes. In these narratives, narrators recalled a specific instance in which a conjurer utilized his/her extraordinary spiritual powers to overcome a threat to the physi-cal, social, or psychological well-being of an individual known by or connected in some way to the performer and/or audience. In the absence of a unified religious worldview and constantly faced with the masters' efforts to impose their values on them, enslaved Africans used these accounts of personal experience of an extraordinary nature to demonstrate in concrete and specific terms that the conjurer's actions reflected a conception of behaviors adaptable to their situation in ways that could be advantageous in securing their interests in a physically and socially healthy community.

Not surprisingly, the African medicine-man's skill in combatting those manifestations of evil that led to illness and disease became the actions most often recounted in conjure tales. Conjurers were portrayed as individuals who, in curing illness, combined their knowledge of the medicinal properties of plants, herbs, roots, barks, animal substances, and so forth with mysticism. In addition, they were revered as individuals whose mystical power made them adept at ferreting out both the mystical causes of illness and the human agents. The following conjure tale contains not only a detailed description of actions characteristically associated with conjurers but also many of the beliefs concerning the practice of conjuration in the black community.

I was conjured once an' don' wan' to be conjured no mo'. I was conjured an' de spell brung big bumps under both my arms. Yes sir, brung fo' big bumps under de rigfht arm an' three bumps under de lef'. I declare dem bumps was so big dat de petticoat what I used to tie roun' me up under my arms, I had to fasten by shoulder straps over top of my shoulders. Couldn't figger out who conjured me. Only one 'oman could git to me. She de only 'oman what ever come in my house an' she didn't hab no cause to conjure me.

My husban' sen' me to de root doctor, ole Dr. Andrews. He made me chew a root, den he tole me what I been donin'. He say dat odder night I dreamed o' a open drawer at home what somebody done put dere. Den he say dar odder night I dreamed o' an open grave. A coffin was put in dat grave an' hit stayed dere nine days. Den he say I waken up an' ax de chillun, "Who done been here?" He tole hit true. Lord, oh so true! Den chillun say, "Nobody." An' I say, "Take dat bucket to de well, rise it out an' bring me a drink." He say I didn't drink 'cause effen I had drinked, I woulda died right den. Den he say, on de ninth day I was 'sposed to die anyway ef I hadn't come to him.

Den he sing out wid his eyes in a trench [trance?], "Give it back to her what gived it to you an' I kin cure you." I opened my mouth an' I say, "I b'lieves in God I aimin' to go to Heaben 'case he 'paring a place dere fo' me, an' I'se goin' to dat place 'case I ain't goin' give no spell like dis one what has done been given to me back to nobody. No sir." De man, he gimme his knife an' say, "Does you want it?" I say, "No, Jesus, I don' wan' hit," an' I han' it right back to him. He say, "Don' you see how you git rid o' de knife what I done put on you? Well, dat de only quickes' way to git rid o' de spell. Jes' put it right back on her dat put it on you."

I say, "No sir, Heaben is promised to me, an' I ain't goin' do nothin' ter break dat promise." Bout dat time cart drove up. He say, "Scuse me. I want to se how far dese people come." Den he take a mule shoe and tie it up in de roof. An' he swing it back an' forth. He look at' shoe an' atter while he say, "You come twenty; dey come thirty. Dey come fo' you." I say, "All right, doctor, dey mus' come fum roun'd Enfield, North Carolina. Den he come back to me an' say, "I ought to give you some medicine an' I is. When you gits home take dis dose. On de ninth day person will come an' confess. She'll come on de ninth day, sometime 'tween noon an' midnight."

I went home an' take de medicine. Sho' 'nough on de ninth day 'tween three and fo' clock, Carolina Crip commence a hollerin' an' runnin' all up an' down her neighborhood. A man what seed me later said, "Dey been a seekin' you all day." Fo' days and days I been dreamin' 'bout thing in trees. De trees was whar two paths cross each other. It was a Sunday, an' me an' Jake, my husban', went down back o' de house an' crossed de branch. Fus' thing we saw was two paths crossin'. On each side o' de paths was trees wid auger holes bored in'em. Dese auger holes had conjure things in 'em. We could hear her voice way cross de woods asingin' all day—singin' an' confessin' 'cause she couldn't he'p it:

Oh yes! Oh yes!
I been conjurin',
Oh yes! Oh yes!
I been killin',
No cause, no cause, no cause
In de worl'.

Her voice kep' a gittin' nearer. . . . Dat medicine sho' workin' strong on her. She stumbles on up in de yard asingin at de top of her voice. . . . I give her my han' an' I been all right ever since, 'ceptin' de place gits sore an' itches a littel ev'y once in a while.[90]

Cloaked in mystery, often distinguished by a striking appearance, possessed of the power of clairvoyance, and steeped in both mystical and practical knowledge of healing and their community, conjurers were repeatedly revealed in conjure tales as individuals of extraordinary powers. In their world, there was no mystery or accident, only human evil that could be blocked and even reversed to destroy the perpetrator.

The telling of conjure tales served to validate the belief that neither illness nor even death was a "natural" occurence but rather the consequences of ill-will or ill-action of one individual toward another. More importantly, the performance of conjure tales allowed enslaved Africans to transmit a conception of the conjurers' actions in fighting the evil of conjuration as behaviors that could be adopted by individuals to protect the spiritual and social values of the black community. As such, the actions of the conjurer in the tales served as an important source of behaviors accepted as the most advantageous in dealing with situations that disrupted the harmony and equilibrium of the individual and the group. For example, a South Carolina planter reported that the white doctor brought in to treat his slaves constantly "complained that his prescriptions were thrown out the window and March's [a conjure doctor] concoctions were taken in their stead."[91] Although many slaveholders forced their slaves to submit to white doctors and strenuously objected to the use of "conjure" medicine in the quarters, they often discovered that their objections held little sway over enslaved Africans. In defiance of the masters, they sought out conjurers and amassed supernatural aids not only to treat illnesses but also to ward off the evil that could result from an act of conjuration. According to the their own testimony, many wore around their necks and hidden under their clothing asafetida bags, buckeyes, rabbit feet, and various objects that had been invested with "vicarious force" by a conjurer. That the wearing of protective amulets involved risks to individuals caught wearing them was often noted by enslaved Africans. "Old Miss wouldn't stand for no such things as haunts or voodoo," recalled a former enslaved African. "When she inspected us once a week, you better not have no charm around your neck, neither."[92] In addition, Levine argues that over a period of time "slaves built up a vast store of remedies and treatments which may not have always cured disease or saved lives but which doubtless gave them a necessary and salutory sense of competence, control and active participation in at least one area of their lives."[93]

While conjure tales could offer individuals a conception of behaviors that protected them from the evil that led to illness and other forms of misfortune, they consistently reinforced the attitude that the practice of conjuration was an evil to be avoided. The possibility that individual enslaved Africans would adopt the attitude toward conjuration most often revealed in these narratives was dramatically increased by the tendency of narrators to concentrate on the experiences of ordinary individuals who found themselves caught up in the extraordinary events that could result from the practice of conjuration. To enhance this possibility, performers often concentrated on the most spectacular effects of an act of conjuration and the most dramatic actions performed by conjurers.

I hab a sistuh name Ida Walker wut wuz fix wid candy. She ate duh candy an den uh ahm swell up an tun blue. Yuh could see lill animals runnin up an down uh ahm. She got a root doctuh name Sherman. Soons he look at it, he know wut it wuz. He come Toosday an he gie uh a rub tuh use, an he say tuh rub down an he would come back Friday. Wen he come, deah tings all done come intuh duh finguhs. He tuk a basin wid some wome watuh, an he put muh sistuh han in it. Den he ketch hol uh duh han an duh tings run out in duh watuh. Dey wuz puppy dogs.
He ax uh did she want em tuh go back weah dey come frum, an she says yes. So he say he know duh man wut sen em, an he went tuh duh windah an tro duh watuh wid duh puppy dogs in it in duh direction uh duh man house an say, "Go." One week latuh duh man wuz in he fiel ploughin an he drop duh plough an fell down. Wen duh people git tuh em, all he could say wuz, "Dis is my wuk. Dis is my wuk." He went plumb crazy and died, but my sistuh got well an fin. She lib neah Millen now.[94]

In most conjure tales, narrators concentrated on the mysterious illnesses and diseases that individual members of the community experienced and the miraculous cures effected by conjurers in these instances. At the same time, individuals learned from these narratives the consequences of being the victim of conjuration and those that awaited individuals who abused this power. As in this tale, the actions of conjurers to affect a cure were sometimes pictured as being as devastating to the original perpetrators as their actions had been on the victim.

Conjure tales had the effect of reinforcing the belief that illness was merely a sprout of the seed of dissension that, if allowed to flower, could destroy the harmony of communal life and thereby the solidarity that they viewed as essential to their overall well-being. However, conjurers, though most often portrayed as champions in the struggle against the evil and evil-doers who, motivated by ill-will, caused illness, were also regaled at times for their efforts to enhance and facilitate behaviors that promoted harmony in the social and domestic lives of enslaved Africans. For example, one former enslaved African observed that conjurers sometimes sold "hush water in a jug. Hush water was jus' plain water what dey fixed so if you drink it you would be quiet an' patient. De men would git it to give to dey wives to make 'em hush up."[95] Conjurers were also noted for their preparation of "hands" to secure the affection of a member of the opposite sex, to assure marital fidelity, to uncover infidelity of a mate, and to protect individuals from theft or intruders bent on causing harm through conjuration or other means. Henry Roger recalled that his parents buried a "conjure bag" under the front of their house to insure that visitors remained peaceful and friendly regardless of their original design.[96]

While many enslaved Africans expressed skepticism concerning the conjurer's power directly to affect the masters, some related incidents clearly revealed that this belief was not universally accepted.

> His master beat him so sevare, so de man went to a witch. De witch said, "Never min'! you go home. To-morrow you will see me." When de man got up in de mornin', de white man was jus' as happy as happy can be; but de more de sun goes down, he commence ter sleep. At de same time he call to his Negro, "Tommorow you go an' do such an' such a tas'." Givin' out his orders kyan hardly hol' up his head. As soon as de sun was down, he down too, he down yet. De witch done dat. He [witch] come, but he stay in his house an' done dat.

Whether or not the majority of enslaved Africans believed that conjurers could be effective in directly affecting the masters, even the most skeptical seemed to have allowed for the possibility that conjurers could provide a means of indirectly affecting them. The often cited story of Frederick Douglass, who expressed skepticism in the powers of conjurers, serves as a perfect illustration. Douglass, who had been repeatedly and brutally beaten by his master, was given a "hand" by a conjurer as protection against future whippings. When his master approached him with the intent of flogging him, Douglass, to his own surprise and that of his master, engaged the man in a fierce fight and was never whipped again.[97] Although Douglass remained skeptical concerning the power of Sandy, the conjurer in this incident, his experience nevertheless illustrates an important aspect of the belief in conjuration. In many instances, enslaved Africans, believing that they were protected by the power of conjurers' spells, embraced actions that they otherwise would never have attempted.

Conjuration, though a potentially destructive practice if allowed to go unchecked, existed because it offered enslaved Africans decided advantages in protecting their values in the repressive environment in which they lived without upsetting the social order. While the conjurers' actions constantly forced them to recognize and accept the need to act in ways that respected the force in all beings, the conjure tales repeatedly reminded them that they lived in a world in which evil was pervasive. Their belief in the power to conjure, in its most often practiced form, offered them a culturally recognizable, if not socially accepted, mechanism for venting frustrations occasioned by the actions of others that they recognized as injustices, indignities, or violations of their rights as human beings, especially when suffered at the hands of a fellow sufferer. In so doing, they avoided seriously damaging the communal bonds or just as important, incurring the wrath and interference of the masters in intragroup affairs. The individual who utilized conjuration to settle a personal score avoided the overt display of anger, hostility, and aggression which both disrupted the harmony of social life in the slave community and threatened to bring the masters' power to bear upon it. The effects of an act of conjuration could only be blocked by a conjurer, an individual whose power to mediate the force in nature emanated from a mystical source. So the slave community, in adapting behaviors associated with conjuration as a means of dealing with interpersonal conflict, expressed its willingness both to define the behaviors that disrupted the harmony of social life and to accept the conjurer's actions as a form of justice in dealing with them.

When viewed from the viewpoint of those factors most influential in shaping black life in America during the slave period, the conjurer can be revealed as a folk hero whose actions offered enslaved Africans a recognizable focus for creating and maintaining behavioral patterns reflecting values traditionally accepted as the most advantageous to their well-being. On the one hand, the power to conjure assured enslaved Africans that the possession of a black skin, contrary to what the masters preached, neither made them inferior beings nor rendered them incapable of influencing the force in nature for their own benefit. On the other hand, conjuration served as the least costly means, in physical terms, by which they could assert their power as beings-with-force in a socio-political system which defined them as animals and, hence, beings-without-force. Conjurers, though often feared and shunned for their extraordinary powers, existed because they offered enslaved Africans a much needed source of power for dealing with the internal affairs of their own community. As enslaved Africans discovered in their socio-religious values ways of defining and controlling those behaviors that they envisioned as disruptions to individual well-being and communal harmony, their turning to conjurers rather than the masters as a model of behavior allowed them to continue the deep commitment of African people to spiritual values. The fear that knowledge of a powerful conjurer's actions could generate facilitated the community's efforts to create a vision of social life in which the most beneficial behaviors were those structured in such a way that offense could neither be given nor taken in the course of interaction. While this vision of social life had the effect of forging a relationship to the masters beneficial for enslaved Africans, its benefits for the slave system must be viewed as more opportunistic than intended. From the point of view of enslaved Africans, the value of their conjure beliefs derived from their ability to facilitate black culture-building based on values which respected the rights of individuals to achieve their fullest potential as human beings without undue interference from others.

Within the folk heroic tradition of enslaved Africans, the conjurer's characteristic actions complemented those most often associated with the trickster. The black conception of the conjurer as a folk hero was, in the most profound sense, that of a trickster possessed of spiritual power. Conjuration itself involved the use of "tricks" that individuals used to minimize the risks of adapting behaviors envisioned as the most advantageous in securing their individual interests at the expense, most often, of a member of their own community. On one level, the belief in conjuration reinforced the lesson inherent in trickster tales that trickery represented the most advantageous behavioral pattern for securing individual advantage within a hierarchical socio-political system. On another level, the actions of conjurers reinforced the lesson most clearly revealed in the John and Old Master trickster tale cycle, that behavior involving trickery against a fellow sufferer, regardless of its motivations or nature, was not in the best interest of their community. Although conjurers characteristically succeeded by using supernatural "tricks" against members of the black community, their antagonists were tricksters of the worst sort—individuals who attempted to manipulate the force in nature to rob others of their very being. Therefore, enslaved Africans justified the conjurer's actions by virtue of their need to act as both protagonist and antagonist in order to protect the community's values against the consequences of supernatural tricksters. In the end, conjurers emerged as champions over the chaos which always threatened to sever the bonds holding human beings to each other in the social world. In so doing, they offered enslaved Africans a conception of behaviors adaptable to their situation which recognized all human beings as a puny force when compared to the supernatural.

Notes

1. W. E. B. Du Bois, *The Souls of Black Folk* (New York: Avon Books, 1964 [1903]) 144.

2. "Tatler On the Management of Negroes," *Southern Cultivator* 9 (June 1851) 84–85.

3. Rev. Charles C. Jones, *The Religious Instruction of Negroes in the United States* (Savannah Ga., 1842) 128.

4. Dena Epstein, *Sinful Tunes and Spirituals* (Urbana: University of Illinois Press, 1977) 107.

5. Eugene Genovese, *Roll, Jordan, Roll: The World the Slaves Made* (New York: Vintage Books, 1976) 221.

6. Julien A. Hall, "Negro Conjuring and Tricking," *Journal of American Folklore* 10 (1897): 241.

7. Alice M. Bacon and Leonora Herron, "Conjuring and Conjure-Doctors," in *Mother Wit From the Laughing Barrel: Readings in the Interpretation of Afro-American Folklore*, ed. Alan Dundes (Englewood Cliffs, N.J.: Prentice-Hall, 1973) 360–61.

8. Louis Pendleton, "Negro Folk-Lore and Witchcraft in the South," *Journal of American Folklore* 3 (1890): 204.

9. Bacon and Herron 360; Newbell N. Puckett, *Folk Beliefs of the Southern Negro* (Chapel Hill: University of North Carolina Press, 1926) 166.

10. Pendleton 204.

11. Puckett 520.

12. Puckett 520.

13. Puckett 174.

14. John Mbiti, *African Religions and Philosophy* (Garden City, N. Y.: Doubleday, 1970) 1.

15. Albert J. Raboteau, *Slave Religion* (New York: Oxford University Press, 1978) 7.

16. Raboteau 11.

17. Vincent Harding, *There Is a River* (New York: Vintage Books, 1983) 5.

18. The evidence that Africans attempted to reconstitute their religions exists in many forms. The existence of quasi-religious and religious practices such as conjuration, obeah, and voodoo based on African religion among people of African descent throughout the new world constitutes the most dramatic evidence. In addition, the prohibitions and restrictions placed on the behavior of Africans which often became codified in law very early in the history of New World slavery were often influenced by suspicions that African

assemblies involved religious rites. For a discussion of the relationship between "slave laws" and African religious suppression, see Epstein 59–62.

19. Epstein 59–62; Genovese 40–41.

20. In this discussion of African religious specialists and worldview, I am mindful of the fact that a relatively minor number of Africans enslaved in America were Islamic. In addition, I write this section in the past tense not to suggest that traditional African religions have died out, but rather to highlight the fact that the vast majority of Africans enslaved in America would have subscribed to a traditional religious worldview at the time of the trans-Atlantic slave trade and that they did not retain them intact in America.

21. Mbiti 252. In different cultures, the class of religious specialists may have included, in addition to, and in some instances instead of, priests and medicine-men, practitioners such as diviners (who usually functioned as medicine-men), rain makers, mediums, prophets, and divine rulers. In almost all instances the principal duties of religious specialists would have included or overlapped with those identified as duties of priests and medicine-men in this discussion.

22. Mbiti 245–46.

23. E. G. Parrinder, *West African Religion* (London: Epworth Press, 1949), 75f.

24. Parrinder 75.

25. Mbiti 221.

26. Mbiti 218.

27. Mbiti 221.

28. E. E. Evans-Pritchard, "The Morphology and Function of Magic: A Comparative Study of Trobriand and Zande Rituals and Spells" in *Magic, Witchcraft and Curing*, ed. John Middleton (Garden City, N.Y.: The Natural History Press, 1967) 11–12.

29. William Bascom, *Ifa Divination* (Bloomington: Indiana University Press, 1969) 122.

30. Bascom 121.

31. Melville J. Herskovitz and Frances S. Herskovitz, *Dahomean Narratives* (Evanston, Ill: Northwestern University Press, 1958) 11–40.

32. Evans-Pritchard 16.

33. Dr. Irving, "The Yoruba Mission," *Church Missionary Intelligencer*, IV(1853):233.

34. John Beattie, "Divination in Bunyoro, Uganda," in Middleton, ed. 211–12.

35. Mbiti 93.

36. E. J. Marais, *African Thought* (Cape Province, South Africa: Fort Hare University Press, 1972) 10–11.

37. What I call "life-force" is also referred to in the literature as the "force in nature," "force," or "mystical power." Therefore, I use these terms as synonyms throughout this discussion and the book.

38. Marais 6.

39. Raboteau 16.

40. Marais 9.

41. E. A. Ruch and K. C. Anyanwu, *African Philosophy* (Rome: Catholic Book Agency, 1984) 129.

42. Ruch and Anyanwu 135.

43. Ruch And Anyanwu 135.

44. Quoted in Ruch and Anyanwu 74, from L. S. Senghor, "Discours Prononcé à l'Université d'Oxford," October 1961.

45. Ruch and Anyanwu 173.

46. Ruch and Anyanwu 173.

47. Mbiti 271.

48. Mbiti 258–259.

49. Ruch and Anyanwu 114.

50. Mbiti 38.

51. Mbiti 218.

52. Mbiti 220.

53. Benjamin C. Ray, *African Religion* (Englewood Cliffs, N.J.: Prentice Hall, 1976) 159.

54. Mbiti 252.

55. Ruch and Anyanwu 113.

56. Georgia Writers Project, *Drums and Shadows* (Spartanburg, S.C.: The Reprint Company, 1974).

57. Evans-Pritchard 16.

58. John W. Blassingame, *The Slave Community* (New York: Oxford University Press, 1972) 160.

59. Blassingame 161.

60. Blassingame 86–88.

61. Blassingame 88.

62. From an interview with Virginia Hayes Shepherd in Perdue et al., *Weevils in the Wheat* (Bloomington: University of Indiana Press, 1976) 259.

63. Blassingame 162.

64. Genovese 632.

65. Raboteau 13.

66. Blassingame 33.

67. Raboteau 96–100; Epstein 100–111.

68. Raboteau 96–100.

69. Genovese 220–25.

70. Epstein 194.

71. Epstein 194.

72. Postell, *The Health of Slaves on Southern Plantations* (Baton Rouge: Louisiana State University Press, 1951) 82. Many of the conclusions reached by Postell concerning the cause and nature of health problems among enslaved Africans have been supported by other researchers: Thomas C. Parramore, "Non-Venereal Treponematosis in Colonial North America," *Bulletin of the History of Medicine* XL(1970): 571–81; Todd L. Savilt, "Smothering and Overlaying of Virginia Slave Children: A Suggested Explanation," *Bulletin of the History of Medicine* XLIX(1975): 400–404; Kenneth F. & Virginia H. Kiple

"Black Tongue and Black Men: Pellagra and Slavery in the Antebellum South," *Journal of Southern History* XLIII (1977): 404–28.

73. Postell 82–83.

74. Postell 85.

75. Postell 73; Blassingame 159.

76. Raboteau 286.

77. Lawrence W. Levine, *Black Culture and Black Consciousness: Afro-American Folk Thought from Slavery to Freedom* (New York: Oxford University Press, 1977) 63; Postell 100.

78. Training and therapeutic practices used by doctors during the era of slavery are discussed by Postell 97–106 and Genovese 225–26.

79. Postell 105.

80. From an interview with Richard Jackson in George P. Rawick, ed., *The American Slave: A Composite Autobiography*, Vol. IV (*Texas Narratives*) (Westport, Conn.: Greenwood Press, 1977) 195.

81. Mbiti 2.

82. Rawick, ed., Vol VII (*Oklahoma Narratives*) 40; Fisk University, *Unwritten History of Slavery: Autobiographical Accounts of Negro Ex-Slaves*, comp. and ed. Ophelia Settle Egypt et al. (Washington, D. C., 1968 [1945]) 46.

83. Bacon and Herron 361; Puckett 276.

84. From an interview with Susan Davis in Rawick, ed., Vol. XI (*Missouri Narratives*) 284.

85. Jones 130.

86. Raboteau 276–77.

87. William Wells Brown, *My Southern Home* (Boston, 1880) 68–69; Blassingame 49; Raboteau 252.

88. Georgia Writers Project 34.

89. Georgia Writers Project 36; Raboteau 278.

90. From an interview with Matilda H. Perry in Perdue et al. 221–223.

91. Henry W. Ravenel, "Recollections of Southern Plantation Life," *Yale Review* 25 (1936): 767.

92. Norman R. Yetman, ed., *Voices of Slavery* (New York: Holt, Rinehart and Winston, 1970) 189–90.

93. Levine 66.

94. Georgia Writers Project 36–37.

95. Rawick, ed., Vol. VI (*Alabama Narratives*) 322; Raboteau 280.

96. Quoted in Levine 78.

97. Frederick Douglass, *Narrative of the Life of Fredrick Douglass: An American Slave* (Boston: The Anti-Slavery Office, 1845) 71–74.

F O U R

Christian Soldiers All:
Spirituals as Heroic Expression

As a prelude to his discussion of the spiritual song tradition of en-slaved Africans, Harold Courlander in his book, *Negro Folk Song U.S.A.*, observes that "the slaves brought to Christian service religious tradi-tions their own, as well as established methods of treating musical and invocational ideas."[1] Of these traditions, he notes that

> They had clear-cut concepts of the role of music in life. Music permeated virtually every important phase of living in Africa, from birth to death. Singing related to religious activity had a specific character and specific requirements... In religious rites, epic and dramatic actions of demigods, as well as their special powers and attributes were recalled and extolled. Those who served such dieties, sang songs of praise which alluded to their various powers, behavior, and noteworthy deeds. Much of the oral religious literature of the African layman consisted less of prayers (as we think of them) than of dramatic statements, in the form of song, relating to the dieties.[2]

Courlander concludes that, in America, "Confronted with new reli-gious patterns, the New World African found in the Bible prolific material adaptable to the dramatic statement and, occasionally, the epic treatment."[3] Although he examines several spirituals as ex-amples of the epic treatment given to the lives of biblical figures by enslaved Africans, he neither indicates how these songs reflect and/ or reveal the influence of African religious traditions nor discusses those aspects of the spiritual song tradition in general which might reveal specific connections with African epic traditions or religious beliefs.

Nevertheless, Courlander's suggestion that the spirituals represent a transformation of African religious ritual and heroic song traditions offers a cogent explanation for the inclination of enslaved Africans to emphasize dramatic and heroic action in the spirituals. In various ways, others have noted the prominent role of biblical heroes in the spirituals as well as the epic-like qualities of the tradition. Sterling Brown, for instance, in a brief examination of the spirituals concludes that

> The spirituals make an anthology of Biblical heroes and tales, from Genesis where Adam and Eve are in the Garden, picking leaves, to John's calling the roll in Revelations. There are numerous gaps, of course, and many repetitions. Certain figures are seen in an unusual light; Paul, for instance, is generally bound in jail with Silas, to the exclusion of the rest of his busy career. Favored heroes are Noah, chosen of God to ride down the flood; Joshua, who caused the wall of Jericho to fall (when the rams' lambs' sheephorns began to blow); Jonah, symbol of hard luck changed at last; and Job, the man of tribulation who still would not curse his God.[4]

Lawrence W. Levine also comments on the the frequent references to biblical figures in the spiritual. He suggests that these references helped enslaved Africans in their efforts to develop one of the most important themes of the songs:

> In the world of the spirituals, it was not the masters or the mistresses but God and Jesus and the entire pantheon of Old Testament figures who set the standards, established the precedents, and defined the values; who, in short, constituted the "significant others." The world described by slave songs was a black world in which no reference was ever made to any white contemporary.[5]

While the spiritual song canon contains numerous songs that do not mention biblical figures at all, an impressive number are developed around their exploits and/or allude to their deeds in a meaningful way. Furthermore, the spirituals that recall biblical personages and events are by no means literal renderings of biblical texts. Rather they present biblical figures and situations creatively in a vernacular which redacts the language of the King James Bible to achieve a lofty poetic style replete with drama and action befitting epic expression.

Although students of the spirituals have frequently alluded to the portraits of biblical figures as a distinctive feature of the songs, with the exception of Courlander they have not viewed the African religious song tradition as a potential expressive model for spiritual song creation. In fact, critical discussion of the spirituals has been dominated by protracted debate and controversy over whether African cultural traditions had any influence at all on the creation of the songs. From an analysis of the complicated and often heated debates over the origins of the spirituals, D. K. Wilgus observes that discussion has revolved around the questions "what elements in the Negro spirituals have been borrowed from North American whites and what are due to an African heritage and/or the Negro's own creation in America."[6] While scholars on all sides of the issue have been willing to concede the possibility of African musical influence to some degree, most have been unwilling even to consider the possibility that the song texts had their roots in African oral tradition. Wilgus, however, views this aspect of the controversy as an indication of the sanity of its participants: "Whatever the confusion in some minds, no serious students has imagined that Negroes disembarked in Virginia singing 'Deep River' or 'Roll, Jordan.' And whatever the confusion in some minds, no reputable scholar who has studied the problem has ever said that Negroes merely imitated or echoed white songs."[7]

The controversy over the original source of spiritual songs, treated by Wilgus as an isolated issue in the scholarship, is far more complex than it has appeared on the surface. Scholars, regardless of their views on cultural influences, have demonstrated as much interest in the meaning to be attached to the existence of a unique body of religious songs among enslaved Africans as in the source of the musical and expressive traditions that influenced their creation. Such an emphasis, in discussions ostensibly devoted to unraveling the mystery of origins, has been neither capricious nor accidental. This controversy developed in the years immediately following emancipation when the collection, publication, and performance of spirituals created a great deal of interest in the society. During this era, many scholars saw the spirituals, along with the other major forms of folklore created by African Americans during slavery, as a way to guage the potential black response to freedom rather than as a source of ideas and behaviors important to an understanding of black culture. In the case of the spirituals, this approach was influenced by the suspicion harbored by many whites that enslaved Africans had somehow perverted Christian religious teachings and made them an expression of their own African cultural values. Throughout the period of slavery, some whites were never able to shake the feeling that, in Frederick Olmsted's terms, black expressions of Christian beliefs represented merely black efforts "to furnish a delusive clothing of Christian forms on the vague superstitions of the African savage."[8] In effect, Christianity in the hands of Africans, some whites suspected, had merely served to revitalize African religious beliefs in America. Others expressed equally strong convictions that enslaved Africans had accepted Christianity, as presented to them by whites, as a religion of submission and compensation and had, in the process, become better slaves, a view propagated by both laymen and scholars of black religion well into the twentieth century.[9] Nevertheless, in the late nineteenth century, lingering suspicions of an essential "savage" (i.e. African) element in the black character created much anxiety in the white community as folklore collectors frequently used black folklore to both prove and disprove accusations that freed African Americans posed threats to white well-being.

At any rate, in discussions of the origins of the songs, the issue was often reduced to whether spiritual songs resulted merely from an imitation of white religious song forms and ideas or were indeed original black creations which expressed ideas and values unique to people of African descent. In the ensuing debate, those who argued most strenuously that black spiritual songs were directly influenced by white religious expression also maintained that the ideas and values embodied in them did not reflect concerns unique to enslaved Africans. For example, Newman I. White compared key images in the songs to those found in white religious songs of the period and concluded that since both black and white spirituals contained expressions such as "freedom," "the Promised Land," and "Egyptian bondage," "without thought of other than religious meaning," the black spirituals which made reference to these ideas could not reflect "the Negro's longing for physical freedom," as some had claimed.[10] George P. Jackson who, with White, was a staunch advocate of white origins, claimed that white spirituals both contained similar ideas and grew out of similar conditions: "I may mention in closing the chief remaining argument of the die-hards for the Negro origin of the Negro spirituals. How could any, the argument runs, but a natively musical and sorely oppressed people create such beautiful things as 'Swing Low,' 'Steal Away,' and 'Deep River?'. But were not the whites of the mountains and the die-scrabble hill country also 'musical and oppressed'?"[11]

However, scholars who argued for strong African influence and/or indigenous creation of spirituals often adopted the position that they did not embody social ideas so much as reflect the peculiar social conditions under which their creators lived. H. E. Krehbiel, for instance, who maintained that the songs contained "idioms that were transported from Africa" suggested that only under the conditions of enslavement could the songs have taken form in America

> Nowhere save on the plantation of the South could the emotional life which is essential to the development of the true folksong be developed; nowhere else was there the necessary meeting of the spiritual cause and the simple agent and vehicle. The white inhabitants of the continent have never been in the state of cultural ingeniousness which prompts spontaneous emotional utterance in music.[12]

James Weldon Johnson, who advocated indigenous creation, contended that, though influenced by African musical tradition, the spirituals revealed the enslaved African taking "complete refuge in Christianity."

> Far from his native land and customs, despised by those among whom he lived, experiencing the pangs of separation of loved ones on the auction block, knowing the hard master, feeling the lash, the Negro seized upon Christianity, the religion of compensation in the life to come for the ills suffered in the present, the religion which implied the hope that in the next world there would be a reversal of conditions, of rich man and poor man, of proud and meek, of master and slave. The result was a body of song voicing all the cardinal virtues of Christianity.[13]

In arguing that the spirituals primarily served enslaved Africans as creative escape and emotional compensation for their oppressive earthly existence, scholars such as Krehbiel and Johnson sought to defend the songs against accusations both of white origins and of social commentary as their dominant function.

John Lovell, Jr., however, virtually stands alone as a strong advocate both for indigenous creation of spirituals and for an interpretation of them as a reflection of the social ideas of enslaved Africans. Lovell argues that spirituals, though created in America under the peculiar conditions of slavery, exhibited some African musical and cultural influence, especially the African practice of using song as a form of social commentary.[14] He rejects the idea that the message of the songs was "otherworldly" or even essentially religious. He contends that enslaved Africans "settled upon Christianity as the nearest available and least suspect and most stimulating system for expressing their concept of freedom, justice, rights, and aspirations."[15] Lovell suggests that the songs should be studied as "folk poetry" and their creators viewed as poets who discovered in Christianity a source of ideas and used spiritual song creation as a creative outlet for expressing their feelings of oppression and injustice both within their situation and toward the masters.

Although scholars who participated vigorously in the debate over the origins and meanings of the spirituals often presented a great deal of evidence to defend their positions and conclusions, they seldom explored outside the texts and music or engaged in any other than formal analysis. In addition, despite their willingness to consider and, in most instances, concede the possibility of African musical influence, they almost universally accepted the Euro-American religious song tradition and/or Christian religious values as the only logical or possible prototype or source for spiritual song texts. Therefore, even those who argued for indigenous creation of the songs merely sought to prove that the texts of spirituals were not based on the Euro-American tradition.

While spiritual song creation was obviously influenced by both the introduction of enslaved Africans to Christian religious expression and their religious, social, and expressive needs in slavery, the existence of the spirituals as a unique body of song oriented toward heroic expression in ways distinct from Euro-American religious songs cannot be explained as creative parody or even indigenous creation. Nor can the cultural origins or influences which made them meaningful to enslaved Africans be fully comprehended through an examination of the texts and music of the songs in isolation from the socio-cultural influences on their creation or the social contexts in which they were performed. Despite the bias toward formal analysis of those who participated in the debate over the origins of the tradition, the socio-cultural *milieu* of spiritual song performance has not been lost. Early collectors of the songs consistently emphasized and described the context of performance as well as the structure of the religious rites in which they functioned as a vital form of expression.

Although early collectors often expressed the view that their primary goal was to preserve a unique body of religious song, they demonstrated a great deal of interest in portraying the context and style of spiritual song performance. Motivated by curiosity and, in some instances, incomprehension, early collectors were often convinced that, even if the singing style was not purely African, they were witnessing something in black religious services and song performances which had no parallel in white tradition. The attitude of Henry C.

Wood, who collected spirituals in the camp meeting setting in the late nineteenth century, was typical of that of many early collectors who believed that without ethnographic detail the songs could neither be understood nor appreciated by white readers. He wrote that "to reproduce them apart from the surroundings is to rob them of much of their wild beauty and the strange impressiveness which they possess to so marked a degree."[16] Wood described the role of song as important to every phase of black religious services. He described the entire service as an extended song, from the chanted sermon with its call-and-response pattern to its parallel in the spiritual song singing which served as a bridge between different parts of the service. Like most early collectors, Wood was struck by the emotional interaction and involvement of the participants with both sermon and song:

> To see the negro at the height of his religious frenzy, however, and in the full enjoyment of its influence, one should attend camp-meeting, where the dusky worshipper yields up himself fully to the spell of the fervor which enwraps him with its intensity and sways him in its peculiar force.[17]

Nathaniel Dett also commented on the emotional involvement of blacks with their songs in his preface to *Religious Folk-Songs of the Negro as Sung at Hampton Institute*. He observed that "In those primitive Negro churches where original songs are still sung, there is often hand-clapping, patting and rattling of the feet, swaying of the body, and sometimes, but rarely now, snapping of the fingers in accompaniment."[18]

While the trance-like states that resulted from the emotional involvement of blacks with song and sermon were not totally unfamiliar to white collectors, who often compared them to camp meeting revival behavior, the "shout" described by Henry Spaulding as "a single outburst and manifestation of religious fervor" caught the attention of many collectors as a uniquely black religious element.[19] In more descriptive terms, Spaulding observed of the "shout" that

> After the praise meeting is over, there usually follows the very singular and impressive performance of the 'shout,' or religious dance of the negroes. Three or four, standing still, clapping their hands and beating time with their feet, commence singing in unison one of the peculiar shout melodies, while the others walk around in a ring, in single file, joining also in the song. Soon those in the ring leave off their singing, the others keeping it up

the while with increased vigor, and strike into the shout step, observing most accurate time with the music. This step is something halfway between a shuffle and a dance, as difficult for an uninitiated person to describe as to imitate. They will often dance to the same song for twenty or thirty minutes, once or twice, perhaps, varying the monotony of their movement by walking for a little while and joining in the singing.[20]

In addition to the "shout" as a unique aspect of black spiritual song performances, early collectors also found remarkable the important role of song leaders and the special recognition accorded them in the black community. William E. Burton, for instance, wrote extensively of his encounters with Sister Bemaugh, a noted spiritual song leader in the community where he collected. He recalled one incident in particular:

> At a meeting which I used to attend frequently, one of the leading singers was Sister Bemaugh, who often started the tune. One night there came from another settlement a famous singer, a man, who quite usurped Sister Bemaugh's place. There was no denying that she felt it, as he stood up before the congregation whenever a hymn was called for, in a most comfortable frame of mind, his head turned well to the left and the thumb and finger of his right hand holding the tip of his left ear, as he sang song after song. Several times Sister Bemaugh attempted to start a song; but each time he was ahead of her. [21]

The spiritual song leader served as "bard" responsible not only for leading songs but also for creating new songs. James Weldon Johnson recalled two noted leaders of songs from his childhood who shared the duties as leader and creator:

> My memory of childhood goes back to a great leader of singing, "Ma" White, and a maker of songs, "Singing" Johnson. "Ma" White was an excellent laundress and a busy woman, but each church meeting found her in her place ready to lead the singing.
> On the other hand, singing was "Singing" Johnson's only business. He was not a fixture in any one congregation or community, but went from one church to another, singing his way. I can recall that his periodical visits caused a flutter of excitement akin to that caused by the visit of a famed preacher. These visits always meant the hearing and learning of something new. I recollect

how the congregation would hang on his voice for a new song—
new, at least to them. They listened through, some of them joining in waveringly. The quicker ears soon caught the melody and
words. The whole congregation easily learned the response,
which is generally unvarying.[22]

Spiritual song leaders were valued for their abilities and talents to
improvise creatively and to make their voices an extension of those in
their community.

To most early collectors of spirituals, there was little doubt, as John
Mason Brown observed, that "The religious songs of the negro slave
were composed and communicated without the aid of writing and
were unmistakably marked in their construction."[23] Brown defined
"their construction" as songs that "abounded to excess in metaphor
of the most striking character."[24] Brown was particularly struck by the
vividness and frequency with which the spiritual song creators turned
to the language and imagery of war to portray their religious ideals.

The saints are styled the "Army of the Lord," led by King Jesus,
the "Captain" and "Conqueror." They were exhorted to hasten
to the summons of silver trumpets, marshaling the faithful to victory, and were described as sweeping down all the obstructions of
evil, and marching foward, with measured tread, up the hill on
which stands the city reserved for their habitation. The banners,
trumpets, drums and other paraphernalia of an army were used
without stint, and often with the most graphic effect.[25]

Thomas Wentworth Higginson also called attention to the frequent
use of martial imagery in the spirituals sung by the black soldiers
under his command during the Civil War. Although he expressed
skepticism concerning whether the military references were improvised to suit the war context of their performance or were originally
part of the songs, he nevertheless concluded that "These quaint religious songs were to the men more than a source of relaxation; they
were a stimulus to courage and a tie to heaven."[26]

In addition, several of the early fieldworkers noted what they considered to be a pronounced secular element in both the texts and
performance of the spirituals. Reverend Barton noted a large number
of what he called "Family Songs" which "in the successive stanzas is
the substitution of "father," "mother," or other relative in order."[27]
Spaulding related that the tradition, to him, seemed to unfold as a
blending of "things sacred and profane" which he attributed to "the

imperfect and fragmentary knowledge of the Scriptures which the negroes have picked up."[28] Even though several collectors commented that they believed there to be no clear-cut distinction in the black community between the sacred and the profane in the performance and creation of spiritual songs, few expressed any doubt that blacks were sincerely religious. Instead they attributed the apparent secular element to either a lack of formal education, poor acculturation under slavery, the innate character of blacks, or the fact that the songs were often performed in settings other than the church. In addition, many early collectors believed that the songs were entirely improvised at the time of their performance or that, at the least, there were no standard texts of spirituals. Since spirituals could be created as well as performed anywhere, their incorporation of non-religious elements was understandable.

However, most described the religious service as the primary context for spiritual song creation. Not uncommonly, the preacher or his sermon was noted as the impetus for spiritual song creation. Marion A. Haskell offered an example to support his contention that they were practically all improvised songs:

> Spirituals are often composed on the spur of the moment by a preacher or a member whose voice can insure the attention of the assemblage. At a meeting held in Columbia, South Carolina, the preacher chose as the subject of his sermon "Paul and Silas Imprisoned," and for an hour or more commanded the strictest attention of his hearers. At the end of this time interest began to flag visibly, and apparently the spirit of exhortation had fled from the minister. After a hard struggle to rouse the audience by another reading of the prison scene, he suddenly burst forth in a loud shout:
>
> > Y'all heah! Do dy-se'f no harm!
> > Y'all heah! Do dy-se'f no harm!
> > Oh-h-h! Y'all heah!
>
> At each repetition additional voices would join in, until the whole house had caught the words and rhythm.[29]

Because they believed that the songs were improvised, most early collectors viewed them basically as the product of an emotionally charged religious atmosphere and not the expression of other than black religious faith.

In these descriptions, early collectors, who often worked as participant-observers, revealed the spiritual song tradition of enslaved Africans as one which combined music, dance, song, and drama into an integrated performance. While they frequently expressed the view that the tradition of religious song performance that they encountered among newly freed blacks had little resemblance to the traditions of religious singing with which they were familiar, they seldom indicated any strong belief in an African influence on spiritual song creation or texts. Nathaniel Dett was uncharacteristic in that he argued that the African heritage of enslaved Africans offered the only logical explanation for the focus of the songs:

> But how, otherwise, should one explain the strong unwavering hope of final recompense, and the assurance of the perfection of another life to come, unless one is willing to admit that the slave brought with him from Africa a religious inheritance which, far from being shaken in any way, was strengthened by his American experience? Does it seem natural to suppose that there could be anything in slave life, not only as it existed in our Southern States, but even in slave life as it has existed anywhere in the world, to inspire such an idea.[30]

In an indirect reference to the biblical heroic tradition embodied in the spirituals, Dett observed that "It was nothing else, then, than this religious inheritance, their Oriental regard for parable and prophecy, which made easy the incorporation of so much of Bible story; for in striving to give voice to his experiences the slave found in the Testaments, in the story of the children of Israel, for instance, much in the way of a text ready made."[31]

Contrary to Dett's suggestion, however, scholars who have attempted to explain the focus on biblical figures and incidents in the spirituals have almost invariably turned to the experience of slavery rather than the African "religious inheritance" to explain its importance. In the process, they have interpreted the spirituals in ways which relegate the heroic tradition embodied in them to the realm of fantasy. In fact, the spiritual song canon as a whole has generally been envisioned primarily as a projection of the psychological and social longings of enslaved Africans for freedom and not as the expressive embodiment of a model of emulative behavior based on spiritual values. In the most focused discussions of biblical heroes in the songs, scholars have suggested that enslaved Africans recreated the actions of biblical figures as a way of projecting their dreams and fantasies about freedom expressively. As projections of "fantasy life [which] was so rich and important to them," according to Levine, the spirituals served as a form of social criticism of and psychological release from their everyday reality.[32] The actions of biblical heroes as portrayed in them, therefore, did not function as a normative model of heroic action because enslaved Africans could not and did not emulate the actions of these figures.

While enslaved Africans permeated the spirituals with a veritable encyclopedic list of criticisms of the conditions under which they lived and infused the songs with a psychologically healthy attitude about the future, their conception of biblical figures as folk heroes in the spirituals did not function merely as the expressive embodiment of their dream or fantasy life clothed in religious garb. As with most interpretations of folklore created by enslaved Africans, this view of the function of the heroic tradition embodied in spirituals is based on speculative retrospection—after all, enslaved Africans endlessly sang about biblical heroes who acted to secure their freedom, but they did not adopt the confrontative style of a Moses, for example, in demanding their own freedom. To uncover the function and meaning that enslaved Africans derived from the biblical heroic tradition embodied in their songs, we must attempt to understand the factors that influenced their transmitting in spirituals a conception of biblical figures as folk heroes whose characteristic actions reflected values guiding action important to them. Spiritual song creation, while undoubtedly serving religious and psychological needs, must also have served the community's cultural needs for recognizability in religious expression and their immanent social needs for a model of behavior. Therefore, it is essential that we consider the possibility that the types of actions performed by biblical heroes were not totally unfamiliar to enslaved Africans and, therefore, could function as a model for heroic actions based on African cultural values.

Although African religious literature has traditionally been discussed almost entirely in terms of the numerous and diverse myths found all over the continent, myths merely serve as the foundation of African religious beliefs and rituals. They neither constitute the whole of African religious expression nor represent the only means of celebrating or conceptualizing the power of the supernatural as a vital force in the African world. Mbiti contends that "Evidence shows that African peoples worship God at any time and in any place, and that there are no rules obliging people to worship at a given time and place."[33] However, mythic performances which often have prescribed rules governing the context and time of performance have attracted

f African religious expression. Dom-
us on myth as the dominant form of
ilts from the bias of western scholars
what he calls "cult buildings."[34] He
n technology and climate militated
in enclosed structures but also that
themselves (which stressed natural
eligious universe) influenced African
e contends that, whether used in the
all African expressive traditions serve
he pervasive influence of religion in

hs which served primarily to explain
creators, Africans also possessed a vast
erature   ich included tales, praise poems, and
arious forms of African heroic literature, the spiritual
on of enslaved Africans in form, content, and perform-
mbles the African heroic epic tradition more closely than it
the mythic traditions or the Euro-American religious song tradi-
on to which it has so often been compared. Heroic epic performances involve more than the recitation in song form of narratives
chronicling in literal or linear terms the exploits of figures recognized as heroes. They are complex events which include music,
dance, drama, and song and involve performers and audiences in a
dynamic interaction to celebrate the deeds of heroes. Scholars have
only recently begun to recognize the extensiveness of heroic epics in
Africa and their function as both religious and heroic expression.
The preliminary evidence suggests that African heroic epics existed as
a vital form of African oral literature at the time of the trans-Atlantic
slave trade and could have easily served as expressive models for spiritual song creation and performance.

THE AFRICAN HEROIC EPIC TRADITION

Heroic epics, according to Daniel P. Biebuyck, have been collected
extensively in West and Central Africa and to a lesser extent in East
and South Africa, where heroic poetry in the form of panegyrics or
praise poems has been the focus of most collecting and study.[36] In
addition to heroic epics which subordinate historical facts to fictional
representation, epic-like narratives and recitations which focus on
genealogies, migrations, places, battles, and group histories are also

performed both as separate narratives dealing with historical personages and incidents and as part of fictional epic performances. Although it is impossible to date the origin of any particular epic, it is
clear from internal evidence that many originated centuries ago.
Furthermore, Biebuyck relates that because of various connections
between different groups, African heroic epics often share "certain
common details in pattern, structure, heroic characters, and
events."[37] In essence, the African heroic epic traditions, though diverse in many ways, shared enough common elements to have facilitated transformation in America under the appropriate circumstances. However, to understand how Africans enslaved in America
discovered in their epic tradition a creative model for transforming
the biblical saga to create an expressive model for spiritual song creation, we must first attempt to understand the nature and meaning of
the African epic tradition within the context of African culture-building.

The heroic epic in Africa is a long narrative poem which "is sung
episode by episode; then the episode is narrated and acted out."[38]
Although singing and music pervade the performance of an epic, the
structure of an epic performance varies from group to group. In
some instances, portions of the epic story are sung and others narrated. In addition, the African heroic epic, though a coherent narrative when performed in its entirety, is multigeneric, or, as Biebuyck
describes it, a "supergenre," in that it "encompasses and harmoniously fuses together practically all genres known in a particular culture."[39]

> There are prose and poetry in the epic, the narrative being con-
> stantly intersected with songs in poetic form. The prose narrative
> to some extent, and the songs to a large extent, incorporate prov-
> erbs, riddles, praises, succinct aphoristic abstracts of tales,
> prayers, improvisations, allusions and references to "true stories"
> and persons.[40]

On the multigeneric nature of the African epic, John W. Johnson
concurs that "It may also be noted that praise poetry is often embed-
ded inside epic poetry as an integral part of its whole. The praise
poem, with the proverb and a few other types of folklore, constitutes
one of the standard modes of Mandekan epic."[41]

The African heroic epic, though overtly neither an historical nor
religious narrative, incorporates and reflects the values of Africans in
regard to both history and religion. Charles Bird observes, for instance, that

In the areas in which they are performed, the epics are universally recognized as a symbol of the origins, growth, and development of the state. As such, an epic frequently includes genealogies of the ruling groups, collapsed with mythological material pertaining to the origin of the world and the like. Often events in which the gods interceded symbolized the favoritism they are claimed to demonstrate toward the culture as a whole. The epic hero is himself a superman empowered by the gods to restore the state to its deserved grandeur in the natural order of things. The strength of the culture is fully reflected in the exploits of its epic hero.[42]

Biebuyck concurs that the epic hero serves an emergent function perceived as important to culture-building: "The advent of the hero is an astonishing phenomenon which is sometimes connected with cosmic turmoil (rain and thunder) or with unusual social and physical situations."[43] The hero, however, is immediately plunged into situations of hardship and trial and must earn the favor of the gods to overcome the obstacles that beset him.

Epic performances are also highly complex events of both ritual and social significance which are "interspersed with long pauses, to eat and drink, for dance performances, for dramatic action, for musical interludes, for praises." The celebratory atmosphere in which epics are performed causes these events to attract "a diverse, and sometimes large participating audience."[44] The performance of an epic in most African societies is not restricted by any temporal requirement or to any particular occasion as is often the case with mythic performances. Bird and Kendall, for example, claim that these "Heroic poems are sung continually in the Mande world. Bards sing them for all social ceremonies—births, baptisms, marriages, funerals."[45] Furthermore, the performance may last for a few hours or for several days depending on the occasion as well as on the bard's inclination during a particular performance. Although epic bards are well-known figures in African communities, their social identities vary from culture to culture. In some cases, they are specialists in a caste-like structure; in others, epic singing may be a family tradition. In any case, the singers almost invariably undergo some form of training to master the musical and verbal skills necessary to perform effectively, even though they usually claim divine inspiration as the most important requirement to sing of the deeds of their culture heroes.[46] Among many groups, the epic singer's artistic ability is clearly seen as a spiritual gift. Biebuyck notes, for instance, that the titles by which bards are known in some societies indicate the group's perception of their abilities as divinely inspired performers: "References to the bard as *Kyanga* seem to emphasize the fact that, in Lega thinking, the bard obtains his knowledge directly from a divine source. The idea of the quasi-divine origins of the bard's knowledge is also found among the Mango."[47] Within some groups, the epic bards' extensive knowledge of the history and culture of the community, displayed in their narrative performances, makes them important sources of counsel and advice outside of their professional duties as storytellers.

In addition to their mastery of a story line, epic bards must be accomplished musicians, actors and poets. While they are often accompanied during a performance by their apprentices as well as the audience who may participate in a performance in various ways, they also are the master musicians who, in some societies, accompany themselves on a variety of instruments. As actors, they dramatize their performances by acting out certain actions of the hero or other actors, both divine and human. Their poetic skills include mastery of the lofty language of the epic and the ability to improvise and create praise and aphorisms:

> The bard is not bound by a rigid text that he must follow with precision. He can introduce into narratives certain episodes or characters, and leave others out. He inserts personal reflections, proverbs, statements. He digresses to speak about himself, his ancestors, his experiences, his clan or caste, his artistry, his musical instruments, his teachers, and predecessors, or about certain members of the audience.[48]

The epic bard must always be conscious of the audience not only because it is for them that he performs, but also because they are not passive observers of the performance. The audience participate by acting as a choir alternatively singing and humming:

> The percussionist and members of the audience sing the refrain of the songs or repeat a whole sentence during each short pause made by the bard. In this capacity, they are called *barisya* (those who agree with; those who say yes). Members of the audience also encourage the reciter with short exclamations (including onomatopoeia) and handclapping and whooping.[49]

Furthermore, because the audience already know the story as well as the values that it embodies, they are critical participants.

The African epic as a narrative form "is not necessarily centered on the deeds of one hero who is always the driving force behind the action," although the epic is developed around the heroic career of a central heroic figure. The actions of other figures aid in clarifying the message of the epic and the historical and cultural information that it contains.[50] The epic hero whose exploits are the subject of the narrative is a national hero rather than one celebrated by a segment or subgroup within a society. He is also usually distinguished by an unusual birth, threatened in his youth, removed from his home, and forced to undergo hardships and trials before returning to his people. Although the epic hero is invariably described as an exceptional person, he is not necessarily an individual possessed of extraordinary physical endowments or stature. For example, Sunjata, the hero of one Mande epic, is described as crippled and infirm, and Fokali, the hero of another, is portrayed as extremely short with a disproportionately huge head and mouth.[51]

The physical stature of the epic hero, however, has no effect on his ability to triumph over his adversaries. The African epic is not a narrative which emphasizes physical confrontations or prowess. Johnson observes, for instance, that the hero's "major battles against his adversaries are not described in epic as great conflicts of weaponry, but rather they are battles of sorcery."[52] Bird and Kendall also note the relative absence of physical confrontations between the hero and his adversary in epics. They claim that epics "contain no extensive references to warfare, and few descriptions of physical prowess, yet they show great attention to details where the particulars of sorcery and its outcomes are at issue and when the tokens of power are described."[53] They argue that "Resolution of conflict in both political and heroic epics involves the recourse to spells and magic."[54] Biebuyck concurs that epic narration does not emphasize physical confrontation to any appreciable degree. He observes that epics "are not simply narratives of battle, tension, and heroic deed, but of appeasement, of resolution, and of harmony."[55]

The source of the hero's magic power with which he confronts his adversary is the focus of the heroic quest in African epics. According to Bird and Kendall, "The quest for strange and esoteric knowledge, for the secret underlying an adversary's *nya* [life-force] defines the content of Mande heroic literature. The degree to which this theme dominates the literature constitutes a striking contrast between European and Mande epic traditions. These differences emanate from different concepts of action and heroic activity."[56] The Mande epic tradition is not alone in portraying the quest for esoteric knowledge and the mystical power that comes with its possession as the focus of heroic adventure in the epic. The content of African epics generally revolves around the efforts of the hero to acquire mystical knowledge and power to succeed against his adversary. This conception of heroic activity in the epic derives, as Bird and Kendall suggest, from the concept of action in African societies. They argue that "The philosophy of action in the Mande world is keyed to the notion of *nya*, 'means,'" or the more general term, life-force, which is believed to provide the individual at birth "with an initial set of means to action, the ability to perform particular acts and, more importantly to be protected from the consequences of these acts." As we have already discussed, the life-force of individuals determines both their being, ontologically and socially, and what they can do as beings. The epic hero is one who literally performs actions beyond his "means."[57] Therefore, he does not naturally possess the "means" to protect himself from the dangerous or evil forces unleashed by his actions. His quest then becomes one of acquiring "fetishes and talismans" to increase his means or to gain the magical protection that he needs to perform the acts that will change his destiny.

In order to acquire the magical protection he needs to eventually defeat his adversary, the hero must violate the tabus of his society governing the manipulation of the force in nature. For this reason, the African epic hero has often been conceptualized in the scholarship as less than an ideal role model. Christiane Seydou argues that "the notion of transgression as the motivation for the action of the plot" constitutes a stable feature of African epic narration.[58] She observes that

> The hero, in point of fact, is always depicted as outside of the norm, as excessive, and as fundamentally inimitable. He, therefore, is not a model but a catalyst who provides the impetus for and instigates the audience toward realizing the commonly held ideology (of which he himself symbolizes a component).[59]

Johnson also suggests that the hero's manipulation of mystical or occult powers to affect his destiny makes him a problematic model of heroic action:

> There is a strong folk belief among many people in Mali that a hero—or anyone for that matter—has a destiny. This belief is not, however, one of predestination, for the hero must correctly identify and attempt to fulfill his appointed destiny. If he undershoots his capabilities, he may lose out altogether. If he advances

too rapidly, he may be consumed by the occult power he needs in order to fulfill his destiny. Although the hero may bring prestige and even wealth to his people, he is not so much admired personally as feared. For example, one major method the hero may employ to gain occult power (nyama), which can be used to assist him in fulfilling his destiny, is to violate the tabus of society. If the hero is strong enough, that is to say if he is in tune with his destiny at that stage of its fulfillment, he will be able to gain control over the occult power for the next step. If on the other hand he has attempted too much too fast, he may be consumed by the power.[60]

Biebuyck, on the other hand, argues that "the hero's uniqueness lies, above everything else, in his ability to reverse his destiny" and that he accomplishes this reversal by violating the social and sacred tabus of his culture. He notes, however, that for the hero to "achieve full *karama* (life-force) and *nkuru* (fame and force)," he must discover the socially approved ways of using his esoteric knowledge and power for the benefit of the community. Therefore, he contends that the hero's adventures should be viewed as a kind of initiation rite in which he learns through his hardships and trials to control his own life-force (which, at the beginning of his adventure, is already accepted by his community as superior because of his unusual birth) for the benefit of his community.[61]

The epic hero's manipulation of occult forces to affect his destiny is obviously a key to understanding the meaning that Africans derived from epic narration. In many ways, the African epic hero's quest for mystical power represents a heightened example of that engaged in by those who participate in the narration of his deeds. Mbiti contends that, in Africa, the quest for mystical knowledge and power constitutes an on-going activity. "Some may even pay fantastic amounts of wealth to have reasonable access to it, in one form or another. This mystical power is not a fiction: whatever it is, it is a reality with which African people have to reckon."[62] Because they believe in the existence of esoteric knowledge and mystical power, Africans neither view its pursuit as a vagarious activity nor hold a simple attitude toward it. Their attitude toward the quest to obtain it is complicated by their belief that the possession of this mystical force is the most potent form of protection for both individuals and the community, and that its uncontrolled pursuit poses the greatest threat to the lifestyle that they believe leads to its increase. In other words, Africans are not so much threatened by the possession of mystical power, since they believe that all individuals are born with mystical power or a life-force, as they are by the consequences of behaviors that individuals adopt to increase their share of it.

For Africans, no threat is posed by the efforts of individuals to enhance their life-force to achieve full ontological being by observing the forms of behaviors recognized by the group as ideal. However, efforts to enhance one's own life-force using magic or witchcraft is a punishable evil. Such behavior is viewed as a violation of tabus that threatens the well-being of the entire group whose collective power is seen as dependent on the strength of the force of those who participate in it. In African cultures, the collective power of the group is measured by its prosperity, which is seen as a sign of favor with the gods and spirits. As we have already noted, Africans view an action which diminishes the life-force of another member of the group or offends against the gods as effectively diminishing the collective power of the entire group. When situations occur that they define as a diminution of life-force, they turn to their religious specialists to cleanse the individual and community of the evil force unleased by the ill-action and to punish those responsible for it. Although religious specialists use the same actions that unleashed the evil forces in the first place, their actions are viewed as morally justifiable, both by virtue of their superior force and because their actions are perceived as beneficial to the community.

The ways in which Africans "reckoned" with the existence of mystical power in their community are apparently what scholars have in mind when they characterize the epic hero as one who acts "outside the norm." The epic hero, however, is not one whose exploits take place primarily within the context of his community. "The hero himself is a restless wanderer who is constantly away from his village." The epic hero's milieu is the forest, and he is often associated with hunting and war. Although "the atmosphere of the forest and the hunt pervades many passages in the epic," hunting is not an important activity of African epic heroes, even though it is an important focus of other forms of African heroic literature.[63] Scenes of the hunting camp merely serve as a background for much of epic action and reveal the interchangeability of the hunter and warrior roles traditionally recognized in African societies. The epic hero, as Courlander and Sako point out, is "a man who accomplished exceptional deeds in war, or in personal combat against other heroes."[64] That Africans would celebrate the deeds of victorious warriors in their oral traditions should not be surprising. Africans have historically confronted war as a recurrent threat and solution to their autonomy and survival. Precisely because they have been frequently faced with war as an obstacle to culture-building, their heroic epic traditions have served as important expressive vehicles for transmitting a conception of the behaviors that they recognize as the most advantageous to their survival and well-being in a warlike or hostile environment. The frequent occurrence of war in African societies accounts in large part for the popularity of the epic as a narrative which recounts the heroic exploits of exceptional warriors. In addition, Biebuyck notes in his summary of African heroic epic traditions that "all epic-producing ethnic groups have elaborate traditions of migration, expansion, and cultural assimilation, or well-established traditions of conquest and warfare."[65] During times of war and armed conflict between African groups, African cultures had to contend with challenges to their cultural identity and values not only from the actions of external foes but also from the actions that they had to employ to meet them.

Although the African heroic epic celebrated the deeds of war heroes, it served as more than an expressive vehicle for transmitting the exploits of these figures, a fact very clearly revealed in its depiction of war and warlike behavior. The heroic epic also served as an expressive vehicle for transmitting African religious values since that played an important role in their view of successful warlike behavior. For example, in African societies, warriors and hunters traditionally sought to enhance their spiritual protection before commencing a hunt or engaging in battle by consulting religious specialists who possessed the power to endow their weapons with "vicarious force." They also traditionally wore protective amulets and received ritual purification after battle to protect themselves from the evil forces unleashed by their actions. Although Africans accepted these as traditional behaviors of warriors, they nevertheless faced a risk in creating expressive traditions to celebrate the deeds of warrior heroes who succeeded as much through magic as physical prowess. That is, in portraying heroes whose success was influenced by magic, individuals, especially uninitiated members of the group, might come to accept the actions performed under extraordinary conditions as normative in everyday life. Therefore, despite the fact that African warfare resulted from various causes and often involved fierce physical confrontations between combatants, the heroic epic depicts war primarily as a threat to and a test of the spiritual or magical power of the group, symbolized by the fictive hero. For example, the heroic epic traditionally portrays the encounter between the hero and his adversary as a test of the magical protection each possesses at the moment of combat. The ensuing battle unfolds as a ritual contest in which they take turns hurling various weapons at each other in a show of confidence in their magical protection. The only hint of the physical nature of war is indicated by the winner's taking the head of the loser in some epics.

Africans obviously did not engage in ritualized combat in actual situations of war. Nevertheless, their portrayal of the epic hero as a ritual actor must be viewed as a functional expression of heroic values within African cultures—one through which they transmitted a conception of behaviors that they envisioned as the most advantageous for protecting their identity and values during times of war. On the most literal level, their conception of the epic hero as one who acted to enhance his life-force to succeed in combat against his adversary reflected behaviors adopted by Africans in times of war. On another level, the conception of the epic hero as one who acts "outside the norm" reflected the reality that war creates a situation in which groups justify the violation of their most sacred tabu—the taking of human life—by virtue of their need to ensure their own physical and spiritual survival as a community.

The African epic, therefore, functions as more than an expressive mechanism for transmitting a conception of heroic warlike behaviors as actions which violate tabus. It is a narrative which, in its portrayal of the hero and heroic action, functions to reinforce the socio-religious values of African cultures. The African epic hero, despite his apparent moral transgressions, characteristically performs actions that African people would view as morally justifiable retaliatory actions in their all-encompassing religious universe. The hero's adventures, in many ways, represent a fictionalized and much more involved example of the procedures used by medicine-men in African communities in dealing with manifestations of evil that arise within the community and threaten its well-being. His adventures, in the end, allow him to discover the secret of his adversary's "means," and acquire the magical protection that he needs eventually to confront and defeat an external adversary whose use of his power threatens him and his group. Johnson, for example, translates two of the praise-names for Sun-Jata, the Mandekan epic hero, as "Sorcerer-Seizing-Sorcerer" and "The Wizard."[66] In essence, these praise-names suggest that Africans conceptualized the epic hero as one who acts against external foes who threaten their collective life-force in much the same way as the religious specialist acts against those witches and sorcerers who behave in a similar fashion in the community. In addition, Biebuyck argues that the epic hero enters the world with traits which mark him as one with divine characteristics. By virtue of his unusual birth, Africans would recognize him as an individual possessed of extraordinary spiritual powers which he enhances through his adventures.[67]

Furthermore, the African epic hero's adversaries employ the same magical tactics and possess magical power. They are usually the heroes of opposing groups and pit their power against that of the epic hero. Johnson notes, for example, that the adversary of the Mandekan hero, Sun-Jata, was not despised, but rather his "spirit" was "revered and worshipped" by the Mandekan people.[68] Courlander and Sako offer that in African societies and in the epic "Young men were cautioned again and again that it was not enough to possess martial skills and valor, but they needed the help of the "mystic sciences" to offset the magic of their enemies."[69] In this regard, the epic hero proves himself to be a master of the "mystic sciences" and capable of harnessing the force in nature for the benefit of his community against external forces bent on its destruction.

The audience for the heroic epic, however, is never left in doubt as to the values that it is to attach to the actions of the hero and other actors in the narrative. Virtually every student of the African epic tradition points out that these narratives are replete with cultural detail and their narration pervaded by moralizing. "Precisely because of the wealth of content," notes Biebuyck, "the epics have, implicitly if not explicitly, strong didactic and moralizing undertones. They uphold a vision of Nyanga culture. Rashness, impetuosity, verbosity, arrogance, intemperance, ruthlessness, thoughtlessness, hardheartedness—all are implicitly criticized. The bard's concluding statements also reveal a moral quality."[70] The epic bard's role in preserving a sense of equilibrium between the actions of the hero and the values of the society is essential to a complete understanding of the meaning and function of heroic epic narration. Johnson claims that "Considered the official 'protector' of his culture, the professional bard who recites the epic mentions multifarious aspects of his society."[71] He concludes that "What is certain is that bards tend to describe society as they believe it ought to be rather than how it really is. The function is, therefore, more didactic than reflective in this aspect."[72]

In a more formal sense, the epic bard has at his disposal numerous conventions of epic performance which facilitate his abilities to influence, reinforce, and validate the moral values of his culture through his portrayal of the hero and his adventures. In addition to the latitude granted him to improvise and digress in the telling of the narrative, the bard incorporates various genres of folklore into the epic text to achieve various effects, especially to comment on the actions and character of the hero and other actors. Because of the frequency with which the bard uses proverbs and praise in these formal digressions, Bird refers to the incorporation of other genres as a shifting into the "proverb-praise mode." He suggests that the singer employs this mode of narration to achieve several effects: to advance the plot by creating a bridge between episodes, to comment on his own values as a performer and member of the community, and to establish his veracity as an interpreter of the culture.[73] At the same time, the values and meanings that members of the audience associate with these folk forms as cultural expression in other contexts are transferred to the fictive epic world. Proverbs and aphorisms, for example, serve to highlight and reinforce the moral and social values of the group by succinctly commenting upon the actions of epic actors and situations. The inclusion of prayers and invocations reminds the audience of its relationship to the supernatural and the modes of worship and sacrifice recognized by the group.

The bard's constant use of panegyrics in the form of praises and praise poems is by far his most effective expressive device for revealing the meanings to be attached to the actions depicted in epics. Seydou relates that the African epic often begins with an extended praise poem which commemorates the historical or legendary figure it celebrates. The praise poem or "motto" which opens the epic performance typifies the hero and evokes the highest attributes of his being. Seydou observes that through the recitation of the praise poem, the bard both "evokes and invokes the person" and attempts, through the magical power of "word," to compel him to live up to his "praises" in the world of the epic. The epic performance, Seydou contends, serves on the group level as a correlate of the praise poem as applied to the individual in that it, in portraying heroes whose actions represent "the ideology and values recognized by the group," calls upon the community to live up to its values:[74]

> The recital of an epic dedicated to a particular hero is announced by that hero's musical motto which is repeated throughout the performance. The musical theme together with the verbal images created by the narration call out to and mobilize the audience, reviving in it an awareness of both its distinctive identity and its unity.[75]

The persistent use of praises and praise poetry in the epic contributes greatly to the didactic and moralistic tone of the narratives. As Kwesi Yankah points out, praise poetry "is known to pervade nearly the entire realm of oral poetry in Africa. It is, indeed, yet to be known if there is a restricted genre in any African culture which is locally acknowledged to hold a monopoly over 'praise'."[76] He also notes that although praise poetry is devoted primarily to "laudatory attribution," it may also be and is quite often used to criticize or otherwise call attention to immoral or socially unacceptable attributes or behaviors:

> It [praise poetry] requires not merely an identification tag, but a cumulative use of artistically framed nominal quotes that telescope the socio-cultural relevance of the referent. The set of strong appellations applied, thus, may be in respect of one's social or genetic identity; worthy, meritorious characteristics or feats; peculiar misdeed, misconduct; or a combination of these.[77]

For this reason, Yankah suggests that the term "referential poetry" may be more descriptive of the content and function of these performed appellations since they serve primarily to point out the actions and attributes of an individual "as deserving attention of society from among a paradigm of peers and co-equals."[78] At any rate, in the context of epics, they serve to facilitate the clarification of moral and social values by identifying various actors and actions as worthy of special attention. In addition, in the rather loose performance of the epic, the bard may use these poetic digressions to comment on members of the audience whose attributes or actions, known to contemporary participants in the performance, aid in clarifying the values to be attached to actions and actors described in the fictional epic.

The heroic epic tradition of Africans offered them a focus for celebrating their history, religion, and cultural identity in an integrated and diverse performance. Seydou characterizes the epic performance as a "mechanism of exaltation in communion" in that Africans celebrate the actions of epic heroes as symbolic of the "ideal forms of behavior" reflecting their values and identity. As such, the epic performance "incites the audience to experience this identity and the desire to actualize it as the result of collective knowledge (the subjects are, in effect, known to everyone) particular to the epic."[79] The "collective knowledge" that Africans envision as "particular to the epic" is nothing less than the "ideal forms of behavior" that reflect their moral values in both their historical and emergent dimensions. The epic hero, who arises at a crucial moment in the group's history, characteristically performs actions which offer his people a model of behavior for protecting their values from both internal and external threats occasioned by their existence in a hostile, warlike atmosphere. In African epics, these values are revealed as inherently religious in the sense that the important actions of the hero have moral implications which, in African societies, have an ontological (and, therefore, religious) dimension. However, the epic hero who, as representative man, is threatened at birth and sets out on a quest to enhance his life-force to change his destiny, offers African groups an important model of behavior for protecting themselves from threats to their survival and well-being by acting to enhance their own collective power. The epic reveals, however, that the most advantageous behavior for enhancing the collective power of the group lies not in violating tabus but rather in clinging tenaciously to the values guiding actions recognized by the group and, in essence, living up to their own image of themselves. In the end, Africans celebrate the superiority of their own religiously defined values and identity in epic performance—an identity and value system which allows them to survive and prosper under the most destructive conditions that human beings can create—war.

THE HERO AS CHRISTIAN SOLDIER

Although Africans enslaved in America did not continue to experience war, in a literal sense, as an obstacle to the maintenance of behavioral patterns by which they defined their identity and values, they nevertheless lived in a hostile environment with enough similarities to their previous one to facilitate transforming their traditions of heroic expression. While the enslavement of the majority of Africans in the New World circumscribed their vision of heroic action, maroons (enslaved Africans who escaped the slave system and established their own communities in isolated areas), sometimes acted in ways that reminded enslaved Africans of their epic heroes. For example, enslaved Africans who lived in the area around New Orleans in the 1830s discovered in the maroon leader, Bras Coupe, a warlike figure whose exploits inspired folk heroic creation reminiscent of that around African epic heroes.[80] They recounted in legends how Bras Coupe terrorized whites in the area around New Orleans with his late night assaults and murderous rampages through the countryside. According to legend mingled with fact, the native-born African who came to be known as Bras Coupe had belonged to General William de Buys, a prominent slave owner in the area. The General took a particular liking to this large and affable enslaved African whom he called "Squire." He taught "Squire" to shoot a gun and often took him along on hunting expeditions into the bayous. "Squire," who was supposedly warned in a dream that he would lose an arm, practiced hard and learned to shoot with either hand. Among other enslaved Africans, he was known as a ladies' man and enjoyed a favorable reputation as a drummer and dancer in the Congo Square festivities. The freedoms accorded "Squire" by his master increased his longing for emancipation. He ran away several times and received only mild punishment when captured and returned. On one occasion he was shot in the arm by a patrol searching for runaways, and his arm had to be amputated. Thus, he became known as Bras Coupe.

When his arm healed, however, Bras Coupe disappeared into the Louisiana swamps, where he organized a maroon colony composed of other runaway Africans and renegade white men. For three years, he led raiding expeditions in which he robbed and murdered whites around New Orleans. Enslaved Africans in the area attributed Bras Coupe's success to the fact that he was a conjurer possessed of extraordinary supernatural powers. His abilities to elude successfully patrols and others bent on his capture for several years caused some to speculate that he could not be killed. Others told of how hunters who spotted him fired bullets at him that bounced off his chest and reversed their course, barely missing those who fired them. Still others told of how an army expedition sent to capture him was lost in a mysterious fog and never found its way out of the swamp. Some even claim that, in the recesses of the swamp, Bras Coupe became a cannibal and enhanced his power by eating human flesh.

On April 6, 1837, however, a party of hunters came across the notorious maroon leader near Bayou St. John. Although he disappeared into the swamp before they could capture him, he was wounded by one of them before he could escape completely. Three months later, a fisherman and supposed friend of the maroon deposited his body at the doorstep of the Mayor of New Orleans. It was later discovered that the fisherman had struck a sleeping Bras Coupe on the head while he was recuperating from his wound in the fisherman's tent. The fisherman's motive for killing his friend was the two thousand dollar reward offered for his capture. For two days, the body of Bras Coupe was exhibited at the Place d'Armes and "all the slaves were required to view it as a warning of what lay in store for them if they should try to follow in Bras Coupe's footsteps."

We should not be surprised that enslaved Africans would react to their enslavement by embracing warlike behaviors nor that black folk heroic creation around an aggressive, warlike figure such as Bras Coupe would culminate in a hero conceptualized as a conjurer. To protect themselves against the consequences of the behaviors that violated tabus against the manipulation of the force in nature within their community, enslaved Africans had transformed in their conjure tradition many of the behaviors that reflected values guiding action traditionally associated with the African epic hero. Therefore, when presented with a figure who aggressively confronted and succeeded against the martial powers of whites, enslaved Africans, turned to their African heritage for an expressive model to transmit a conception of Bras Coupe as a folk hero. In this sense, the attribution of mystical or magical powers to Bras Coupe by enslaved Africans reflected the continuing influence of the values associated with the African heroic tale and epic traditions on the conception of heroic action.

The legend of Bras Coupe, however, is somewhat deceptive as a basis for understanding how enslaved Africans transformed their heroic epic tradition in America to create a model of behavior to protect their identity and values from the threats posed by the actions of slavemasters. From available evidence, the Bras Coupe legend was not known to or, at least, does not appear to have become a part of the oral tradition of, enslaved Africans outside the area surrounding New Orleans. Of equal importance, Bras Coupe was a maroon. For the majority of Africans enslaved in America, a maroon terrorizing farms and plantations would have represented an unusual specter. Genovese notes, for example, that physical conditions in the United States did not support the creation of maroon colonies or the maroon lifestyle as an advantageous one for Africans enslaved in America. He points out that "the rapid development of the southern back country confronted slaves with a formidable white power and reduced possibilities for sustained warfare to a minimum. Thus, the slave might know of groups of desperate holdouts here and there, but he had no example of an autonomous movement to guide him."[81]

While enslaved Africans were undoubtedly influenced by the absence of an "autonomous movement" of successful warlike behavior against their enslavers in determining how they would transform their tradition of heroic expression, they were also influenced by the differences in both the social and cultural factors which influenced their lifestyle in America from those they had experienced on the African continent. In the African world where religion pervaded every aspect of life, Africans had depended on their religious institutions to define the ideal forms of behavior that protected their identity and values from both external and internal threats. Although they transformed many aspects of the expressive and ritual traditions surrounding the African religious specialists to create the conjure tradition, enslaved Africans did not envision conjuration as a source of behavior that protected their identity or values from the physical aggression of the masters. Their conception of the power of conjuration was defined by their existence in the slave system, a hierarchically ordered socio-cultural environment which they shared with the masters. Regardless of how they may have viewed the masters as the power brokers within the system, they nevertheless existed in an interdependent relationship with them—one in which they were ultimately dependent on the enslavers' benevolence for the quality of their lives. Therefore, enslaved Africans found themselves confronted with a situation in which, at least perceptually, the practice of conjuration as a form of aggression against the masters threatened rather than facilitated the maintenance of the values that they associated with conjurers and conjuration. In addition, acts of conjuration as a form of protection against the consequences of aggressive actions directed at the masters not only all too often resulted in failure, but also created a potential (and, in most cases, actual) increase in the oppressiveness of existence for the entire community. The masters, for their part, repeatedly demonstrated their ability to control the behavior of both conjurers and those supposedly protected by the power of conjuration with physical power. Their effectiveness led many enslaved Africans to adopt the view that the masters' lack of belief in its power protected them from its effects. Therefore, for enslaved Africans to associate the actions of individuals who acted aggressively against the master with the conjure tradition would have jeopardized their ability to maintain the values that they associated with its practice—values ultimately important to the social well-being of their community.

In essence, the illusion of shared identity and values created by existence in the slave system severely limited the vision of the powers of conjurers and conjuration as a source of behavior that could protect enslaved Africans from the powers of the masters. Despite the extraordinary powers attributed to conjurers in tales of their exploits, their power was envisioned as capable of protecting enslaved Africans from the consequences of intragroup behaviors that threatened the social and spiritual values of the community. Nevertheless, the conjure tradition allowed enslaved Africans to maintain the belief that behaviors reflecting spiritual values were the most advantageous to their well-being. But their belief that the enslavers did not share their spiritual values and could not be affected by behavior reflecting them left them vulnerable to the external threat posed by the masters.

Despite the enslavers' attitudes and behaviors toward Africans and their religious practices and beliefs, many were reluctant initially to allow enslaved Africans to receive the religious instruction necessary for the creation of a shared system of spiritual values between the enslaved and the enslaver.[82] While the Church of England worked diligently throughout the seventeenth and eighteenth centuries to convince slaveholders of the importance of Christian conversion for their slaves, the masters' responses to these efforts were often less than enthusiastic. However, the masters were not always at fault in the failure of Africans to become Christians during this period. Even when masters consented to conversion of their slaves, cultural and linguistic barriers between Africans and Christian clergy and missionaries sometimes proved insurmountable in providing the religious instruction considered a prerequisite for baptism by the Anglican church.[83] While the language barrier was obviously a great impediment to African comprehension of Christian religious teachings, the cultural barrier was undoubtedly an equally if not more important factor for enslaved Africans. In particular, the abstract, moralistic teachings of Anglican clergy and missionaries remained at odds with the slaves' African mode of religious perception.

In the cultures where enslaved Africans had their roots, they were constantly confronted with and acknowledged the presence of God in all things, especially their own lives. "In the traditional religions of West Africa," notes Raboteau, "the power of the gods and spirits was effectively present in the lives of men, for good or ill, on every level—instrumental, social and cosmic. Aspects of reality seen as impersonal from a modern scientific viewpoint were not only personified but personalized, i.e., placed within the context of human relationships."[84] Through constant prayer, sacrifice, and participation in the mythic and ritual performances of their religions, Africans had made their relationship to the gods and spirits both immediate and personal. For enslaved Africans, the Anglican church offered them neither a concrete focus for apprehending the power of God in Christianity nor a religious ritual commensurate with their African religious practices.

In addition, Anglican religious instruction, which usually involved the teaching of "the Ten Commandments, the Apostles' Creed and Lord's Prayer" did not present Christianity to enslaved Africans in a way that highlighted any benefits, communal or individual, of structuring their behavior according to its literal dictates.[85] In many ways, these tenets of Christianity emphasized moral values that ran directly counter to their view of the behavioral demands of living in the slave system. Therefore, as Raboteau has argued, "Not all slaves who could understand religious instruction were eager to accept Christianity."[86]

Furthermore, there is evidence to suggest that the issue of the benefits to be derived from conversion was important in the decision of enslaved Africans as to whether they accepted religious conversion. For example, Rev. James Blair, official representative in Virginia to the Bishop of London, reported in 1731 that "notwithstanding all the precautions which the ministers took to assure that baptism did not alter their servitude, the negroes fed themselves with a secret fantasy that it did, and that the King designed that all Christians should be made free. And when they saw that baptism did not change their status they grew angry and saucy, and met in the nighttime in great numbers and talked of rising."[87] The inability of enslaved Africans to discover in the abstract doctrine of the Anglican church a model of moral behavior or a system of spiritual values either commensurate with their African religious worldview or capable of advancing their interests in slavery must be viewed as an important reason for their initial reluctance to openly embrace Christianity.

Opportunistically, however, the wave of religious fervor known as the Great Awakening, or Christian Evangelical Movement, which began sweeping the country in the mid-eighteenth century offered enslaved Africans a vision of Christianity commensurate with both their African religious sensibility and their individual and communal needs in slavery. "By stressing the conversion experience instead of the process of religious instruction," the Christian Evangelists overcame many of the external and internal obstacles to conversion of enslaved Africans that the Church of England had been unable to circumvent.[88] On the one hand, the Christian Evangelical Movement claimed among its earliest converts many slaveholders whose own new-found "religion" made them more receptive to conversion for their slaves. In addition, most slaveholders found the almost instantaneous individual conversion experience more adaptable to the economic requirements of slavery than the process of religious instruction to which one of their objections had been the time it took away from work. On the other hand, the Christian Evangelists' emphasis on the conversion experience as well as biblical gospel made Christianity more accessible to enslaved Africans. For enslaved Africans who had their roots in cultures which had personalized their relationship to God through spirit possession, the ecstatic conversion experience bridged the gulf between Christianity and their African religious modes of worship. Furthermore, revivalist preachers who, in their sermons, stressed the biblical saga rather than abstract doctrine as the foundation of Christianity, offered enslaved Africans a concrete focus for apprehending the moral and spiritual tenets of Christianity.

More importantly, "the Methodist and Baptist exhorters [who] visualized and personalized" the plight under Egyptian slavery of the Israelites, whose obedience to a powerful and wrathful God had caused Him to send them a deliverer–hero, offered enslaved Africans a conception of an historical situation with obvious parallels to their own.[89] As an essential part of their Christian indoctrination, not only were they challenged to identify with biblical situations and personages, whose legacy of persecution, oppression, and deprivation was presented to them as exemplary of the plight of Christians, but they were also offered the opportunity through conversion of establishing a relationship with the God which had allowed biblical figures to be delivered in dramatic ways from the evils of this world. Of equal importance, in the evangelical religious services in which singing and holy dancing were prominent and, especially, in the animated, extemporaneous oral performances of evangelical ministers who dramatized the biblical saga, enslaved Africans were presented with the celebration of a religious and ancestral history with obvious conceptual, expressive, and performance parallels to their own African heroic epic traditions.

The enthusiastic response of enslaved Africans to Christianity as presented by evangelists was undoubtedly influenced by their discovering in it a source of spiritual power greater than that wielded by both their conjurers and the slavemasters, and one to which even these figures were subject. Therefore, in being converted to Christianity, they embraced the opportunities that it offered them for creating an identity and lifestyle based on values alternative to those fostered by existence in the slave system. As Christians, they no longer had to define their values or structure their behavior to propitiate the slave system's power brokers. Rather, like their religious ancestors, they could base their identity on, and develop behavioral patterns which reflected values appropriate to, their view of themselves as the children of God whose dehumanization in slavery was an evil that He did not sanction. Moreover, as enslaved Africans in large numbers accepted God as a source of spiritual power capable of affecting their destiny as the persecuted victims of the slave system, they turned to the actions of biblical figures to create oral expressive traditions to transmit a conception of ideal religious behavior. Furthermore, in creating oral expressive traditions to portray the characteristic behaviors of biblical figures as the most advantageous for protecting their identity and values as Christians, enslaved Africans transformed the biblical saga into an heroic tradition based on values guiding action that they had traditionally associated with the African epic hero.

While the expressive response of enslaved Africans to Christianity was undoubtedly influenced by the ritual and expressive parallels that they saw between Christian religious worship and their African heroic and religious traditions, their transforming of the biblical saga into an heroic tradition based on values associated with the African epic hero must also be seen in terms of the situation that they faced in slavery. Inasmuch as Africans enslaved in America did not freely submit to their enslavement, they continued to experience intergroup conflict and the behaviors necessary to fend off an external threat to their identity and values as major obstacles in their efforts to maintain cultural autonomy. In America, their enslavers, who constantly subjected them to physical and psychic abuse in efforts to destroy their ability to resist enslavement, created an environment of endless strife with the enslaved. From the moment that Africans arrived on the North American continent, their enslavers mounted a campaign of abuse, the goal of which was to convince them that slavery was their destiny and that white power was the only important one in their lives. By stripping Africans of their personal autonomy and basic human rights, the enslavers revealed that their objective was not merely to dominate Africans politically and physically but to redefine black identity by destroying their sense of humanity.

To achieve their objective, the enslavers constantly heaped upon enslaved Africans physical abuse, most often in the form of brutal whippings. The frequency with which the enslavers resorted to the lash was paralleled only by the intensity and cruelty with which some laid on these floggings. Genovese reports that "On some Sea Island plantations every slave's back had scars, and the narratives of ex-slaves revealed many stories of slaves whipped to death."[90] In addition, some enslavers literally poured salt into the open sores left by these beatings to prolong and intensify their effects. Escott reports that other methods were also employed to enhance the effects of a flogging:

> To add painful refinement to this cruelty, some masters cut open the blisters on a slave's back, dipped sealing wax into them, poured a solution of fiery peppers onto the sores, or aggravated the lacerations by striking them with a hand saw. Suspending a slave on tiptoe during and after the beating increased the pain, and some masters whipped pregnant women after making them "lie face down in a specially dug depression in the ground." Quite often in any of these situations all the slaves were made to watch when one was whipped, and the terror of punishment surpassed its incidence for the individual.[91]

In addition to the frequent whippings that they administered, the enslavers devised and implemented various other punishments with even more threatening consequences for black survival. In some cases, "nigger boxes" were used in which an enslaved African was placed for prolonged periods of time in a cell-like structure which allowed barely enough room for a shift in position while standing. For those accused of rape or murder, burning alive without trial or hearing was a common form of punishment. Although outlawed by the nineteenth century except in the case of accused rape, public castration was a not uncommon form of punishment for black males during the early years of slavery. Even after it was outlawed in most southern states, "Privately inflicted castration did not disappear; scattered evidence suggests that some masters continued to apply it especially to slaves who had become their rival for coveted black women."[92] Not only did enslaved Africans suffer immensely from the physical cruelty inflicted on them by their own masters, but they were also subject to abuse from any white person, all of whom saw themselves as "policemen" of slave behaviors.[93]

Furthermore, the enslavers subjected enslaved Africans daily to conditions which tried and tested their moral and spiritual stamina as human beings. They were subject to the "whims and passion of every member of the [enslaver's] family,"[94] dependent for food, clothing and shelter, forced to work long hours under the watchful eye of master, mistress or overseer and experience the trauma of separation from family and friends at the masters' discretion and pleasure. The masters degraded them constantly by forcing them to participate in what Blassingame has called the "ritual of deference" to all whites. In addition, they carefully regulated their movements (both as individual masters and overseers and as part of patrols constituted for the purpose of enforcing the restrictions imposed on their movements).[95]

As devastating as the enslavers' physical treatment was for the maintenance of the values that Africans had traditionally recognized, and came to accept as Christians, as the most advantageous to their well-being, they, at the same time, attempted to use their physical advantage over enslaved Africans to force them to accept a value system revolving around behaviors that constantly confronted the black community with the possibility of moral and spiritual degeneration. For instance, a Florida slaveholder who opposed Christian religious instruction for his slaves declared that "I never interfere in their connubial and domestic affairs." However, he "encouraged as much as possible dancing, merriment, and dress, for which Saturday afternoons and night, and Sunday morning were dedicated."[96] The encouragement of "merriment" among enslaved Africans by some slaveholders undoubtedly led to the kind of scene described by a visitor to St. Louis in 1818. He reported that "Here the negroes were accustomed to assemble in the pleasant afternoons of the Sabbath, dance, drink, and fight, quite to the annoyance of all seriously disposed persons."[97] While the practice of some slaveholders to provide enslaved Africans with opportunities to vent their frustrations and hostilities supported their interests in maintaining a contented work force, it did little for the maintenance of the moral and spiritual values that Africans had traditionally recognized or came to view as definitive of their identity. Blassingame notes, for example, that the types of behavior given license on these public occasions sometimes spilled over into the slave quarters: "Many slaves tried to drown their anger in the whisky bottle, and if not drowned, the anger welling up was translated into many other forms. Sometimes the slave projected his aggressions onto his fellow slaves: he might beat up, stab, or kill one of his fellow sufferers."[98]

In addition, unlike this Florida slaveholder, most masters did interfere in the "connubial and domestic affairs" of enslaved Africans, and in the process, created conditions among them which made it extremely difficult for them to maintain or infuse a sense of morality into their social and domestic lives. Postell notes, for instance, that "There was nothing the master was more interested in than the increase of his slaves through the birth of children."[99] The birth of a child was a form of material acquisition for slaveholders that could significantly enhance the productivity of their enterprise with little or no economic commitment from them. Although many slaveholders apparently resented the comparison between slave and stock breeding leveled against them by opponents of slavery, they nevertheless "carefully watched birth statistics, and within the medical knowledge of the time, took pains to promote conditions conducive to the rearing of large families."[100] However, African women, though encouraged to produce large numbers of children, basically had no control over the circumstances surrounding the conception, rearing, and fate of their offspring. Black women were expected to return to work as soon as possible after giving birth, while the care and rearing of their children were decisions made by the slaveholder. In addition, the masters had the right to sell slave children as well as the parents at their discretion. The indiscriminate breaking up of black families was one of the initial and most traumatic experiences faced by Africans enslaved in the New World—one which tugged constantly at the moral and spiritual fabric of the black community.

Whether slave breeding was a conscious goal of slaveholders or not, most did not interfere with sexual promiscuity in the slave quarters, especially when it produced large numbers of children to black women. On the contrary, many slaveholders were active sexually with black women themselves and frequently fathered children by them. "The white man's lust for black women," according to Blassingame, "was one of the most serious impediments to the development of morality" among enslaved Africans.[101] In addition, some slavemasters not only conceived children by forcing themselves upon black women, but also controlled the pairing of black men and women to insure fertile unions. In some instances, especially in situations where women outnumbered men, the masters employed "studs," referred to by enslaved Africans as "stockmen," "travelin' nigger," or "breedin' nigger."[102]

The interference of slavemasters in the domestic and family life of enslaved Africans was demoralizing, especially for African men, who had traditionally viewed the protection of their families as sacred duties. Against the power of their enslavers, they had to stand by helplessly and watch the rape of their wives and daughters and the separation of their families. For this reason, many black men had little incentive to marry and establish monogamous sexual unions. "They did not want to marry a woman," concludes Blassingame, "and be forced to watch as she was beaten, insulted, raped, overworked, or starved without being able to protect her." Therefore, many black males, if they married at all, preferred to "marry abroad," that is, take a mate from a neighboring plantation so that they would not be forced to watch her humiliation. Even so, because masters were free to pair enslaved Africans as they saw fit, they sometimes severed such unions, especially if they did not produce a child, or even as a form of punishment.[103] Consequently, sexual and cohabitational arrangements characteristic of polygamy became of part of the moral dilemma that enslaved Africans faced as they sought to live by Christian values. Polygamy, however, did not usually exist in the form of one spouse sharing two or more mates. A report issued by a South Carolina congregation described a situation more typical of the kinds of arrangements that the slave system created:

It has been found, upon examination that some of them [slaves] had been living with a second companion in the familiar intercourse of husband and wife, often having separated from one or more that were still living & in the same neighborhood.[104]

Arrangements that were polygamous by Christian religious standards were often foisted upon enslaved Africans by forced separation and represented a serious threat to the moral values of converted Africans.

The enslavers' constant displays of physical aggression and interference in the social and domestic lives of enslaved Africans constituted only one of several aspects of the intergroup conflict that influenced the process of folk heroic creation which culminated in a conception of biblical figures as epic heroes. In reality, the enslavers' behavior toward Africans as fellow Christians had an even more profound influence on their turning to biblical heroes for a model of religious behavior. While most slavemasters were apparently more receptive to the idea of conversion for their slaves with the advent of the Evangelical Movement, they were not willing to allow them total religious freedom.[105] In some instances, slavemasters continued to exhibit a great deal of hostility toward the idea of religion for enslaved Africans. "My boss didn' 'low us to go to church, er pray er sing," recalled Gus Clark of his slavemaster. "Iffen he ketch us prayin' er singin' he whupped us. He didn' care fer nuthin' 'cept farmin.'"[106] On the other hand, some pious slaveholders not only encouraged their slaves' religion but actually required them to attend church or participate in religious services on the plantation. However, they insisted on the right to determine who or what the slaves heard at such services by choosing ministers who would deliver an acceptable message and by allowing slave religious worship only under white supervision. In addition to their efforts to control black religious worship, slavemasters also frequently attempted to reduce Christianity to an ethic of submission. William Wells Brown wrote in his narrative of slavery, for instance, that some slavemasters came to prefer religious slaves because they believed that in the sermons that the slave heard, he learned that "God made him for a slave; and that, when whipped he must not find fault—for the Bible says, 'He that knoweth his master's will, and doeth it not shall be beaten with many stripes.'"[107] The general import of the message most often delivered to enslaved Africans by the "white folks preacher" was summarized by Lucretia Alexander:

The preacher came and he'd just say "Serve your masters. Don't steal your master's turkey. Don't steal your master's hawgs. Don't steal your master's meat. Do whatsomever your master tells you to do." Same old thing all the time.[108]

The efforts of the enslavers to define ideal religious behavior as submission to white authority served merely to weaken any identification of converted enslaved Africans with the masters as fellow Christians.

In addition, the enslavers' attempts to manipulate Christian religious ideals to secure their interests served to intensify identification of enslaved Africans with each other, as well as biblical figures and situations.

In part as a result of their attitude toward the masters as Christians, enslaved Africans rejected not only the religious values that the masters attempted to foist on them but also the expressive forms that embodied them and, often, their religious service as a model of religious worship. The attitude that enslaved Africans developed toward their masters' religion was often revealed in their refusal to join the same religious denomination when given a choice. Moses Roper reported in his narrative of slavery, for instance, that the enslaved Africans on his master's plantation "thinking him [the master] a very bad example of what a professing Christian ought to be, would not join the connexion he belonged to, thinking they must be a very bad set of people."[109] When converted Africans evaluated the conditions under which they were forced to practice their religion, they came to realize that if they were to change their destiny through spiritual empowerment by God they must violate the masters' rules by refusing to accept the masters' definitions of ideal religious behavior or to allow their own behavior to be governed by it.

While most enslaved Africans were not given the option of separating themselves denominationally or even of worshiping without white presence, they nevertheless defied the masters and created their own worship services. Although black religious worship without white supervision was generally prohibited during the period of slavery, enslaved Africans routinely defied the masters' prohibitions and proscriptions and worshiped together in the absence of whites. Peter Randolf, who was enslaved in Virginia, described the general nature of such religious meetings:

> Not being able to hold meetings on the plantation, the slaves assemble in the swamp, out of reach of the patrol. They have an understanding among themselves as to the time and place of getting together. This is often done by the first one arriving breaking boughs from the trees, and bending them in the direction of the selected spot. Arrangements are then made for conducting the service.[110]

Although enslaved Africans devised elaborate schemes to avoid detection of their secret religious meetings (such as turning pots over in the center of the gathering, a practice that they believed muffled the sounds of their praying and singing), those who attended these meetings did so with the knowledge that they faced great dangers from white patrols, who frequently broke them up and flogged the participants. In addition, masters could be extremely harsh with members of the slave community who defied them by attending religious meetings without permission. Charlotte Martin, for instance, reported that her brother "was whipped to death for taking part in one of the religious ceremonies."[111]

The willingness of enslaved Africans to risk their personal well-being and attend clandestine religious meetings over the objections of the masters was directly influenced by their transforming the biblical saga into an heroic tradition based on values guiding action traditionally associated with African epic heroes. In these meetings in the recesses of southern swamps, upland thickets, and drafty cabins, enslaved Africans created the spirituals and transmitted through them a conception of the behavior of biblical heroes as the most advantageous for affecting their destiny as a community. They called upon the most creative members of their community to use their poetic and vocal talents to transform the biblical saga into an heroic tradition reminiscent of their African epics. Under the inspiring leadership of these talented bards, enslaved Africans witnessed and participated almost nightly in expressive and ritual performances that recalled the great epic celebrations of their homelands. In their religious services, they acted neither as passive observers nor as simply receptive congregation members; they participated in a religious experience in which they combined song, sermon, dance, and drama into an integrated performance. They created and performed spirituals as well as sermons in their traditional African fashion, using call and response in which a leader's narration was often overlapped or echoed by the lyric response of the group. In the process, they engaged in a continuous dialogue concerning the rewards of a personal relationship with God and the punishments that awaited those who violated his laws. In short, didactic songs, the spiritual song bards dramatized through the lives and deeds of biblical heroes the benefits of adapting behaviors exemplary of the religious life as a source of values for protecting their identity from both internal and external threats.

In the spirituals, enslaved Africans conceptualized enslavement and persecution as the greatest obstacles for Christians in their efforts to live up to their image of themselves as the children of God, and enslavers and persecutors of God's faithful as their constant adversaries. Throughout the spiritual song tradition, they portrayed biblical heroes who confronted enslavers and persecutors and who were forced by circumstances to protect their identity and values as well as their physical well-being in situations not unlike those known to the African slave community. With the African heroic epic as an expressive model for spiritual song creation and their own struggles in the slave system as a context for creation, it is not surprising that, of all the heroes who appear in the Bible, Moses, whom God empowered to lead the Israelites out of Egyptian slavery and into the Promised Land, dominates the action. In the spiritual song tradition, Moses appears in numerous songs devoted to his heroic deeds as well as others in which his attributes and deeds are alluded to. Of all the biblical heroes, the life and deeds of Moses were the most reminiscent of those of African epic heroes: he was born under unusual circumstances, was exiled and grew up away from his people, underwent great trials and tests, and acquired the spiritual knowledge and power to affect his community's destiny. In the various songs devoted to him, the spiritual song bards reconstructed Moses' life and career as an epic adventure. He emerged as a hero at a time when his people faced a great threat to their physical and spiritual well-being:

When Israel was in Egypt's land,
Oppressed so hard they could not stand.[112]

Although his destiny was placed before him as that of leading his people out of bondage, Moses initially refused to accept it and, therefore, was tried and tested by God:

When the Lord call'd Moses
Moses 'fused to answer.

When his head was achin' with the fever,
Moses say, "Here I'se Lord."

From his ordeals, Moses acquired the spiritual knowledge and power to confront the powerful Pharaoh:

Go down Moses
Way down in Egyptian land
Tell Ole Pharaoh
To let my people Go.
When spoke the Lord;
Bold Moses said;
Let my people go.

In his confrontations with Pharaoh and throughout his adventures, Moses succeeded entirely through the use of spiritual knowledge and power communicated to him by God. In various spirituals, the bards dramatized Moses' parting of the Red Sea, extracting of water from stone, and various other magical feats.

In their spirituals which recreated the story of Moses and the Israelites in their heroic struggle with the Pharaoh and the Egyptian enslavers, enslaved Africans found a narrative core around which they could develop an heroic epic. In the songs which dealt with the exploits of Moses, enslaved Africans did not transmit merely their conception of an historical situation with obvious parallels to their own. They also depicted the situation which justified their turning to Christianity as a source of values and behaviors for dealing with the situation that they faced in the slave system. The empowerment of Moses to deliver the Israelites out of slavery epitomized for them the rewards of establishing and maintaining both an individual and a communal relationship with the Christian God. Inasmuch as converted Africans believed that "de God that lived in Moses' time jus' de same today," they also believed that He would answer their prayers and empower a deliverer hero from one among their number. The didactic and often proselytizing tone of many of the spirituals was greatly influenced by the belief of enslaved Africans that they, like the biblical Israelites, would collectively be freed by remaining steadfast as a community in their obedience to God. Therefore, in their songs, they repeatedly portrayed Moses' as an answer to the collective prayers of the faithful:

Old Pharoah said, "who is de Lord
Dat I should him obey?"
"His name it is Jehovah,
For he hears His people Pray."

Their vision of Moses as an epic hero and their spirituals as a form of epic expression in which the triumph of the Israelites was the central focus is crucial to an understanding of the meaning that enslaved Africans derived from spiritual song creation and performance. As they came to believe that God would empower a Moses to deliver them if they maintained their faith in His power, enslaved Africans created spirituals based on the exploits of various biblical figures to serve as models of behavior for living a Christain life under conditions which constantly tempted them to abandon their spiritual values. Their singing of these biblical figures served to reinforce the values that they believed led to Moses' triumph in defeating the enslavers of their biblical ancestors. They characteristically portrayed biblical figures as individuals who confronted situations and moral dilemmas which served as heightened examples of those that they faced in the slave system. For example, the portrayal of Daniel is typical of this approach to spiritual song creation:

Daniel faithful to his God,
Would not bow down to men,
An' by god's enemy he was hurled
Into the lion's den.
God locked the lion's jaw, we read,
An' robbed him of his prey.
An' de God dat lived in Daniel's time
Is jus' de same today.

Daniel, who is persecuted for placing his relationship to God above that with men, reflected a type of situation familiar to enslaved Africans. Their very lifestyle was one in which they were constantly expected to accept a relationship to the masters above all others in their lives. However, in the spirituals, enslaved Africans used Daniel's stance to transmit a conception of the rewards of remaining firm in one's faith in the face of earthly trials and adversaries. In typical African heroic epic style, the spiritual song bard also capitalizes on Daniel's heroic example in another, more subjective spiritual to personalize the didactic message of the narrative:

I thought I heard them say
There were *lions* in the way.
I don't expect to stay
Much longer here.

In the spirituals, enslaved Africans turned to the actions of various biblical figures to constantly reinforce the idea that living a lifestyle based on religious values led to the kind of spiritual empowerment which resulted in earthly deliverance. Moreover, they characteristically conceptualized biblical heroes not as individuals of exceptional personal or physical attributes but rather as ordinary persons like "Moses, an infant cast away" or "Lit'le David" a "sheperd boy," who, by virtue of their respect for the power of God, were empowered by Him to perform extraordinary feats of moral and spiritual courage. As in the example of Daniel, they often recalled the exploits of biblical figures in songs which emphasized the events with which they were identified, and in others, more subjective in nature, reinforced the didactic message. For example, in retelling the story of Joshua in the spiritual, "Joshua Fit the Battle of Jericho," the bard expresses unbridled enthusiasm and admiration for Joshua, whom God empowered to lead a successful assault which brought down the walls of Jericho with an army of warriors armed with ram's lamb's horns:

Joshua fit the battle of Jericho, Jericho
Joshua fit the battle of Jericho, Jericho
Joshua fit the battle of Jericho, Jericho
An' de walls come tumblin' down.

You may talk about yo' king of Gideon,
You may talk about yo' king of Saul,
Dere's none like good ole Joshua
At de battle of Jericho.

Up to de walls ob Jericho
He marched with spear in han'
"Go blow dem ram horns, " Joshua cried,
Kase de battle am in my han'.
Den de lam' ram sheephorn begin to blow,
Trumpets begin to sound.
Joshua commanded de chillen to shout,
An' de walls come tumblin' down.

In the spiritual, "That Suits Me," enslaved Africans called upon members of their community to embrace the religious life with the same spiritual zeal displayed by Joshua and his band of valiant religious soldiers:

Come on mamma le's go roun' the wall,
Come on mamma le's go roun' the wall,
Come on mamma le's go roun' the wall,
Don' wanna stumble and don' wanna fall—
An' that suits me.

Most of the biblical heroes of the Old Testament emerged in the spirituals as folk heroes whose faith in God was so strong that they stood fast in the face of evil and, thereby, were empowered by Him in their time of need to overcome personal trials at the hands of enemies of the faithful. Their heroic stances served as models of behaviors for achieving the rewards of maintaining a personal relationship with the God who had empowered Moses to overcome enslavers and persecutors of God's faithful. Such biblical figures were most often portrayed not only as unyielding in their faith but also as maintaining it in the midst of times and situations which tried them as human beings. Noah, for instance, persisted in his task appointed by God while unbelievers made him the object of ridicule:

> They called Noah a foolish man,
> Oh! didn't it rain.
> Cause Noah built de ark on dry land.
> Oh! didn't it rain.

God's elevation of Noah above others as a reward for his faith was paralleled in the version of the story of Joseph as recreated by enslaved Africans:

> Joseph by his false brethern sold,
> God raised him above all.

Converted Africans needed and found in the stories of biblical heroes such as Daniel, Noah, and Joseph an ideal focus for transmitting a conception of the rewards and benefits of maintaining faith in the power of God in their everyday lives as evil and evil-doers, both within and outside their community, ridiculed and tempted them. Under the conditions that they practiced their religion in slavery, they required constant reassurance that the persecution that they endured both in their daily lives and in trying to worship God in their own way entailed the kinds of benefits that justified the personal suffering and risks that they faced. In their spiritual songs that dramatized the heroic struggles of biblical figures, they were able to constantly present believers and, more importantly, unbelievers, with dramatic evidence that the benefits of their establishing a relationship to God and remaining faithful to Him outweighed the temporary costs that they paid.

While enslaved Africans undoubtedly envisioned God's empowerment of Moses who delivered his faithful followers from the earthly evils that beset them, especially slavery, as the greatest benefit of maintaining a proper relationship with Him, they also found in the biblical saga a figure who had been empowered by God both to transcend earthly suffering and to confer on them the ability to do so. In the spirituals, God's gift of Jesus symbolized His continuing love of His faithful, His power as a Deliverer, and the assurance that their faith would be rewarded—if not on earth then in Heaven. As the Son of God, Jesus' power was God's power made manifest on earth. It was a benevolent power that could not only confer on the "blin' man [who] stood on the road an' cried" the ability to see but it could be called upon in times of need:

Lord help the po' and the needy,
Lord help the widows and orphans.
Lord help the motherless children
Lord help the hypocrit members.

In addition, the life of Jesus as portrayed in spirituals was one through which God constantly displayed His power both to perform miracles and to reward Christian suffering. Jesus' death, which he faced without ever saying "a mumbalin' word," his miraculous resurrection, and his ascension to Heaven were all offered as proof of God's power and promise.

By transforming the biblical saga into an heroic tradition based on values guiding actions traditionally associated with the African epic heroic tradition—redefined as Christian religious values—enslaved Africans were able to embody in their spirituals a conception of the actions of biblical heroes as the most advantageous for protecting their identity and values from both external and internal threats in a hostile environment. On the one hand, they emphasized the heroic battles and dramatic confrontations that these figures participated in to evoke the physical nature of their struggle both as Christians and as human beings. Regardless of how biblical figures may have been portrayed in the Bible, they could suddenly emerge in the spirituals as soldiers;

Moses was a soldier,
In the army of the Lord.

Daniel was a soldier,
In the army of the Lord.

Even Jesus, "the lamb of God" could be depicted as a warlike figure in the spirituals:

Jesus, walkin' down de heabenly road,
Out of his mouth came a two-edged sword.

In addition, their religious ancestors, the biblical Israelites, all became soldiers in the spirituals:

> When Moses an' his soldiers f'om Egypt lan' did flee,
> His enemies behin' him, An' in front of him de sea,
> God raised de water like a wall, An' opened up de way,
> An' de God dat lived in Moses' time is jus' de same today.

While they constantly praised biblical figures for their heroic deeds
and accomplishments as Christian soldiers, they took delight in the
defeat of their adversaries:

> Didn't Ole Pharaoh get drowned, get drowned,
> In the red sea.

On the other hand, enslaved Africans, in their spirituals, constantly
reiterated that the rewards garnered by biblical heroes derived from
their remaining faithful to religious values in situations and under
conditions which tried and tested their moral and spiritual stamina as
human beings:

> My Lord delivered Daniel, Daniel,
> My Lord delivered Daniel, Daniel,
> Why not every man.

Although enslaved Africans created in their spirituals an heroic
epic based on the biblical struggle of Moses and the Israelites, they
clearly envisioned in their own situation not so much a parallel as a
continuation in which the values and behaviors of biblical figures
could still serve as model for their community. In the spirituals, enslaved Africans revealed their view of their own situation as a warlike
struggle for spiritual empowerment to meet a common foe nowhere
more clearly than in their constant portrayal of religious conversion
as a military induction and the religious convert as a soldier in the
army of God:

> I am goin' to join in this army of my Lord,
> I am goin' to join in this army of my Lord.
>
> Takes a humble soul to join,
> In this army of my Lord.
> . . . .
> I won't 'treat back in de army ob de Lord,
> I won't 'treat back in de army ob de Lord.

I'm a solger in de army ob de Lord.
I'm a solger in de army ob de Lord.

Goin' t' fight agains' satan in de army ob de Lord
Goin' t' fight agains' satan in de army.
I'm a solger in de army ob de Lord.
I'm a solger in de army ob de Lord.

I'm singin' wid a sword in ma hand, Lord.
I'm singin' wid a sword in ma hand.

The battlefield on which the convert waged war was not remote historically or geographically; it was the world of everyday reality endured as a "troubled world," an "unfriendly worl'," and a "roarin' hell" where one's enemies were all around. The religious convert as soldier waged an on-going battle with Satan whom enslaved Africans conceptualized as a familiar figure:

Satan is liar and conjurer too,
If you don't mind,
He'll conjure you.

Armed with the assurance that they served a more powerful Being, converted Africans took delight in the fact that they served a God capable of empowering them to defeat Satan.

The conception of Satan as a conjurer in the religious oral literature created by enslaved Africans did not necessarily indicate a rejection of conjurers or the values that they associated with conjuration in their community. While some enslaved Africans, after conversion to Christianity, maintained vehemently that the practice of conjuration and Christianity were incompatible, others held as strongly to the belief that God as a source of spiritual empowerment could and did empower individuals to perform acts of conjuration.[113] Inasmuch as conjurers had no association with any power beyond that granted them by the belief of individual enslaved Africans, their presence in the black community was almost sure to become a source of debate as Christianity offered them an alternative source of spiritual power. In the struggle of black Christians to project their values as the most advantageous for the black community, they obviously found it advantageous to portray as evil incarnate a figure familiar to the community. In an important sense, among members of their community, conjurers and the power that they wielded over the imagination of enslaved Africans represented the greatest internal threat to their values as Christians. However, by portraying conjurers as the primary example of Satan's power in the world, the spiritual song bards offered certain proof to unbelievers that Satan's was a limited power—one ultimately incapable of empowering individuals to overcome enslavers.

In a more profound sense, black Christians' portrayal of Satan as a conjurer was more directly influenced by the fact that they shared Christianity as a source of spiritual empowerment with the slavemasters than by the existence of conjurers in their community. In other words, Christianity, as a source of behavior reflecting values guiding action shared by both the enslaved and enslaver, offered enslaved Africans a way of conceptualizing the behavior that would allow them to defeat their adversaries. In their interpretation of Christianity, enslaved Africans envisioned both God and Satan as beings capable of empowering individuals to affect their destiny. However, in their view of themselves as the chosen of God and in their acceptance of biblical example, enslaved Africans clearly saw God as a superior source of spiritual power. Nevertheless, Satan was a power to be reckoned with and an ever-present threat to those who tried to live according to God's laws. Their realization of the complexity of their situation was revealed nowhere more clearly than in their portrayal in the spiritual of Satan as an everpresent threat who, despite his recognition of God's power, was unwilling to desist from his efforts to hold them in chains:

> The Devil he thought he had me fast...
> But I thought I'd break his chains at last.
> . . . .
> What make ole Satan hate me so?
> Because he got me once and he let me go.
> . . . .
> The Devil's mad and I am glad,
> He lost this soul, he thought he had.
> And I won't stop praying,
> That's what Satan's a grumbling about.

Enslaved Africans in their spirituals revealed that they, like their ancestors, accepted their religious beliefs as a source of values and the most potent weapon in the struggle to protect their identity and physical well-being from the threat posed by their adversary's constant efforts to undermine them. However, to achieve victory in their situation, they had to act valiantly in the midst of their enemies to enhance their spiritual power as a community.

In this respect, the spiritual song tradition's focus on the religious converts was not capricious. As they came to accept spiritual empowerment by God, in a collective sense, as the most important reason for adopting, as their model, behaviors based on Christian religious values and the actions of biblical heroes, the reality of their situation in the slave system and the behavior that they routinely adopted to deal with it created an incredible obstacle to their realizing God's promise. On one level, their conception of the warlike and confrontational actions of some biblical heroes as ideal models of religious behavior for their community created the potential that individuals would come to accept physical confrontation as the values guiding action to be derived from Christian conversion. Consequently, although enslaved Africans often infused the spirituals with a warlike tone and depicted successful heroic confrontations as the greatest reward of religious faith, they also constantly expressed the importance of the heroes' faithful service to God and the morality of their behavior rather than their physical acts as the most important prerequisite for success in these events.

The necessity to emphasize the spiritual dimensions of biblical heroism represented not only the influence of their African heroic epic and cultural values on spiritual song creation but also their concern for the well-being of members of their community. Despite the masters' incredible displays of physical force, enslaved Africans could and did sometimes respond to the harsh and brutal punishment meted out to them by their enslavers with behaviors which temporarily turned the slave system into a battlefield. While the majority of enslaved Africans did not choose physical aggression or armed conflict as a way of dealing with the oppression of the masters, over 250 documented attempted slave revolts in the United States reveal that large numbers regarded physical confrontation as a possible solution to their plight. Not only did enslaved Africans repeatedly attempt to organize revolts of different sizes and with varying degrees of success, but they also escaped the slave system, sometimes in large enough numbers to establish maroon colonies from which they engaged the enslavers in guerilla warfare, in some instances, over extended periods of time.[114] In addition, frustrated and abused Africans frequently unleashed their anger and hostility in spontaneous and contemplated individual acts of rebellion and violence.

The warlike struggle of enslaved Africans against their enslavers and its potential impact on the identity and values of black Christians, however, cannot be comprehended merely in terms of the number of times that they engaged the enslavers in physical confrontations.

Whether or not they participated in the physical confrontations and violence that caused the slave system to be pervaded by an atmosphere of suspicion and tension, enslaved Africans routinely adopted retaliatory behaviors against the enslavers which promoted a warlike view of existence. To circumvent the masters' control and physical power, enslaved Africans routinely resorted to lying, cheating, and stealing to obtain material necessities, avoid work, and escape punishment for various actions which violated the rules of the system and their own communal values. They cheated by putting rocks in their cotton baskets to reach the required weight, breaking the masters' plows and tools, mistreating livestock, and slowing down work at every opportunity. To buffer themselves against the masters' wrath when caught, they either lied or feigned ignorance, humility, and illness.[115] The ever-present threat of the masters' power also made them adept at masking their feelings in all types of situations. For example, Austin Steward reported in his narrative of slavery that when his mistress died, they pretended to be "deeply affected" by it publicly. One fellow sufferer who was unable to fake tears "went to the pump and wet his face, so as to appear to weep with the rest." In private, however, they all "rejoiced that she was no more."[116]

In turning to Christianity as a source of values guiding action, enslaved Africans did not abandon either aggressive actions or the trickster-like behaviors that they viewed as important to their well-being in the slave system. Instead, they discovered a basis on which they could conceptualize both aggressive and subversive behaviors as justifiable retaliatory actions as long as they were directed against the masters. As soldiers in God's army, they became justified in fighting the evil system of slavery in any way that enhanced the possibility that God would send them a deliverer-hero. While the spirituals counseled obedience to God and the morality of behavior in dealing with fellow Christians, this morality was also based on the view that they, as the enslaved, were the only true Christians in the slave system. Therefore, the behaviors that they adopted in dealing with the masters were not actions that threatened their values as Christians or their identity as moral human beings but rather behaviors that protected them from the assaults of their earthly adversaries empowered by Satan—a power that, as Christians, they were morally justified in fighting against.

On another level, despite the warlike tone of many of the songs, as heroic expression based on the African epic tradition, the spirituals were not intended to provide enslaved Africans with a literal model of aggressive warlike action. In an important sense, spiritual song performances revolving around the actions of biblical heroes served as rituals to evoke the power of God and the heroes of the past and to invoke members of the contemporary slave community to be prepared to seize the heroic moment should it be offered by God. For enslaved Africans, the ritual significance of spiritual song performance was as crucial and integral to their realizing God's promise of deliverance as the physical battles that they fought daily and the one which they knew would come. In their songs, and the frequency with which they created opportunities to perform them, they revealed a strong belief in the power of word and ritual to both evoke and invoke not only the power of God and the heroes of the past but the power inherent in members of their community to realize the rewards of this power in their lifetimes. In essence, singing about the heroes of their religion represented for them a way of invoking a sense of their own collective past as the oppressed children of God, and renewing that past in the present. Their conception of biblical heroism served constantly to remind them that they had an identity and values worthy of protection, and that only by living up to their own image of themselves as Christians and as human beings could they garner God's promise.

For enslaved Africans, their belief that, by acting to enhance their collective spiritual power through ritual recreation, God would send them a deliverer-hero did not appear to them as a vain hope. In the Christian religious tradition, they discovered a figure whose role and responsibility for protecting their religious values from both external and internal threats offered them the possibility for realizing the rewards of their faith. "Nigger preachers in dem times wuz mighty-nigh free," declared a former enslaved African. Despite heavy restrictions placed on their efforts to minister to their flocks during slavery, black preachers embodied spiritual attributes and often performed actions which exemplified the values that Africans had traditionally associated with heroic action. While black preachers were usually limited to presiding over baptisms, funerals, weddings, and preaching under white supervision, they routinely defied white prohibitions on their activities and organized clandestine religious meetings, mediated on behalf of their fellow sufferers with the masters as best they could, and served as moral and spiritual advisors under the trying conditions of slavery.[117]

Despite the importance of the black preacher as a "leader of the slave religious life and an influential figure in the slave community,"[118] the black preacher does not appear to have served as a focus for folk heroic creation during slavery. Although preachers were occasionally mentioned in spirituals, no body of folklore devoted to the exploits of preachers during slavery appears in collections. Whether the absence of a folklore of black preachers reflects the reality of the situation or the bias of early collectors for spirituals as the only form of black religious expression during slavery is difficult to determine. Nevertheless, the role of black preachers in the slave system and the descriptions that exist in slave narratives suggest that many served as emulative models for enslaved Africans. Many noted that, despite the restrictions placed on black preachers during slavery, they often risked their personal well-being by defying the prohibition of the masters to preach biblical gospel to their fellow sufferers. Furthermore, the evidence suggests that they were preferred by enslaved Africans both as nascent Moseses and as preachers of the "word" that would empower them. To the black religious community, their sermons represented a desirable alternative to the "white folks preachers'" constant reiteration of the "Servants obey thy master" text.[119] Nevertheless, because most black preachers were closely supervised, they were often forced to stick close to the masters' approved text for sermons preached in their presence. As one black preacher noted of his experiences as a minister during slavery: "When I started preachin', I couldn't read or write and had to preach what massa told me. And he say tell them niggers iffen they obeys the massa they goes to heaven, but I knowed there's something better for them, but I doesn't tell 'em except on the sly. That I done lots. I tell 'em iffen they keeps prayin' the Lord will set 'em free."[120] Enslaved Africans were well aware of the risks faced by their preachers. One former enslaved African recalled that the black preacher on her plantation on orders from the mistress and under her supervision reiterated the "obey thy master" theme in his sermons. However, when she was not present "He come out from straight preaching from the Bible."[121] Obviously, black preachers who were caught "straight preaching from the Bible" had to face the consequences of their rebellious actions. Nevertheless, the example of religious persistence in the face of persecution that enslaved Africans gained from the actions of their preachers enhanced their confidence in pursuing their own vision of the possibilities of their faith.

Even if black preachers did not serve as an important focus for black folk heroic creation during slavery, their existence kept alive the potential that enslaved Africans could realize the conception of biblical heroism embodied in the spirituals. Although black preachers tended not to be revolutionaries, they were men called by God to deliver His message of suffering and faith as preludes to heroic action. Furthermore, to enslaved Africans, they were potential Moseses and their persistence in the face of the enslavers' persecution of them and their community reinforced the power of the biblical vision. The perception of the preachers as nascent Moseses was often heightened by the tendency of black preachers to recount their dramatic calls to the ministry in which they compared their callings to those of biblical figures. For example, a black preacher from Virginia, reported that "one day when I was working in the field all by myself, God told me he wanted me to [be] a leader for my people like Moses. I complained that I was not prepared. And God said, 'You go an' I'll go with you an' speak for you.' From that day I became some sort of leader of my people."[122] Furthermore, as Genovese points out "the preacher did not typically call for revolt and violence, for conditions overwhelmingly discouraged insurrectionary ideas among sober black men. But many could turn into revolutionaries if conditions changed. There was little in their temperament or in the quality of their religious faith to inhibit a call to arms."[123] He also notes that the message of slave religion itself "counseled patience and realism but did not destroy the possibility for revolutionary daring." When enslaved Africans did turn to revolutionary daring, they conceptualized and actualized it almost entirely within the model of heroism that they had created in their spiritual song tradition. Moreover, their religious leaders could usually be found in the thick of it.

Although the role of religion in the covert rebellion against enslavement has been discussed frequently, the relationship between overt rebellion and the conception of biblical heroes has not been treated. Albert Murray in a rare and brief allusion to the importance of biblical heroes states that "No one can deny to Moses, great emancipator that he was, the position of epic hero to anti-slavery movements." However, from his contemporary integrationist's perspective, Murray questions the wisdom of enslaved Africans' "identifying with a nationalist who defined freedom and fulfillment in terms of leading his people out of the land of their actual birth into some exclusive territory."[124] From the contemporary perspective of enslaved Africans who had to endure the daily hell of slavery and who had faith in the "word" of God, Moses' action offered them a conceptual model of behavior for achieving their goal of freedom. More importantly, their conception of Moses as an epic hero allowed enslaved Africans to embrace their own Moses when she appeared in the person of Harriet Tubman to lead her people out of the land of their birth and scene of their degradation. Like Moses, Harriet Tubman risked her own freedom to answer the call of God to lead her people out of slavery. As Vincent Harding describes her, she "grew up on stories of the Hebrew children, sang the songs of impossible hope, she saw visions and dreamed the dreams of struggle and conflict and searching for freedom. She prayed and talked with God and became fully convinced that her God willed freedom."[125] For the hundreds of enslaved Africans who risked their lives to follow this diminutive woman out of the slave South into the free North, Harriet Tubman was the Moses of her people.

The ability of the biblical heroic tradition to offer enslaved Africans a model of adaptive behavior was nowhere more obvious than in slave revolts. The major revolts during the nineteenth century not only relied on the biblical tradition to frame their appeal for followers but also involved religious leaders in major roles. While few details are known about Prosser's Rebellion which took place in Henrico County, Virginia in 1800, it is clear that religion played a key role in the heroic attempt of the Prosser brothers to achieve black liberation.[126] Although Gabriel was apparently the mastermind of the plan, which enlisted anywhere from a dozen to a thousand recruits, Martin, a preacher, led the effort to recruit black followers at funerals and other religious gatherings. Gabriel, whose plan called for a midnight attack on Richmond "to capture arms, burn warehouses, and perhaps take the governor hostage" drew his inspiration from the revolt of enslaved Africans in Haiti.[127] Nevertheless, he recognized the importance of religion among Africans enslaved in America and yielded to Martin's knowledge of the Bible to frame an appeal. Martin is reported to have used the faith of enslaved Africans in biblical example and prophecy to assure them that God would assist them in their efforts as He had the Israelites. To quell fears of potential recruits, Martin preached to them and told them that "their cause was similar to [the] Israelites." And he read to them from the Bible that "if we worship him . . . five of you shall conquer an hundred and an hundred thousand of your enemies."

Despite apparent months of recruiting and planning, the Prossers' plan was foiled by torrential rains which flooded rivers and creeks en route to Richmond on the appointed day. In the meantime, their plan was betrayed and white search parties eventually captured many of the conspirators. The Prossers along with many others were executed. However, as Harding notes, "It is not known how deeply this appeal from the Old Testament moved the persons who gathered in those secret meetings, nor which of them joined the attempted rebellion in response to it. But the analogy to the Israelites was a traditional one in the black community and it continued to have great force among the slaves. Therefore, it would not be too much to expect that some of the men who set themselves on the path of rebellion in those Virginia meetings were responding to a profoundly religious call."[128]

What is clear, even from the scanty evidence that we have of the Prossers' attempted rebellion, is that the biblical heroic tradition of enslaved Africans could and did enhance the possibility for heroic action among them and that even failure did not significantly dim their vision of it. In 1822, for example, Denmark Vesey, a class leader in the Methodist church in Charleston, South Carolina, attempted to take advantage of a black secession movement from the white Methodist church to organize a general rebellion against slavery.[129] Vesey, who had purchased his freedom in 1800, refused to return to Africa so that he could remain and fight for the freedom of his people. Although Vesey was familiar with the slave revolt in Santo Domingo from his travels around the Caribbean, as a church leader, he believed that a religious appeal would be more meaningful to potential recruits than a political one. However, he did apparently use the Haitian uprising to supplement his religious appeal by suggesting that it was proof that the time was ripe for them to realize biblical prophecy. He read to his followers from the Bible that "Behold the day of the Lord cometh, and thy spoil shall be divided in the midst of thee. For I shall gather all nations against Jerusalem to battle; and the city shall be taken." He attempted to convince his followers that "Santo Domingo and Africa will assist us to get our liberty, if we will only make the motion first."[130]

Like the Prossers' attempted rebellion, Vesey's plan was betrayed by a potential recruit before it was realized. However, his use of the heroic potential in the religion of enslaved Africans was undeniable. At Vesey's trial, a deposition was read against him which stated that "His general conversation was about religion which he would apply to slavery, as for instance, he would speak of the creation of the world, in which he would say all men had equal rights, blacks as well as whites, all his religious remarks were mingled with slavery."[131] After the capture of Vesey and his confederates, authorities found a letter in the trunk of Peter Poyas, a co-conspirator in the plot, which indicated the depth of faith of Vesey's followers in the power of God as a deliverer. The letter, apparently addressed to Vesey and the other organizers, stated: "Fear not, the Lord God that delivered Daniel is able to deliver us." Despite the faith of the letter's writer, Vesey and his band were not delivered from execution. Many believed, however, that the slave spiritual, "Go, Down Moses," was created and first sung at one of his recruiting meetings.[132]

Interestingly, the most successful slave revolt of the nineteenth century was not only based on a deeply religious and biblical foundation, but was also led by Nat Turner, a man who clearly saw himself and was seen by his followers as a prophet of God.[133] Turner's story of his life and rebellion clearly shows the influence of the conception of both the Old Testament prophet/warrior and the New Testament Messiah traditions on his efforts. Like the Old Testament prophets, Turner believed that he was called by God to serve His will as a deliverer of his people. He claimed that while he was praying one day, the Spirit spoke to him. According to Turner, it was "the Spirit that spoke to the prophets in former days." In the years to come, Turner not only continued to hear the voice of the Spirit, he also dreamed prophetic dreams and had visions until he was convinced that he was indeed called by God as a deliverer. Like Moses and Christ, Turner went through his own wilderness experience. He spent thirty days in the woods as a runaway but returned to his master of his own free will. Of his experience, he said: "But the reason of my return was, that the Spirit appeared to me and said I had my wishes directed to the things of this world, and not to the kingdom of heaven, and that I should return to the service of my earthly master—'For he who knoweth his Master's will, and doeth it not, shall be beaten with many stripes, and thus have I chastened you.'"

For Turner, there was no question as to who the Master was that he must obey. In 1831, Nat Turner, inspired by his visions and fortified by his faith in God, led a band of enslaved Africans through the countryside of Virginia and killed between sixty and seventy white children, women, and men. Unlike the Prossers and Vesey, Turner did not attempt to recruit large numbers of followers. He was convinced that God would give momentum and numbers to his fight as it developed. When he was eventually captured, he pleaded "not guilty" because he was following the commands of God. Even though wholesale slaughter of blacks followed Turner's revolt, he nevertheless became a hero in the eyes of many. Legends and rumors circulated widely that when he was removed from the gallows after his execution, it was discovered that "he had prints under his feets and in his hands say 'Jesus'." Others told that the limb of the tree on which he was hanged died at the same moment that he did. Stories also circulated that, like Christ, Nat returned to appear to selected ones in the community.

Despite the inability of bold individuals to mount successful rebellions against the enslavers, their failure did not threaten the values that enslaved Africans associated with biblical heroes. If anything, it strengthened their resolve to continue acting to enhance their collective spiritual power as a community. Clearly, the value of the conception of biblical heroism created by enslaved Africans cannot be measured solely on the basis of its serving as a model of successful aggressive action. In many ways, the conception of biblical heroism embodied in the spirituals did not prepare enslaved Africans to act in overtly aggressive ways against their enslavers. It did, however, both facilitate and justify their maintaining a system of moral and spiritual values alternative to those fostered by existence in the slave system—a system of values that they believed offered them advantages in overcoming the power of slavemasters. In addition, despite the enslavers' treatment of them, enslaved Africans were able to use spiritual song performances constantly to evoke and invoke their biblical heroes to remind members of their community of their differential identity and the values on which it was based. While singing about their adopted biblical ancestors, they could present members of their community with objective proof that their existence as "slaves" was not a reflection of their identity, and slavery was not their destiny as human beings. In addition, they were able to constantly remind members of their community that the rewards of "living up" to their values far outweighed the sufferings that they were experiencing at the hands of the masters.

In the end, by turning to their African heroic epic tradition as a model for spiritual song creation, enslaved Africans were able to transform the biblical saga into an heroic tradition based on values guiding action both recognizable to them and important in their efforts to protect their identity and values as African people from both internal and external threats. To members of their community, they were able to transmit through spiritual songs a model of behavior for enhancing their moral and spiritual well-being under incredibly adverse conditions. In addition, in songs that recreated the lives of biblical heroes, they were able to constantly present members of their community with a conception of behaviors reflecting values that justified their struggle against their enslavers as a moral necessity. Biblical heroes came to serve not merely as models of emulative behaviors but as objective proof that faith in the power of an unseen God led to spiritual empowerment and, ultimately, earthly freedom. As a shared source of values and behaviors, Christianity and the heroic tradition embodied in the Bible became potent weapons in the arsenal of enslaved Africans as they sought a means of protecting their identity and values as African people and their well-being as human beings from the evil being done to them by slavemasters.

Notes

1. Harold Courlander, *Negro Folk Song U.S.A.* (New York: Columbia University Press, 1963) 38.

2. Courlander 38.

3. Courlander 38.

4. Sterling A. Brown, "Negro Folk Expression: Spirituals, Seculars, Ballads and Worksongs," *Phylon* 14(1953): 46.

5. Lawrence W. Levine, *Black Culture and Black Consciousness: Afro-American Folk Thought from Slavery to Freedom* (New York: Oxford University Press, 1977) 37.

6. D. K. Wilgus, "The Negro-White Spirituals," in *Mother Wit From The Laughing Barrel: Readings in the Interpretation of Afro-American Folklore*, ed. Alan Dundes (Englewood Cliffs, N. J.: Prentice-Hall,1972) 68.

7. Wilgus 68.

8. Frederick Olmsted, *A Journey in the Back Country, 1853–1854* (New York: Mason, 1860, repr. 1970) 64–65.

9. Two influential works from this perspective are Benjamin E. Mays, *The Negro's God as Reflected in His Literature* (Boston: Chapman and Grimes, 1928) and E. Franklin Frazier, *The Negro Church in America* (New York: Schocken Books, 1964).

10. Newman I. White, *American Negro Folksong* (Cambridge: Harvard University Press, 1928)11–13.

11. George P. Jackson, "The Genesis of the Negro Spirituals," *The American Mercury* 26(1932): 248.

12. H. E. Krehbiel, *Afro-American Folksong* (New York: Schirmer, 1914) 4.

13. James Weldon Johnson and Rosamond Johnson, *Books of American Negro Spirituals* (New York: Dacapo Press, 1969 [1925, 1926]) 20.

14. John Lovell, Jr. *The Forge and the Flame* (New York: Macmillan, 1972) 111.

15. Lovell 111.

16. Henry C. Wood, "Negro Camp Meeting Melodies," *New England Magazine* (March 1892): 61.

17. Wood 61.

18. Nathaniel Dett, "Preface" to *Religious Folk-Songs of the Negro as Sung at Hampton Institute* in *The Social Implications of Early Negro Music in the United States*, ed. Bernard Katz (New York: Arno Press, 1969) xli.

19. Henry Spaulding, "Negro 'Shouts' and Shout Songs," *Continental Monthly* (August 1863): 196.

20.Spaulding 196.

21. William E. Barton, "Old Plantation Hymns," *New England Magazine* 19 (December 1898), reprinted in Katz 80.

22. Johnson and Johnson 22–23.

23. John Mason Brown, "Songs of the Slave," *Lippincott's Magazine* 2(December 1868):618.

24. Brown 618.

25. Brown 618.

26. Thomas Wentworth Higginson, "Negro Spirituals," *The Atlantic Monthly*, 19(June, 1867): 695.

27. Barton 77.

28. Spaulding 197.

29. Marion A. Haskell, "Negro Spirituals'," *The Century Magazine* 36 (August 1899): 578.

30. Dett xli–xlii.

31. Dett xlii

32. Levine 37.

33. John S. Mbiti, *African Religions and Philosophy* (Garden City, N. Y.: Doubleday and Co., 1970) 93.

34. Dominique Zahan, *The Religions, Spirituality and Thought of Traditional Africans* (Chicago: University of Chicago Press, 1979) 18.

35. Zahan 18–19.

36. Daniel P. Biebuyck, "The African Heroic Epic," *Journal of the Folklore Institute* 13(1979):18.

37. Biebuyck 28.

38. Daniel P. Biebuyck, "The Epic as a Genre in Congo Oral Literature" in *African Folklore*, ed. Richard M. Dorson (Bloomington: Indiana University Press, 1972) 263.

39. Biebuyck, "The Epic as a Genre" 266.

40. Biebuyck, "The Epic as a Genre" 266–67.

41. John W. Johnson, "Yes Virginia, There is an Epic in Africa," *Research in African Literature* 11(1980): 310.

42. Charles Bird, "Heroic Song of the Mande Hunters," in *African Folklore*, ed. Richard M. Dorson (Bloomington: Indiana University Press, 1972) 290.

43. Daniel P. Biebuyck, *Hero and Chief* (Berkeley: University of California Press, 1978) 93.

44. Biebuyck, "The Epic as a Genre" 262.

45. Charles S. Bird and Martha B. Kendall, "The Mande Hero: Text and Context," in *Explorations in African Systems and Thought*, ed. Ivan Karp and Charles S. Bird (Bloomington: Indiana University Press, 1982) 22.

46. Biebuyck, "The African Heroic Epic" 20–21.

47. Biebuyck, "The Epic as a Genre" 262.

48. Biebuyck, "The African Heroic Epic" 23.

49. Daniel P. Biebuyck and Kahombo C. Mateene, eds., *The Mwindo Epic* (Berkeley: University of California Press, 1969) 13.

50. Biebuyck, *Hero and Chief* 9.

51. Bird and Kendall 19.

52. Johnson 317–18.

53. Bird and Kendall 18.

54. Bird and Kendall 16.

55. Biebuyck, *Hero and Chief* 4.

56. Bird and Kendall 18.

57. Bird and Kendall 16.

58. Christiane Seydou, "A Reflection on Narrative Structure of Epic Texts: A Case Example of Bambara and Fulani Epics," *Research in African Literatures* 14(1983): 314.

59. Seydou 314.

60. Johnson 117.

61. Biebuyck, *Hero and Chief* 104.

62. Mbiti 258.

63. Biebuyck, *Hero and Chief* 36.

64. Harold Courlander and Olismane Sako, *The Heart of the Ngoni* (New York: Crown Publishing, Inc. 1982) 4.

65. Biebuyck, "The African Heroic Epic" 6.

66. Johnson 116.

67. Biebuyck, *Hero and Chief* 99–101.

68. Johnson 116.

69. Courlander and Sako 8.

70. Biebuyck, *Hero and Chief* 5.

71. Johnson 320.

72. Johnson 319.

73. Bird 284.

74. Seydou 131.

75. Seydou 131.

76. Kwesi Yankah, "To Praise or Not to Praise the King: The Akan APAE in the Context of Referential Poetry," *Research in African Literatures* 14(1983): 381.

77. Yankah 382.

78. Yankah 382.

79. Seydou 113.

80. This sketch of the life and legend of Bras Coupe is based on accounts offered in the following: Herbert Asbury, *The French Quarter* (New York: A. A. Knopf, Inc., 1936) 244–47; Frederick W. Turner, III, "Badmen, Black and White," dissertation, University of Pennsylvania, 1965, 358–65.

81. Eugene Genovese, *Roll, Jordan, Roll: The World the Slaves Made* (New York: Vintage Books, 1976) 591.

82. Raboteau 97–128.

83. Raboteau 11.

84. Raboteau 11.

85. Raboteau 133.

86. Raboteau 121.

87. Jerome W. Jones, "The Established Virginia Church and the Conversion of Negroes and Indians, 1620–1760," *Journal of Negro History* 46(1961): 12–23.

88. Raboteau 132; Genovese 183–84.

89. Raboteau 132.

90. Genovese 65.

91. Paul D. Escott, *Slavery Remembered* (Chapel Hill: University of North Carolina Press, 1979) 42.

92. Genovese 65.

93. John W. Blassingame, *The Slave Community* (New York: Oxford University Press, 1972) 162–163.

94. Lewis G. Clarke, *Narrative of the Sufferings of Lewis G. Clark . . .* " (Boston, 1859) 17.

95. Discussions of the day to day conditions experienced by enslaved Africans from their point of view as presented in their writings and recollections can be found in several studies, e.g., Blassingame 154–83, Genovese 597–647, and Escott 36–70. In addition, see Charles H. Nichols, *Many Thousand Gone* (Bloomington: Indiana University Press, 1963).

96. Zephaniah Kingsley, *Treatise on the Patriarchal or Co-operative System of Society as it Exists in Some Governments, and Colonies in America, and in the United States, under the Name of Slavery, with its Necessitites and Advantages, by an Inhabitant of Florida* 2nd ed., 1829, excerpted in Dena Epstein, *Sinful Tunes and Spirituals* (Urbana: University of Illinois Press, 1977) 194.

97. John Mason Peck, *Forty Years of Pioneer Life,* Memoir (Philadelphia, 1864).

98. Blassingame 209. For a more in-depth study of the problems created by the use of alcohol among enslaved Africans consult Genovese 642–43.

99. Postell 111.

100. Postell 111.

101. Blassingame 82.

102. Escott 45.

103. Blassingame 85–86.

104. Welch Neck Baptist Church Minutes, 1738–1932, South Caroliniana Library, University of South Carolina, excerpted in Raboteau 187.

105. Blassingame 62; Raboteau 213–14.

106. George P. Rawick, ed., *The American Slave: A Composite Autobiography* (Westport, Conn.: Greenwood Press, 1977), Vol. VII (*Mississippi Narratives*) 24; Raboteau 214.

107. Brown 83–84.

108. Rawick, ed., Vol. VIII (*Arkansas Narratives*), pt. 1, 35.

109. Moses Roper, *A Narrative of the Adventures and Escape of Moses Roper from American Slavery* (London 1840) 62.

110. Peter Randolph, *Sketches of Slave Life or, Illustrations of the Peculiar Institution* (Boston 1855) 30.

111. Fisk University, *Unwritten History of Slavery: Autobiographical Accounts of Negro Ex-Slaves*, comp. and ed. Ophelia Settle Egypt, J. Musuoka, and Charles S. Johnson (Washington D.C.: 1968[1945]) 60.

112. Spiritual song lyrics used throughout these texts are traditional and were taken from the following sources: E. A. McIlhenny, *Befo' De War Spirituals* (Boston: Christopher Publishing House, 1933); William F. Allen, Charles P.

Ware, and Lucy McKim Garrison, *Slave Songs of the United States* (New York: Peter Smith, 1951[1867]); William A. Fisher, *Seventy Negro Spirituals* (Boston: Oliver Ditson Co., 1926); Christa K. Dixon, *Negro Spirituals: from Bible to Folksong* (Philadelphia: Fortress Press, 1976); Johnson and Johnson, *Books of American Negro Spirituals*; John Lovell, Jr., *The Forge and the Flame.*

113. Raboteau 287.

114. Eugene Genovese, *From Rebellion to Revolution* (Baton Rouge: Louisiana State University Press, 1979) 1–83; Blassingame 119–124.

115. Blassingame 211–213; Escott 73–79.

116. Austin Steward, *Twenty-Two Years a Slave, And Forty Years A Freeman* (Rochester, N.Y., 1861) 93.

117. Raboteau 232.

118. Raboteau 231–232.

119. Raboteau 234; Eugene Genovese, "Black Plantation Preachers in the Slave South," *Louisiana Studies* (1972): 188–214.

120. Rawick, ed., Vol. IV (*Texas Narratives*) 9.

121. Norman R. Yetman, ed., *Voices of Slavery* (New York: Holt, Rinehart and Winston, 1970) 106.

122. Charles L. Perdue et al., eds. *Weevils in the Wheat* (Bloomington: Indiana University Press, 1976) 10.

123. Genovese, "Black Plantation Preachers" 193

124. Albert Murray, *The Hero and the Blues* (Columbia: University of Missouri Press, 1973) 61.

125. Vincent Harding, "Religion and Resistance Among Antebellum Negro, 1800–1860," in *The Making of Black America* Vol. I, ed. August Meier and Elliot Rudwick (New York: Atheneum, 1969) 192–93.

126. Harding 182–183; Harvey Wish, "American Slave Insurrections Before 1861," *Journal of Negro History* 3 (July 1937): 331.

127. Harding 182.

128. Harding 183.

129. Harding 184–86; John W. Lofton, Jr., "Denmark Vesey's Call to Arms," *Journal of Negro History* 4 (1948): 395–417; Sterling Stuckey, "Remembering Denmark Vesey," *Negro Digest* 4 (February 1966): 28–41.

130. Harding 185.

131. Harding 185.

132. Harding 185.

133. Herbert Aptheker, *Nat Turner's Slave Rebellion* (New York: Humanities Press, 1966).

"You Done Me Wrong": The Badman as Outlaw Hero

In 1893, Morris Slater slung his gun across his shoulder at the end of a long week as a turpentine worker in rural Alabama and headed into town to unwind in the local jooks.[1] When he arrived in town, he was accosted by a white policeman who demanded that he hand over his gun.

> Standin' on corner didn't mean no harm,
> Policeman grab me by my arm,
> Wuz lookin' fer Railroad Bill.[2]

When Slater refused to relinquish his firearm, a struggle ensued in which the policeman was killed.

> Railroad Bill was mighty sport
> Shot all the buttons off high Sheriff coat
> Den holler, "Right on desparado Bill."[3]

Slater jumped on a passing train and escaped. For the next three years he thwarted all efforts to capture him and secured his survival by robbing freight trains of canned goods and other merchandise. Slater became well known for breaking into crates on trains, removing their contents and throwing them out along the tracks only to return later to pick them up. He then sold his bounty to poor African Americans who lived along the railroad tracks. His train robbing exploits earned him the name of "Railroad Bill."

> I went down on Number One,
> Railroad Bill had jus' begun,
> It's lookin' for Railroad Bill.

> I come up on Number Two,
> Railroad Bill had jus' got through
> It's lookin' for Railroad Bill.
>
> I caught Number Three and went back down the road,
> Railroad Bill was marchin' to and fro.
> It's that bad Railroad Bill.[4]

According to legend, Railroad Bill's success in eluding his would-be captors was due to the fact that he was a conjure man who could transform himself into almost any shape at will. Some African Americans told stories of how Bill on different occasions eluded policemen and railroad detectives by turning himself into various animals including a black sheep, a fox, and a bloodhound.

Regardless of what African Americans saw as the source of Bill's success in eluding the law, agents of the law considered him a desperate criminal whose apprehension was inevitable. In fact, in the counties that surrounded Escambia, Alabama, candidates for sheriffs made and were elected on the promise that they would capture him. One in particular, E. S. McMillan, became one of Bill's victims when he engaged the outlaw in a desperate gun battle in 1895.

> Railroad Bill, he went down Souf,
> Shot all de teef, out o' de constable's mouf,
> Wa'n't he bad, wa'n't he bad, wa'n't he bad.[5]

According to legend, Bill was a deadly shot and killed as many as a dozen men during his career. And the longer he remained at large, the bolder and more daring he became. In one story, Bill even robbed a train carrying a posse sent to capture him.

> Talk about yo' five an' ten dollar bill,
> Ain't no Bill like old desparado Bill,
> Says, right on desparado Bill.[6]

In 1896, Railroad Bill was killed. According to legend, he was lured to Tidmore's store by a note he received from an erstwhile friend, where he was ambushed by law enforcement officers.

> Railroad Bill eatin' crackers and cheese,
> Long came a sheriff, chipper as you please,
> Wuz lookin' fer Railroad Bill.

Railroad Bill lyin' on de grocer floor,
Got shot two times an' two time more—
No more lookin' fer Railroad Bill.[7]

After his death, law enforcement officers carried his body from town to town in rural southern Alabama for public viewing and to demonstrate the power of the "law" to others who might try to follow his example. Nevertheless, many of the black folk in rural southeast Alabama refused to accept the fact of his death. They chose instead to believe that Railroad Bill still roamed the forests in one of the numerous animal forms that he, as a conjure man, could assume.

Railroad Bill was just one of many badman heroes to capture the black folk imagination during the 1890s and whose exploits became the subject of songs, legends, and folktales. Stackolee, John Hardy, Harry Duncan, Devil Winston, and other lesser known figures all emerged during the last decade of the nineteenth century and served as important catalysts for black folk heroic creation.[8] Although the oral traditions surrounding individual badmen were known to a greater extent in some localities than others, they were based on strikingly similar exploits and shared important conceptual elements. In many ways, the personal attributes and characteristic. behaviors associated with badmen seemed quite divorced from those identified with black folk heroes during the period of black chattel slavery. However, to African Americans who celebrated them as folk heroes, neither the personal traits nor the actions associated with these figures in folklore were totally unfamiliar. Although black badmen were invariably conceptualized as individuals who, like Railroad Bill, were accused of breaking the law and became heroic because of their crimes, their acts of lawlessness were conceptualized within a tradition of folk heroic creation that African Americans recognized and accepted as normative expressions of their heroic ideals.

In studies of the black badman as a folk hero, folklorists have consistently painted a portrait of this figure as a champion of violence, directed primarily at the black community. Black badmen heroes are described by Levine as individuals who "preyed on the weak as well as the strong, women as well as men. They killed not merely in self defense but from sadistic need and sheer joy."[9] Abrahams describes them as rebels whose rebellion "is consciously and sincerely immoral." The action of black badmen, according to Abrahams, "is not directed in positive terms" but rather "against anything that constrains" them.[10] Bruce Jackson describes the "ultimate badman" as "one who fears and respects nothing" and is, therefore, "dangerous to his community."[11] As a result of their portrayal of the black badman as a source of unrelieved violence in the black community, folklorists have repeatedly suggested that the black conception of the badman as hero derives from the fear such figures generate among African Americans. Therefore, the folklore of black badmen offers African Americans merely an expressive outlet for their feelings of hostility and violence, (presumably resulting from their oppression in the society) and not a model of emulative behavior adaptable to real-life situations.

Most critical discussion of the badman as a folk hero, however, has been based on the conception of this figure in the toast tradition, a more recent expressive embodiment of the exploits of badmen. Although folklorists generally acknowledge that the conception of the badman in the toast tradition has its roots in folk heroic literature created around the turn of the century, they have not dealt critically or systematically with this earlier tradition, which portrays the exploits of badmen primarily in ballads. A consequence of ignoring the earlier manifestations of the badman tradition in black culture is evident in folkloristic discussions of the tradition, where there is a constant emphasis on the destructive and unproductive nature of badman heroes. In drawing this portrait of the badman, folklorists have basically relied on early fieldwork reports which suggested that a character-type known in black communities as the "bad nigger" served as the prototype of the badman of folklore. The uncritical acceptance of the "bad nigger," who most often acted as a neighborhood bully, as the real-life prototype for the badman of folklore not only has distorted the basis on which African American accept badmen as folk heroes, but has also led to unproductive searches for the factors that have been most influential on folk heroic creation surrounding badmen in black culture.

Because black badman folk heroes characteristically act within the black community, folklorists have suggested repeatedly that conditions and situations in the black community have served as the primary catalyst for folk heroic creation surrounding badmen. In the process, they have basically ignored the fact that an act of lawlessness constitutes the central event in the folklore of badmen. This is not to say that folklorists have not recognized lawlessness in this folklore. However, they have most often suggested that lawlessness functions as the source of the threat of these individuals, to society and the back community, rather than as the most important influence on folk heroic creation surrounding these figures. Therefore, when folklorists have noted the law as a possible influence, they have offered no extended analysis of its role as a catalyst for black folk heroic creation.

G. Malcolm Laws, for example, offers rather tentatively that one reason for the emphasis on criminal activity in black ballads created around the turn of the century to chronicle the exploits of black badmen is the fact that African Americans "so often have been the victims of the white man's laws."[12] Roger Abrahams concludes that the black badman "As a social entity is rebelling against white men's laws;" however, because he envisions the black badman basically as a rebel against social and familial values in the black community, he does not discuss the law as particularly relevant to an understanding of the badman as a folk hero in black culture.[13] Perhaps owing to the vagueness of Abrahams's assertion or his presentation of it as one in a catalogue of influences on the development of folk traditions surrounding black badmen, Bruce Jackson takes exception to it and insists that "one would be hard put to find a focus for him [the black badman], from his point of view or the teller's perception of his point of view in the 'white man's laws.'"[14]

Levine, on the other hand, approaches discussion of the black badman tradition from the perspective of outlaw folk heroic traditions—those in which lawlessness serves as a normative response to oppressive conditions created and maintained, in most instances, by the law or, at the least, the socio-political system that it upholds. However, he examines the black badman tradition ethnocentrically by comparing it to the American outlaw tradition of the late nineteenth century. As a result, he concludes that the black badman cannot be considered an outlaw hero by the standards that he associates with the outlaw hero. He notes that

> The "good bad man," the "noble robber," the "gentleman killer," the "social bandit," who dominated the outlaw legends of the United States and of many European countries from which American immigrants came, shared characteristics which black outlaws generally lacked. Such romanticized bad men turned to lives of crime only under the most extreme provocation, often to avenge a wrong by the authorities. Their crimes are selective, aimed against those with economic or political power.[15]

By constrast, black badmen, according to Levine, are "pure force, pure vengeance; explosions of fury and futility." Therefore, he concludes that "Black singers, storytellers and audiences might temporarily and vicariously live through the exploits of their bandit heroes, but they were not beguiled into looking to these asocial, self-centered, and futile figures for any permanent remedies."[16]

To reevaluate the meaning and function of the badman in black folk heroic literature, a necessary first step must involve an examination of the black conception of the "bad nigger," especially in terms of the evolution of the relationship between this character-type and the law. While a black character-type referred to as the "bad nigger" has existed in American society since the days of slavery, whether these figures served as prototypes for badmen heroes in African American folk tradition is certainly debatable. From the evidence left by enslaved Africans, they were familiar with real-life individuals that they, as well as whites, referred to as "bad niggers."[17] These individuals characteristically adopted aggressive behaviors in the slave system and refused to accept either the masters' physical powers as a match for their own physical prowess and mental determination, or to accept the values of the black community as binding on them. They sought through open defiance, violence, and confrontation to improve their lot in slavery regardless of the consequences of their actions for their own or the slave community's welfare. Although enslaved Africans undoubtedly derived a certain amount of pleasure from the actions of those bold individuals who refused to accept whippings, sauced masters and mistresses with impunity, ran away at the slightest provocation, and even killed masters and overseers who abused them, they did not embody the exploits of "bad niggers" in oral traditions celebrating them as folk heroes.[18] "Bad niggers" who, from the perspective of enslaved Africans, knowingly placed the acquisition of status above their own personal well-being and that of their fellow sufferers posed serious threats to the welfare and values of the entire slave community. Not only did their flagrant disregard for the masters' rules constantly threaten to bring the masters' power down on the entire community, but they were also as likely to unleash their fury and violence on their defenseless fellow sufferers as on the masters. Although enslaved Africans undoubtedly evaluated the actions of "bad niggers" differently than the masters, they also realized that it was not in their best interest to promote such actions as heroic.

Some folklorists have suggested, however, that conditions during slavery inhibitive to a conception of the "bad nigger" as a folk hero somehow changed after emancipation. H. C. Brearley, for instance, notes in his discussion of the folklore of the badman that "open expression of admiration of a 'ba-ad nigger' is doubtless of a comparative recent development. Even if his type existed during slavery, the singing of ballads in his honor was not a very politic method of securing the favor of masters and overseers."[19] Obviously, the black view of what constituted "bad nigger" behavior in slavery was destined to undergo a change after emancipation, since many of the actions associated with this character type during slavery were defined by and directed against the unfair control and authority of slavemasters. Therefore, it is reasonable to assume that, in many cases, behaviors defined by whites during slavery as those of the "bad nigger" came to be viewed by African Americans after emancipation as the free and open expression of citizenship. Certainly, the majority of African Americans approached their freedom with the attitude that they could refuse to accept white abuse, to participate in the "ritual of deference," or to allow whites to circumscribe their movements or behavior—refusals that would have garnered them reputations as "bad niggers" during slavery.[20] In addition, most individuals who had acted as "bad niggers" in the slave community had not been abnormal personalities; they had been individuals motivated by a keen desire for freedom and frustrated by the lack of constructive opportunities for self-advancement within the restrictive slave system. After emancipation, they were often able to find other avenues into which they could channel their energies and apply their physical prowess to make new lives for themselves.[21] In some instances, these individuals, because of their superior strength and courage became the natural leaders of their people and aggressively fought for black civil rights as political organizers. In these cases, they became "men" and "women" in the eyes of black people and provided a model of aggressive action for achieving the dreams of freedom through political action.

Nevertheless, regardless of how African Americans may have perceived themselves in relation to whites, or the behavioral options available to them as citizens after emancipation, whites continued to view almost any black person who challenged their authority or right to define black behavior and social roles as a "bad nigger." They also persisted in believing that they had the right to apply personal sanctions against African Americans who challenged their superiority in the society. Therefore, as many African Americans routinely tested their freedom immediately after emancipation by adopting behaviors and attitudes toward and in the presence of whites that would have been expressly forbidden during slavery, many African Americans quickly garnered reputations with whites as "bad niggers."[22]

Although southern whites reacted swiftly at the close of the Civil War to reestablish their right to deal personally with such individuals under the law—most notably with the passage of the Black Codes—they were unable to press their notions of proper racial etiquette and black social roles into law under the restrictions placed on them by reconstruction governments.[23] Nevertheless, as white frustrations mounted toward a black population intoxicated with notions of freedom and equality, white physical attacks against African Americans, most often unprovoked, escalated in the years immediately following emancipation, as whites increasingly used violence as a means of reminding blacks of the consequences of being branded a "bad nigger" by them. "Neither a freedman's industriousness nor his deference necessarily protected him from whites if they suspected he harbored dangerous tendencies or if they looked upon him as a 'smart-assed nigger,'" observes Leon Litwack of the precarious situation in which African Americans found themselves during the reconstruction era.[24] Litwack further notes that of the uprovoked acts of violence against African Americans during reconstruction the "largest proportion related in some way to that broad and vaguely defined charge of conduct unbecoming black people—that is 'putting on airs,' 'sauciness,' 'impudence,' 'disrespect,' 'insubordination,' contradicting whites and violating social custom."[25] Furthermore, whites viewed and made the object of their most violent and organized aggressive actions those "bad niggers" who took on leadership roles in the black community.[26]

Moreover, with Redemption and the resumption of Home Rule in the South, criminal laws and punishment emerged as the primary means by which whites dealt with individuals that they considered "bad niggers." Regardless of its stated purpose, the criminal punishment of African Americans in the late nineteenth century had as a primary function the "breaking" of recalcitrant "bad niggers"—individuals who refused to submit to white authority and control in the society. The most dramatic evidence that criminal punishment of African Americans had a function different from that meted out to the majority of whites resided in the disparity observable in the forms to which they were subject. Although blacks and whites were presumably subject to the same forms of punishment, few whites were ever sentenced to the two most common forms of punishment meted out to the vast majority of blacks in the late nineteenth century: the chain gang and convict lease system. Both forms of punishment were characterized by forced labor, inhuman living and working conditions, and an extremely high mortality rate.[27] Benjamin Brawley notes of the chain gang system in Texas, for instance, that "from 1875–1880 the total number of prisoners discharged was 1651, while the number of deaths and escapes for the same period totaled 1608.[28] With their legs chained together while at work during the day and their bodies chained together at night, few prisoners ever "escaped" the chain gang.

In addition, as cruel as it was, criminal punishment for the majority of African Americans resulted primarily from minor offenses against

whites or violence against blacks. African Americans accused of violent crimes against whites were more often tried, convicted, and punished not by the courts but by white lynch mobs.[29] Tindall notes, for
example, that in post-Civil War South Carolina, "few Negroes charged
with murder of whites were ever punished by the law and practically
none charged with the rape of white women."[30] By the late nineteenth century, being the victim of a lynch mob was the most likely
consequence of being branded a dangerous "bad nigger." In addition, whites retained, through their control of the judiciary system,
the extralegal right to deal personally with African Americans who
breached racial etiquette or violated their personal property. In
many instances, they simply used the threat of prosecution in the
courts as a means of maintaining control over African Americans who
exhibited behaviors that they defined as those of the "bad nigger."[31]
In addition, the Ku Klux Klan developed as a powerful extralegal
force in the post-reconstruction South for controlling black behavior
that many whites considered a threat to their supremacy within the
society.

While African Americans in the late nineteenth century, as during
slavery, did not adopt the same view as whites of those who challenged white authority or became the victims of white legal persecution or violence, they nevertheless had to be concerned with the re-
percussions for their well-being both with whites and within their own
communities of condoning behavior which facilitated the occurrence
of these situations. For instance, Charles S. Johnson has argued in his
study, *Shadow of the Plantation*, that because of the arbitrary, brutal,
and unfair treatment that African Americans received at the hands of
the law in the years following emancipation, they made avoidance of
the law a "virtue," especially in their own communities.[32] However, in
attempting to keep the "law" out of the black community, African
Americans assumed an enormous amount of responsibility for maintaining peace and harmony among themselves. Therefore, individuals in black neighborhoods who routinely indulged in gratuitous violence and bullied and preyed on other blacks posed a serious dilemma for the community. These individuals, who garnered reputations as "bad niggers" among blacks, were also likely to become well
known to the "law" as "bad niggers," inasmuch as their violent eruptions often provided the "law" with a reason to enter black neighborhoods. To African Americans, individuals who acted as "bad niggers"
in their communities were not heroes, but rather individuals whose
characteristic behavior threatened their abilities to maintain the
value that they placed on harmony and solidarity as a form of protection against the power of the law.

In essence, African Americans approached folk heroic creation in the late nineteenth century under socio-cultural and political conditions which militate against their finding in the "bad nigger" a focus for folk heroic creation. In creating an oral tradition to transmit a model of heroic action accepted as advantageous for securing their interests in the repressive social environment of post-emancipation America, African Americans had to balance the demands of living with the constant threat of white violence and the failure of the law to provide a standard of justice for all against their own communal values and welfare. "Bad niggers," whose undirected fury and violence in the society constantly threatened the well-being of blacks with individual whites and the law, had not during slavery and did not in freedom exhibit characteristic behaviors which could offer adaptive advantages for protecting black communal values. Even when "bad niggers" made the law their target, black freedpeople still faced the reality that whites controlled too much legal and extralegal power to allow for a reign of black lawlessness directed against them.

Obviously, I am not suggesting that a character-type referred to as the "bad nigger" disappeared from the black lexicon after slavery, and certainly not from that of whites. What I am suggesting is that folklorists who have unquestioningly accepted the "bad nigger" as the prototype for the badman in black folk heroic literature have considered neither the factors important to an understanding of black culture-building after emancipation as they relate to the law and white violence, nor the subtleties of black verbal usage in the folklore embodying their exploits. Most often, students of the black badman tradition have used the terms "badman" and "bad nigger" interchangeably, despite the fact that, in the folklore embodying the exploits of these figures, they are almost never referred to as "bad niggers." In addition, scholars who have used the terms "badman" and "bad nigger" as synonyms for a black character-type have almost invariably supported their view by reference to the inverted meaning that African Americans give to the word "bad" when they prolong the "a" sound in pronouncing it. Brearley, for example, reaches the improbable conclusion that "This use of bad as a term of admiration is quite likely an importation from Africa."[33] While it is unlikely that the inverted meaning of the word "bad" found in black usage occurred in Africa, it is clear that at some point in the history of black people in America a denotative inversion developed associated with how African Americans enunciate the word "bad" as well as how they view the behaviors that it characterizes. Based on the ambivalent feelings that enslaved Africans must have held toward individuals that whites designated as "bad niggers," they undoubtedly accepted the term as an ambiguous description during slavery.

Of equal importance to an understanding of the badman as a folk hero, at some point in the history of black culture-building in America an important contextually defined difference developed associated with how African Americans use and understand the word "nigger." Although enslaved Africans had no control over how they were addressed or referred to by whites, even in bondage, they showed a marked preference for titles of address among themselves such as "Bro" and "Sis" rather than "nigger" to indicate race in referring to other African Americans.[34] Especially after emancipation, "they almost all detested its use by whites, but the very fact of emancipation appears to have increased its popularity in white circles."[35] The popularity of the term "nigger" with whites after emancipation was undoubtedly influenced at least in part by the concerted effort that African Americans made to eradicate its use as a neutral racial identity label in the society. "Even without the benefit of organized or coordinated action, freedmen and freedwomen made known their objections to these relics of bondage," concludes Litwack of the black effort to discard such commonly used white references as "aunt," "uncle," "boy," "girl," and, most especially, "nigger" during the reconstruction era.[36] Nevertheless, in their own communities, African Americans retained and used the term "nigger" with widely different applications. On the one hand, the word was used in intragroup settings as a nominal to refer to another black person to indicate a special and often intimate relationship between the speaker and the other. On the other hand, adjectivally, it was most often used as a pejorative description, to indicate that an individual's actions reflected behavioral norms inconsistent with the aspirations and values of the majority of black people.[37] In other words, African Americans seldom express admiration for those whose behavior they describe as "niggerish."

Folklorists, in accepting the "bad nigger" as the prototype for the badman of folklore, have simply not considered the impact of the law on black life after emancipation or, more importantly, the traditional values of the black community as the most important influence of black folk heroic creation. For example, the absence of a careful consideration of the impact of the law on black life is very obvious in Levine's discussion of black badmen from the vantage point of outlaw folk heroic traditions. While there existed, as Levine emphasizes, some important differences in the conception of black badmen and Anglo-American outlaws in the folklore embodying their exploits, these differences were not sufficient or of the sort to indicate that black badmen were not perceived as acting to protect values in ways traditionally associated with outlaw heroes. For example, Levine stresses the importance of an act of persecution by the law in the folklore of outlawry as important to a conception of a figure as an outlaw hero.[38] While this motif is generally absent in the folklore of the black badman, its absence does not necessarily indicate that African Americans did not perceive the "law" as the catalyst for the actions embodied in the folklore. Outlaws in Anglo-American tradition did not achieve their celebrated status because they literally responded to an act of individual persecution by the law, but rather because their existed among their "people" a general perception of the law and the institutions that it supported as persecutorial. Furthermore, the Anglo-American outlaw tradition was based on a European tradition in which a conception of outlaws as folk heroes was made palatable to their people, who accepted the law as the arbiter of fairness and justice, by presenting in the expressive forms embodying their exploits a motif which justified their actions as retaliatory.

On the other hand, the historical relationships of blacks and whites to the American legal system have been so radically different as to affect their views of how lawlessness in expressive traditions would be conceptualized as heroic. While white Americans have had every reason to view the law as supportive of their interests and rights, and to conceptualize outlaws as heroic only under extraordinary conditions and within well-defined situations, African Americans have had few reasons to view the law as anything other than antagonistic to their interests. They arrived on the North American continent under conditions which placed them outside the law; since during slavery, blacks literally had no legal rights, they could not look to the law for protection of rights or redress of grievances. In post-Civil War America, African Americans hardly had the opportunity to develop a positive view of the law, because the legal rights granted them upon emancipation were rapidly usurped by new laws designed to limit and deny them their basic human and civil rights. More importantly, the folklore of the black badman did not develop within a tradition of folk heroic creation in which retaliatory actions against the established power structure required expressive justification. It had its cultural and expressive roots in the folk heroic tradition that enslaved Africans transformed from their African cultural heritage. Furthermore, the folk heroic traditions of enslaved Africans developed in an atmosphere where destructive material and physical conditions were ubiquitous; persecution was the norm of existence and behaviors against it were accepted as essential to the well being and survival of black people.

In arriving at his conclusions concerning the badman as outlaw, Levine bases his analysis on Eric Hobsbawm's argument that outlawry and the celebration of outlaws as heroes are almost universal cultural phenomena.[39] Although Hobsbawm uses a model which recognizes the universality of outlaw heroic traditions, he also recognizes that the heroic figures that emerge at particular times and in specific cultures often perform strikingly different actions. In addition, he suggests that the socio-political conditions which spawn outlaw heroes are as important as the actions themselves in determining which figure's actions a group will accept as heroic. His analysis must thus be accepted as appropriate to an understanding of the socio-political climate which spawns outlaw folk heroic traditions, rather than as a definitive model for study of specific folk heroic traditions.

Particularly useful to an understanding of the black badman tradition is Hobsbawm's argument that outlaw heroic traditions have historically served as models of heroic action under socio-political conditions that threaten a group's ability to maintain its values, and where the "law" is viewed as in some way responsible for and/or unresponsive to these conditions. The affected group turns to outlaw folk heroes, according to Hobsbawm, because it perceives the law and/or its representatives not only as ineffectual in alleviating the situation but also as supportive of the interests of a segment of the population which remains unaffected or even benefits from the oppressive conditions.[40] "Insofar as bandits have a programme," writes Hobsbawm, "it is the defense or restoration of the traditional order of things 'as it should be' (which in traditional societies means as it is believed to have been in some real or mythical past)."[41] To defend group values or restore "things" to their proper order, outlaw heroes are characteristically portrayed as benefactors of their "people" and act against those individuals and/or institutions who appear to be the beneficiaries of the oppression.

Consequently, if we focus on the actions of black badmen and neglect the conditions which influenced the black conception of them, we cannot reveal the basis on which African Americans accept their actions as those of outlaw heroes. Of the programmatic goals of black badmen in the late nineteenth century, for example, Levine argues that the actions of these individuals revealed that "The simple restoration of things as they had been held no allurement. Society had to be unhinged, undone, made over."[42] While African Americans certainly had no desire for things to return to the way they had been during slavery, they did have a clear idea of what the "traditional order of things" should be, a view that they had defended even before emancipation. "Even those who accept exploitation, oppression and subjection as norms of human life dream of a world without them: a world of equality, brotherhood and freedom, a totally new world without evil," writes Hobsbawm of the vision of those who create outlaw heroes.[43] While such a world had never existed for blacks in American society up to the late nineteenth century, their vision of it had been a primary influence on black folk heroic creation during slavery and would be the most important influence on black folk heroic creation and culture-building in freedom. The failure of this world to come into being, and the black perception of the law as a primary obstacle to its doing so had a dramatic influence on the black conception of the badman as an outlaw folk hero in the late nineteenth century.

In essence, folklorists who have studied the black badman tradition have either implicitly or explicitly made Anglo-American cultural norms and heroic values the standards by which the black badman tradition is to be evaluated. In the process, they have concluded that the black badman's characteristic actions threaten rather than support American values. Obviously, they have based their conclusions concerning the destructive and unproductive nature of the tradition on values guiding action inappropriate to an understanding of it both as a normative model of heroic action in black culture and as an outlaw heroic tradition. To understand the folklore of the black badman as a normative model of heroic action in black culture, it is essential that we view the black badman not only within the tradition of black folk heroic creation begun during slavery but also as an outlaw folk hero. While African Americans clearly experienced changes in their lifestyle after emancipation, they did not abandon values that they had traditionally recognized as advantageous to their well-being, nor the expressive forms which embodied them. Consequently, we must turn to the folk heroic traditions created by enslaved Africans to discover the prototype for the black badman as an outlaw folk hero and the socio-cultural environment of the late nineteenth century to discover the basis on which African Americans evaluated the actions of this figure as heroic.

THE TRICKSTER AND THE BADMAN

In the folklore of enslaved Africans, the trickster tale tradition embodied a conception of behaviors based on values guiding actions that in the late nineteenth century would have been considered those of an outlaw. Although the trickster tale tradition functioned primarily as a normative model of heroic action for securing the material means of survival under the restrictive and repressive conditions of slavery, it was also a tradition in which the central figure's actions were motivated primarily by the socio-political oppression of those who celebrated his action as those of a folk hero. In addition, the trickster who could adeptly step inside his dupe's sense of reality and manipulate it through wit, guile, and deception to secure material rewards could also be boldly aggressive and a minister of violence, especially when cornered or threatened. Moreover, the trickster tales offered a model of behavior for equalizing conditions between masters and slaves by breaking the rules of the system that gave the slave-masters a clear economic, political, and social advantage. It, in essence, functioned as an outlaw tradition within the value system of slavery.

Although some folklorists have envisioned a relationship between the black conceptions of the trickster and the badman, they have not discussed the badman tradition as a transformation of the trickster tradition or the trickster as proto-outlaw. For instance, both Abrahams and Jackson have offered analyses which envision the badman and trickster traditions as reflections of different levels of black acculturation to social norms. Abrahams notes, for example, that

> Where the trickster is a perpetual child, the badman is a perpetual adolescent. His is a world of overt rebellion. He commits acts against taboos and mores in full knowledge of what he is doing. In fact he glories in this knowledge of revolt. He is consciously and sincerely immoral.[44]

Jackson, on the other hand, describes the trickster and the badman in almost opposite terms:

> Although trickster is traditionally the more childish, badman is more childlike. He often acts gratuitously, seems more anxious to display his badness or his 'coolness' than attain any particular goal or need. Trickster is practical. He is goal oriented. Badman focuses on process only; his is a surface pose and counterpose. He rarely considers consequences, while trickster is always conscious of them.[45]

Not only do Abrahams and Jackson approach the trickster and badman traditions as disparate rather than as the product of a continuous tradition of black folk heroic creation, but they also interpret both traditions ethnocentrically. In the process, they fail to reveal either the dynamic continuity of the black folk tradition or the Afrocentric nature of black folk heroic creation in America.

From an Afrocentric perspective, the trickster as conceptualized by enslaved Africans represented a more appropriate focus than the "bad nigger" for folk heroic creation based on a figure whose characteristic behaviors challenged the authority and unfairness of the existing power structure. However, the trickster tale tradition created by enslaved Africans had been wedded to a perception of powerful individual control over both the lives of the enslaved and the means of material survival. In addition, folk heroic creation in regard to the trickster had been based on repetitive face-to-face interaction between enslaved Africans and the slavemasters in situations in which the enslavers' power and control over both their lives and the material means of survival were very much in evidence. As enslaved Africans determined that the masters' powerful control created conditions destructive to their individual and collective well-being and was the only thing standing between them and the material rewards that they required to enhance the quality of their lives, they had opportunistically discovered in their African animal trickster tale tradition an ideal model of individual behavior. It offered adaptive behavioral advantages for attaining what they perceived as their fair share of the system's rewards through individual acts of subversion and manipulation. Consequently, they transformed their conception of the African animal trickster to create an expressive model of behavior which they transmitted in trickster tales.

However, the differences between the lifestyles of enslaved Africans and of black freedpeople were destined to influence perception of the adaptability of behaviors associated with the trickster under the conditions imposed on African Americans in the late nineteenth century. In essence, as the law emerged as the institutional framework within which whites defined and dealt with African Americans in the society, it had a dramatic impact on their ability to accept behaviors embodied in trickster tales as adaptable to real-life situations. In freedom and under the law, African Americans discovered that many of the behaviors associated with the trickster of folklore and adaptable under the conditions of slavery had become, after emancipation, behaviors associated with the criminal, and adopting them in real-life situations no longer in their best interests.

Although African Americans continued to perform trickster tales

well after emancipation, the tellers of the tales in some instances included in their performances a recognition of the law as the factor
most inhibitive to the adaptability of trickster-like behavior.

> Pa'tridge an' Ber Rabbit dy wen' to buy a dawg to hunt deer. So
> Ber Rabbit he bought a dawg could run de deer down. Cos' a pile
> of money, de dawg did. So Pa'tridge didn't have dat much
> money. Pa'tridge stud'ed to 'isself. Pa'tridge beat eve'ybody all
> the time, so he study a plan to beat Rabbit. So jus' have money
> enough to buy a dawg-head, one od dese sham. So he bought his
> dawg-head, an' Rabbit bought his dawg. So dey conclude dey go
> out huntin' togeder. Buy dawg togeder; law so fix, dey had to go
> huntin' togeder. Rabbit take his dawg, go in de swamp. Pa'tridge
> have to tote his dawg-head. When de deer get out de reach of de
> Rabbit, Pa'tridge flew up an' stick his dawg-head on de deer. Fly
> de deer dwon, an' dat deer couldn' get off. Ran to de judge.
> Judge had to decide. Judge say, "Dawg-head on de deer." So he
> [Pa'tridge] get half o' de deer.[46]

As the law became "so fix" as the primary means by which whites
defined and controlled the behavior of African Americans in the society, it also created conditions which curbed dramatically the effectiveness of the animal trickster tale tradition as a model of emulative
behavior, especially for securing the material means of survival.

Nevertheless, the continued performance of trickster tales in freedom suggests that, despite the insertion of the "law" between African
Americans and the types of rewards often associated with the trickster
during slavery, they still discovered situations and ways in which the
subversive and manipulative behaviors associated with the trickster
could be advantageous in dealing with white power. For example, the
ease with which black storytellers after emancipation substituted Old
Boss for Old Master without altering the plots of tales in which John
served as the central character strongly suggests a black perception of
the work situation as one little changed from slavery. Certainly individual whites still maintained and exercised enough control over the
economic lives of African Americans to make aggressive behavior in
dealing with them extremely costly. In addition, the work situation
remained one in which the kinds of face-to-face interaction between
African Americans and whites which made the trickster an effective
model of behavior were little altered. However, in ways basic to the
perpetuation of the trickster as a folk hero, the role of the law in
black life after emancipation precluded their utilizing trickster tales

to transmit a conception of heroic action to retaliate against white legal exploitation and social persecution.

Upon emancipation, the fact of freedom alone altered the relationship between blacks and whites in ways that influenced the adaptability of behaviors embodied in the trickster tales so radically that transformation became almost inevitable. Freedom brought with it both an end to individual white control over African Americans and the right and responsibility of providing for their own material and physical needs. Many of the behaviors that reflected values guiding actions on which the trickster as folk hero had been justified were simply not in the best interests of African Americans. For example, enslaved Africans had embodied in trickster tales a plethora of dissembling and manipulative behaviors to avoid work and other exploitative behaviors of slavemasters under the restrictive and economically unrewarding slave system. However, freedpeople who worked as sharecroppers, for instance, had nothing to gain by dissembling, feigning illness, or pretending ignorance to avoid work, since they technically worked for themselves. The same reality confronted black wage earners generally, since, for the majority, the compensation that they received for their labor was the only means for legally providing for their physical well-being. The threat of being fired meant not only the loss of a means of livelihood, but also, under the vagrancy statutes in many areas, the real possibility of imprisonment.

In addition, when whites turned to the law after emancipation to regain economic control of blacks, they created a climate decidedly unfavorable for black trickster-like activity, especially against their property—a favorite target of African Americans during slavery. "Under slavery theft of food belonging to the owner had been all but universal," observes Eric Foner. "Virtually every planter complained of the killing of poultry and hogs, and the plundering of corn cribs, smoke houses, and kitchens by the slaves."[47] After slavery, these landowners realized that if they allowed former enslaved Africans to continue using such behavior successfully against them, African Americans would have little incentive to submit to white economic controls. White landowners in particular who had countenanced what they considered innate black immorality during slavery strongly supported laws designed to protect their property against the extralegal claims of their former slaves. That many laws enacted after emancipation were designed to eliminate black trickster-like activity to gain economic control over African Americans was reflected in the stiff penalties imposed on behaviors closely identified with enslaved Africans as well as in the emphasis placed on defining property rights. The legal sanctions imposed on theft of livestock in particular made even the most adept trickster apprehensive. Under the Redeemers in South Carolina, for example, the penalty for stealing livestock was a fine of a thousand dollars and a maximum of ten years in prison. In North Carolina and Virginia, a person could be sent to the penitentiary for stealing a chicken. And under Mississippi's "pig law," the theft of a pig or cow was punishable by five years in prison.[48] In addition, "trespass laws" to prohibit fishing and hunting on private property and "fence laws" to end free grazing of domestic animals on open range were aimed primarily at landless blacks who, by these means, might secure a livelihood at the expense of white landowners.[49]

The impact of white manipulations of the law on the economic and social life of African Americans in the late nineteenth century is crucial to an understanding of how and why African Americans transformed their conception of the trickster to create the badman as an outlaw hero. If, as Hobsbawm relates, "Banditry tends to become epidemic in times of pauperization and economic crisis,"[50] then African Americans had every reason to turn to bandits or outlaws for a model of adaptive behavior in the years following emancipation. In fact, the power of the law came down nowhere with greater force than on the economic lives of African Americans—a blow which kept large numbers in abject poverty. Although African Americans had greeted their freedom with a great deal of optimism that they would be able to achieve the kind of prosperity enjoyed by whites at their expense during slavery, they had come to realize by the last decade of the nineteenth century that the material, physical, and social conditions under which they lived were little different from those endured by enslaved Africans. One important difference, however, which dramatically influenced the black creative response to these conditions, was that, as the enslaved, the physical power of the slavemasters had deprived them of the ability to provide for their own human, material, and physical well-being. As freedpeople, the master's power had been replaced by laws which robbed them of both their civil and human rights and the ability to provide for their own material and physical needs. In fact, African Americans in the years following emancipation experienced an actual resurgence of patterns of social control and material scarcity similar to those endured by enslaved Africans at the hands of slavemasters.

The situation for African Americans in the late nineteenth century was made all the more desperate by the fact that the majority had heeded the advice of federal authorities, northern benefactors and missionaries, and their own black leaders and remained in the South to pursue their dreams of working hard and becoming prosperous members of the society.[51] "We thought we was goin' to get rich like the white folks," recalled a disillusioned former enslaved African of the black attitude toward freedom. "We thought we was goin' to be richer than the white folks, 'cause we was stronger and knowed how to work, and the white folks didn't and they didn't have us to work for them anymore. But it didn't turn out that way. We soon found that freedom could make folks proud but it didn't make 'em rich."[52]

In reality, African Americans, while experiencing changes in their lifestyle after emancipation, especially in the nature of their relationship to whites, continued to encounter numerous situations similar to those which had initially influenced enslaved Africans' turning to the trickster as a folk hero. Under Redeemer governments after reconstruction, southern white legislatures launched an effective legal offensive to achieve black economic dependence which, by the 1890s, had created material conditions which posed serious threats to black physical survival. Benjamin Brawley, for instance, has described the decade of the 1890s as "one of the darkest the race has experienced since emancipation. It seemed to the rural southern Negro that the conditions of slavery had all but come again."[53] For African Americans in the rural South, the conditions under which they lived at the end of the nineteenth century had turned the dream of freedom into a nightmare in which their lives were an unrelenting struggle for both fiscal and physical survival at subsistence level. Sharecropping, a system of contract labor which had promised independence and a better economic return than a wage system, had a stranglehold on large numbers of African Americans. Although black farmers had initially embraced the sharecropping system as a solution to landlessness, the majority found that they were barely able to eke out an existence under this exploitative labor system as it became increasingly regulated by laws that clearly favored the white landowner and storekeeper. Through a series of Tenant and Landlord and Lien Vendor Acts, southern legislators created a system of credit and crop mortgages that plunged black sharecroppers each year, "deeper into dependency and debt, pledging [their] future crops to sustain [themselves] during the current crop."[54] Most black sharecroppers found themselves not only in debt after settling their accounts with landowners each year but also unable to provide adequate clothing and food for their families.

Some African Americans who could escape the subsistence level of existence on farms and plantations moved to town. "The principal attraction of the city [was] the greater feeling of security that it afforded and the chances for more remunerative employment and more active social life."[55] While African Americans did often find a more lively social atmosphere in the city, they seldom procured the types of jobs that substantially changed their economic situation. Although southern industrialization was well underway by the 1880s, the best paying jobs rarely went to black workers. According to Greene and Woodson

> The poor whites took the cotton mills and the iron and steel factories as their own; and, with the exception of the rough work in the blast furnaces and sweeping, scrubbing, and the like in cotton factories, there was virtually no work for the Negroes in the plants.[56]

In the cities in both the North and South, African Americans were literally locked out of the industrial revolution sweeping the nation. African Americans in urban areas, in most respects, fared no better than African Americans in rural areas. They worked primarily in domestic and personal service jobs.[57] They found themselves barred, by laws which supported discriminatory practices, from the better paying jobs, and were therefore forced to accept menial tasks to eke out a living. In addition, they were often forced to pay high rents for substandard housing which, in many urban areas, consumed most of their meager salaries.[58] Thus, for food and clothing many African Americans had to make do with the bare minimum. Tindall notes in his study of African Americans in South Carolina from 1877–1900 that "Because of the general prevalence of poverty Negro indigence was scarcely recognized, although the *News and Courier* noticed that many Negroes regularly visited the Charleston city dump, taking therefrom scraps of meat, old ham bone, stale bread, or anything in the shape of food that could be found."[59] In addition, African Americans in the cities were most often segregated in the most rundown areas in which they seldom had streetlights, access to water and sewer lines, or police protection. In some instances, black neighborhoods were allowed to become centers of vice as much for the convenience of white patrons as for the economic benefit of black residents.[60]

The desperate economic and material conditions under which many African Americans lived in the late nineteenth century posed serious problems to their physical well-being. During the thirty years following emancipation, African Americans experienced a substantial decline in birth rates and an increase in mortality.[61] On the one hand, the decline in the birth rate can be seen as a natural consequence of black women being given the choice of having children rather than having childbirth forced upon them by slavemasters eager to increase their work force. On the other hand, the higher mortality rate was an expected result of the higher levels of poverty among African Americans which caused higher incidence of diseases associated with malnutrition and unhealthy living conditions. Although some prominent white thinkers of the period considered the decline in the black population to be certain proof of the unfitness of African Americans for freedom and heralded the demise of the black population on the North American continent, the general decrease in the black population resulted from the deplorable material and physical conditions forced upon African Americans during the period.[62] As in slavery, pneumonia, influenza, and tuberculosis continued to be major causes of death among African Americans until well into the twentieth century, with a mortality rate twice as high for them as for whites from these illnesses. In the late nineteenth and early twentieth centuries, the life expectancy for blacks (both males and females) was substantially lower than that for whites in similar age groups.[63]

With the proliferation of Jim Crow laws in the late nineteenth century, which, in many instances, simply codified into law social practices which had been maintained through custom and coercion since slavery, African Americans found themselves struggling desperately not only to provide for their fiscal and physical well-being but also to maintain the basic rights and privileges of citizenship as whites increasingly used the law to dominate and exclude them from the economic, social, and political life of the country.[64] Consequently, by the last decade of the nineteenth century, black advancement in American society was being strangled and choked off by ever tightening legal and extralegal patterns of segregation and exclusion. African Americans were segregated in separate schools which received only a small fraction of state funds for public education. To make black children available for farm work during planting and harvesting seasons, the school year was shortened for them in many areas. Although blacks demonstrated an almost unquenchable thirst for education and placed a high premium on its potential for improving the quality of their children's lives, the teachers in the classrooms were often undertrained and incapable of providing the kind of education that they needed to compete in the society.[65] In the society as a whole, African Americans were treated as second-class citizens in almost every area of life. They were relegated to separate entrances to public buildings, separate seating in public places (usually in the back or in separate balcony areas), and back or separate cars on public conveyances. They could also be legally denied service in most white owned restaurants, hotels, and places of entertainment.[66]

Due primarily to white manipulations of the law in the decades following emancipation, many African Americans would have found it difficult to point to significant differences in their economic and social positions relative to whites from the conditions that had existed during slavery. The resurgence of white social and economic domination over African Americans, supported and maintained by unfair laws, influenced their sense of well-being not only in the society but also in their own communities. As such, the law thus had a profound impact on black culture-building in the late nineteenth century. At the dawn of freedom, black culture-building reflected the view of many African Americans that individual well-being in the society could be best served by cooperating to develop a strong collective economic and political base in the society. To achieve these ends, they could build on the strong communal values and traditions of mutual support that they developed during slavery. In various ways, African Americans attempted to capitalize on the protection afforded them by the presence of federal troops and their newly acquired political rights under the constitution to prepare collectively for their participation on all levels of society. They formed cooperatives, mutual aid societies, benevolent associations, political education clubs and conventions, and various self-help organizations to care for indigent members of their community, bury their dead, promote social growth, amass funds for their economic well-being, and develop political awareness and influence political decisions relevant to them.[67] African Americans envisioned these efforts both as essential to the development of a strong black community and as a means of creating a relationship to whites in which economic and political power would allow them to prevent a resurgence of white domination of the sort that they had experienced during slavery.

While African Americans succeeded to varying degrees in mobilizing and maximizing their collective power, and lobbied for some of the most pressing economic, political, and social issues facing free black people, their eventual abandonment by the federal government allowed their former enslavers, both through violence and the creation of new laws, to virtually destroy black collective efforts to resist white domination. As long as federal troops had remained in the South, African Americans had been able to capitalize on their collective strength, especially in using their votes to put black and sympathetic white Republicans into political offices. More importantly, they had been able to keep the hope alive of influencing changes in the structure of the society important to their survival and prosperity as a people. With their virtual disenfranchisement by the end of the nineteenth century, African Americans lost the most important source of power that would have allowed them to avoid once again being totally dominated by whites. Without the vote, and the political power that it gave African Americans as a group, they stood little chance of influencing the kind of institutional and structural changes in society that would have gained them equal access to its resources.

In addition to being disenfranchised, African Americans witnessed a proliferation of racist laws and Klan violence which often made collective action not only futile but also often fatal. "Black solidarity, especially in interracial confrontations, frightened whites and, by extension furnished a pretext for their binding together in white leagues and Ku Klux Klans," notes Nell Painter of the white reaction to black community organization and cooperation.[68] She also points out that those African Americans who "appeared concerned with the political well-being of their people" in the late nineteenth century were increasingly "picked off one by one" by nightriders.[69] She further argues that the genocide commited against black secular leadership by the Klan contributed to the rise of preachers to political leadership roles in the black community. While preachers sometimes made effective political leaders, their primary emphasis continued to be spiritual and their concern directed more toward the moral behavior of individuals rather than the collective economic and political welfare of the community.[70]

The effect of the social climate of the late nineteenth century on black communal values was nowhere more evident than in the growing emphasis placed on social distinctions within the black community itself. Although social distinctions had been recognized during slavery, their functional significance had been limited by the commonality and universality of suffering in the oppressive slave system. While the life possibility for the majority of enslaved Africans had been established by their status as "slaves" within the system, the social distinctions that enslaved Africans recognized among themselves were neither an irrational nor a pathological response to enslavement. They were based on a perception that certain physical and social similarities to the masters enhanced individual material and physical well-being—a perception supported by the advantages apparently enjoyed by mulattos and house servants in particular. For example, mulattos, who were often the offspring of the master, were more frequently assigned positions as house servants or artisans while those with more African features usually found themselves relegated to work in the fields. In addition, in the presence of field hands, house servants often flaunted the material and social advantages that their more intimate contact with the master's family afforded them. They sometimes appeared at religious and social gatherings in the slave quarters in the cast-off finery of the masters and mistresses, boasted of the higher standard of living in the "big house," sometimes learned to read, and impressed the others with their intimate knowledge of the morals and manners of the master's family.[71] Naturally, many enslaved Africans came to assume that physical and social similarities to the masters garnered individuals certain advantages and material rewards denied those who did not possess them.

In the atmosphere of cooperation immediately following emancipation, the social distinctions that enslaved Africans had recognized among themselves receded in importance. As to be expected, those who had benefited from their more intimate contact and identification with the masters during slavery had an advantage in negotiating the system over those who had not. They were looked to for leadership and most often provided it as African Americans sought to consolidate an economic and political base in the society.[72] Regardless of previous condition of servitude, African Americans during the era of reconstruction found it more advantageous to ally their interests with members of their own race than with their defeated and politically alienated former enslavers. For instance, the promise of land redistribution, free education, and full civil and political rights seemed to offer African Americans equal, if not greater, economic and poilitical power, especially in the South, than former slaveholders. But the failure of reconstruction to bring about meaningful change in either the economic or political situation of the majority of African Americans, and the resurgence of white domination over them, severely weakened the bonds of cooperation between them as the law and white violence increasingly made black solidarity difficult to sustain.

In the repressive climate of the late nineteenth century, social distinctions among African Americans took on renewed importance as individuals sought to minimize the impact of racism on their lives and achieve prosperity in the society. In the black community, the lack of economic diversity among African Americans led to the development of a caste system in which social status was based on criteria similar to those recognized in the slave community.[73] In many ways, the black community became a microcosm of the larger society in which an absence of color and fidelity to white social values became important in determining how African Americans viewed their social position relative to others and their prospects for success in the society. While the development of an intragroup caste system created a perception of a diverse black community, it merely reflected the reality that African Americans adopted diverse strategies for dealing with their oppression by the law. Nevertheless, the perception of a socially diverse black community influenced folk heroic creation, especially the basis on which different segments of the black population would justify the actions of the badman as a folk hero.

In essence, African Americans found themselves confronted with conditions strikingly similar to those they had experienced during slavery both within the society and within their own community. However, their creative response, from the vantage point of folk heroic creation, could not be the same as that embraced by enslaved Africans. There were important differences in their situation that created obstacles to the ability of African Americans to maintain patterns of behavior that they had embraced as both actual and creative solutions to white power during slavery. Although individual whites may have been responsible for the persistent economic and social persecution and exploitation experienced by African Americans, the law had become their antagonist and was used by whites as a shield between themselves and black claims of unfairness. Furthermore, the law was invisible and, therefore, not easily manipulated—a situation decidedly unfavorable for successful trickster-like behavior of the sort associated with the trickster of enslaved Africans.

Opportunistically, however, as the creation and strict enforcement of laws inhibitive to the economic, political, and social aspirations of African Americans became the dominant expression of white power over them, the "law" became increasingly personified to the black community in the white policeman or sheriff. The proliferation of Jim Crow laws by the end of the nineteenth century had segregated African Americans in their own communities, which facilitated the control of black behavior by duly empowered officers of the law. In black neighborhoods, the white law enforcement officer often appeared as the solitary and visible embodiment of white power. Such officers were given broad authority not only for enforcing the law among African Americans but also for upholding white interests against them. To the black community, the law enforcement officer stood "not only for civic order as defined in formal laws and regulations, but also for white supremacy and the whole set of social customs associated with this concept."[74] Under the law enforcement system that developed after emancipation, law enforcement officers enjoyed the right "not only of arresting, but also sentencing and punishing the culprit" with the endorsement of judges who wanted to be "spared from cases embarrassing to them as professional lawyers."[75] Even though their authority was often limited in situations involving blacks and whites, in the black community and in situations involving blacks only, white lawmen often became the sole arbiters of justice and fairness.

The emergence of the white law enforcement officer as the most visible symbol of white power to the black community (and its "most important contact" with the white power structure) dramatically influenced black people's perceptions of their relationship to whites.[76] From the vantage point of black folk heroic creation, the nature of the contact between lawmen and African Americans was very similar to that between masters and enslaved Africans which had influenced their finding in the trickster a model of heroic action. They encountered each other most often in situations where the white "peace officer" was exercising his power, which included policing black behavior, enforcing white claims against blacks, interceding in domestic and social disputes, and exacting punishment.[77] The tremendous amount of power vested in white law enforcement officers in the late nineteenth century caused many African Americans to view them as the embodiment of the "law" and, by extension, white power. White lawmen were also often extremely rigid and brutal in their treatment of African Americans, because, in most instances, they had no vested interest in the physical well-being of black people. They owed their jobs to the white political brokers in the community and not to disenfranchised African Americans.

The relationship which developed between African Americans and the "law," personified in the white law enforcement officer, greatly facilitated the transformation of the black conception of the trickster to create the badman as an outlaw folk hero. African Americans in the late nineteenth century, like enslaved Africans, came to realize through their repeated one-on-one encounters with the white "lawman's" power that this power was one that could be subverted and manipulated. In many ways, this realization was influenced by the fact that despite the white lawmen's almost unlimited power to control and regulate black behavior, they rarely entered the black community except in the performance of their duty. In addition, the brutality of black treatment by the law, in both its abstract and personified forms, provided African Americans with sufficient justification to envision behaviors which subverted the power of the law for black gain as a justifiable response to its persecution of them, and to transmit a conception of these behaviors in tales and songs of badmen—individuals who succeeded with such behaviors to a superlative degree.

While the relationship that developed between African Americans and the law in its personified form created on the surface a situation perceptually similar to that between masters and enslaved Africans, it was, at a deeper level, dramatically different. Although the personified "law" was perceived as a real adversary in black communities, the white lawman did not control the kinds of material rewards that would have enhanced the quality of black life. In fact, the brutality of the individual lawmen was due in part to the fact that they most often came from the lowest socio-economic strata of the white community, where African Americans were often seen as an economic threat. At the same time, the development of a powerful law enforcement system geared toward the protection of white interests in the society made black retaliatory actions against individual whites, legal or otherwise, virtually impossible, especially in their own communities.

Consequently, the black community became the primary arena in which the trickster-like behavior that came to be associated with black badmen could offer individuals adaptive behavioral advantages in retaliating for their economic exploitation and persecution. However, the black community's becoming the primary arena in which the trickster-like actions associated with these figures could serve as a model of adaptive behavior confronted African Americans with both an actual and creative dilemma. On one level, the trickster-like activities that could significantly enhance the quality of life in a material sense were defined in the society as illegal, and therefore their pursuit entailed risks from the law. At the same time, the relative absence of the "law" in black neighborhoods allowed for the creation of a socio-cultural environment in which certain types of illegal activities involved relatively little risk to personal well-being from the "law" while enhancing the potential for extraordinary economic gain at its expense. In addition, the pervasiveness of destructive material and physical conditions in the black community attributed to the power of the "law" over the lives of African Americans created an atmosphere in which the social restraints against certain types of actions which violated the law were greatly diminished. On another level, African Americans faced the reality that in transmitting, in an expressive form, an heroic conception of an individual whose trickster-like behavior unfolded in their own community and involved its members as

dupes threatened the values that it had traditionally placed on solidarity and harmony in social life.

In other words, in transforming their conception of the trickster to
create a folk hero whose actions unfolded primarily in the black community, African Americans had to be concerned with the consequences of condoning behaviors that potentially threatened both
their communal values and the well-being of its members. Traditionally, African Americans had not accepted trickster-like actions in their
community as advantageous to their well-being. In the slave community, for example, individuals who had adopted behaviors associated
with the trickster against other members of the community walked a
fine line—the wrong side of which was the "bad nigger." For example, although theft of the master's property for their own use had
been a favorite trickster-like activity of enslaved Africans, theft from
fellow sufferers had been strongly frowned upon. Lewis Clarke, for
example, wrote in his narrative of slave life that

> They [enslaved Africans] think it wrong to take from a neighbor,
> but not from the master. The only question with them is, "Can
> we keep it from the master?" If they can keep their backs safe,
> conscience is quiet enough on this point. But a slave that will
> steal from a slave, is called mean as master. This is the lowest
> comparison slaves know how to use: "just as mean as white folk."
> "No right for to complaining of white folks, who steal us all de
> days of our life; nigger what steal from nigger, he meaner nor
> all."[78]

In many ways, the communal attitude toward individuals who
adopted behaviors of the trickster against members of the black community was the same as toward individuals who adopted behaviors of
the "bad nigger" in dealing with other enslaved Africans. In both instances, the community's attitude toward the behaviors was
influenced by the reality that these actions threatened the solidarity
and harmony of communal life in ways that created the potential of
external intervention.

Despite important changes in their lifestyle in the late nineteenth
century, especially the development of a more socially diverse community, African Americans faced a very similar dilemma with trickster-like behaviors which victimized members of their community.
Such behaviors threatened both the values of the black community
and created opportunities for the law to intervene in its internal affairs. Creatively, however, African American singers and storytellers

resolved this dilemma and offered their community a model of heroic action which did not threaten the values of the community. They combined their conception of the trickster with that of the conjurer to create the badman—a folk hero whose characteristic actions resembled those of a trickster but unfolded in the black community. To African Americans, the conception of the badman as a supernatural trickster did not represent cultural novelty, but rather a recognizable heroic type. One of the roles in which enslaved Africans had cast the conjurer was that of a folk hero whose characteristic actions involved the use of supernatural "tricks." Furthermore, the conjurer's use of tricks differed from animal and human tricksters in that the actions of conjurers served as a model of behavior for dealing with subversive actions directed primarily against other members of the black community, whereas tricksters had offered a model of subversive and manipulative behavior for dealing with the powers of the masters—an external threat to the well-being of the black community.

In the black community, both during and after slavery, conjurers were envisioned as individuals whose characteristic behaviors maintained behavioral patterns which protected the values of harmony and communality. The worldview which supported the practice of conjuration (the belief that individual misfortune was caused by ill-will or ill-action of one individual toward another, usually through the agency of magic) made the conjurer's use of supernatural trickery socially if not morally justifiable retaliatory actions against a member of the community. In addition, because any individual could literally buy into the conjurer's power and, thereby, acquire the powers of a supernatural trickster, individuals who felt aggrieved in a situation could always retaliate without direct confrontation, thus preserving, at least perceptually, communal harmony.

In this regard, Railroad Bill, whose actions often were those associated with a trickster and to whom was attributed the supernatural powers of a conjurer, was a representative badman hero. Railroad Bill, however, was not the only black badman of his era whose image as a folk hero became intertwined with the supernatural. The black conjure tradition, especially the belief that the Devil was the source of the conjurer's power, assumed a central role in the black conception of the badman as folk hero in the late nineteenth century. Almost invariably, the behavior of black badmen was portrayed as having a supernatural source, not uncommonly in powers acquired from the Devil or his influence in the world.

For instance, Stackolee, who is generally described as the most notorious of all black badmen, was reputed to have been born with supernatural powers which he enhanced later in life by selling his soul
to the Devil:

> Gypsy told Stack's mother,
> Told her like a friend
> Your double-jinted baby
> Won't come to no good end.

And the gypsy woman shore said a hatful, cause it all come out
that very way. And how come Stackalee's mother to call in the
Fawchin Teller was cause he come kickin into this wide world
double-jinted and with a full set of teeth. But what scared her
most was he had a veil over his face, and everybody knows that
babies born with veils on their faces kin see ghosts and raise 41
kinds of hell.

And so when Stackalee growed up he got to be an awful rascal
and rounder wit lots of triflin women and he staid drunk all the
time. One dark night as he come staggerin down the road the
devil popped up real sudden, like a grinnin jumpin jack. He carried Stackalee into the grave yahd and bought his soul. And
that's how come Stack could go round doin things no other livin
man could do.[79]

Stackolee's powers were so great that he was sometimes described as
not human but rather a being with "ways lak a natural man."[80] Moreover, in most versions of the Stackolee legend, especially as told in
ballads, his shooting of Billy Lyons, the incident which propelled him
into the black folk imagination, resulted from a dispute over his
"magic stetson hat" which was generally believed to be the source of
his power as a badman.

While the legends of Railroad Bill and Stackolee contain the most
explicit indications that African Americans conceptualized badmen
as individuals possessed of supernatural powers, other badmen of
their era have similar elements attached to their legends. George
Winston's demonic nickname, "Devil," for example, was apparently
derived from the belief of African Americans in the area around
Paducah, Kentucky that his behavior was influenced by supernatural
possession. The belief that he was controlled by demons was enhanced by his dramatic and violent conversion after his conviction for

the brutal murder of Vinnie Stubblefield. Mary Wheeler describes this sudden conversion, as told to her by local residents, as an exorcism:

> A few days after Devil's trial and conviction he "got religion" in the county jail, and his weird chanting and frienzied shouting in his small cell throughout the following days and nights created a superstitious awe and terror among the other Negroes in the jail, as well as those gathered on the sidewalk outside.[81]

Whether the ballad of Devil Winston contained references to supernatural possession is not known. Mary Wheeler, the only scholar to have collected the ballad, prints only a fragment, concluding that "Many versions of it contain lines that are not suitable for publication."[82] She offers, however, that based on her interviews with residents of Paducah "Devil seems to have become vested in their minds with some of the qualities of the supernatural."[83]

On the other hand, the legend of John Hardy suggests that he was a man possessed both of and by supernatural powers. Like Stackolee, John Hardy is often portrayed as having been born with supernatural abilities. As a baby, he was able to predict his own fate in life:

> John Hardy was little farmer boy,
> Sitting on his father's knee;
> Says he, "I fear the C & O Road
> Will be the ruination of me, poor boy!
> Will be the ruination of me."[84]

One of the most consistent elements in ballads embodying the exploits of John Hardy is the emphasis placed on his conversion and baptism prior to his hanging for the murder of a man in a card game:

> I've been to the East and I've been to the West,
> I've been this wide world round;
> I've been to the river and I've been baptized,
> And now I'm on my hanging ground, O Lord![85]

This emphasis placed on his conversion stands in stark contrast to descriptions of him in the same songs as "a desperate little man" who "carried a pistol and a razor every day."

While both the conjurer and trickster traditions influenced folk heroic creation surrounding badmen, the black characterization of badmen as "bad" derived from their association with a kind of secular anarchy peculiar to the experience of free black people. Black badmen invariably became associated with the secular lifestyle which developed in the black community after emancipation and became centered primarily in jooks and saloons. Within these establishments and the areas in which they were often situated, the free flow of alcohol and an atmosphere of license often led to violent confrontations among those who frequented them. For example, Tindall notes in his study of African Americans in South Carolina in the late nineteenth century that a "serious law enforcement problem grew out of the prevalence of shootings and cuttings in the settlement of disputes and insults. The problem became especially concentrated and acute in towns on Saturday afternoons and evenings."[86] The lively atmosphere and often violent confrontations which could erupt among black weekend revelers in particular could transform a black neighborhood into a carnival-like environment.

Although violence often became associated with this lifestyle, it had little to do with the real reason that African Americans found the activities which characterized it satisfying. For some of the black population, entertainments to be had in jooks and saloons offered much needed respite from the cares and responsibilities of living in a racist society. These establishments provided a context within which they could celebrate the more human side of their beings free from intrusions from the white world. For others, however, these establishments offered the opportunity of turning their meager paychecks into the American dream. For in addition to good music, dancing, and corn whisky, many bars also had separate rooms or lacked prohibitions against gambling.[87] The illegal games of chance were an incredible temptation for individuals who wanted a fast trip to wealth. At the same time, the existence of gambling games in which individuals could lose their whole week's earnings on the toss of the dice or the turn of a card increased the tension which sometimes led to violence.

In many instances, however, bars and saloons merely served as a convenient focus for both African Americans and the "law" who wanted to ferret out the types of illegal games and activities that came to be associated with secular entertainment in the black community. Some black communities had areas, sometimes known as "bottoms," in which a lack of social restraints against certain types of illegal activities became well known. Brochert, for instance, suggests in his study of turn-of-century alley communities in Washington, D. C. that the attitudes of the residents in economically depressed neighborhoods allowed certain types of illegal activities to become widespread. He states, for example, that in alley communities "Many activities viewed as criminal by the larger community were not viewed as such by the residents. Many of these 'crimes' were in fact forms of recreation and enjoyment." He mentions playing the numbers and craps, as well as bootlegging and drug peddling, as illegal activities commonly tolerated in these communities. "Seldom was anyone injured" he concludes, "and in very few cases did they involve 'outsiders' not known to alley residents."[88] The nature of illegal activities as well as their potential for economic enhancement undoubtedly influenced a laissez-faire attitude toward them among many African Americans. Nevertheless, whether individuals participated in the more violent side of the secular lifestyle or the illegal activities which became associated with it, they were considered "bad," at least by the religious and more socially conscious members of the black community.

The development of an institutional focus for secular pursuits in the black community where illegal activities and violent confrontations often occurred is crucial to an understanding of the black conception of the badman as a folk hero in the late nineteenth century. Within the establishments and areas that catered to the taste of individuals who sought in illegal activities a means of enhancing their economic well-being, individuals who participated in such activities recreationally or sporadically faced little risk from the "law" and posed little threat to the values that the black community placed on harmony to avoid unwanted intrusions from the "law." Despite the black community's general attitude toward these activities, its level of tolerance and its values were sometimes tested by the fact that some individuals increased the risk of an unwanted encounter with the "law" or being involved in a serious violent incident by pursuing illegal activities not simply as recreations but rather as professions. The presence of professional gamblers, pimps, and bootleggers greatly increased the potential that the "law" would crack down on such activities which many individuals in the community valued as a way of enhancing their economic well-being.[89] In addition, professional criminals who became skilled in manipulating the odds in illegal games of chance to increase their advantage often found themselves at risk not only from the "law" but also, on occasion, from willing victims. The double jeopardy in which professional criminals plied their trade exerted a profound influence on the attitude and behavior that they adopted in pursuit of games as well as the community's attitude toward them. On the one hand, they had to be prepared at all times to defend themselves both from the sporadic incursions of the "law" into the black community and from frustrated losers and dissatisfied customers who, as willing participants in illegal activities, had few options for retaliation other than violence. On the other hand, the victims stood little chance of succeeding against professional criminals whose frequent violent assaults against other African Americans had already garnered them reputations as "bad niggers."

In evaluating the badman tradition as a model of heroic action in the black community, the distinction between the "bad nigger" and the badman, recognized by African Americans, must be considered. For African Americans in the late nineteenth century, their perception of important behavioral differences between these two character types served as an important influence on their association of badmen with the conjurer in the folklore surrounding the badman. Although the characteristic behaviors of both "bad niggers" and conjurers involved aggressive manipulation of others, the conjurer's aggression was not perceived as disruptive to the orderly functioning of the community. Furthermore, within the worldview which supported the practice of conjuration in the black community, the belief that individual misfortune resulted from the surreptitious use of supernatural power by one individual against another made the conjurer's use of aggressive trickery socially acceptable retaliatory action. In other words, the conjurer's use of aggressive behavior was considered not gratuitous, but rather designed to restore a natural balance or harmony in the socal world perceived as important to the well-being of the individual and ultimately the community. Consequently, the black association of badmen with the conjure tradition suggests that African Americans perceived their behavior as both justifiable retaliatory action and in the best interest of the community. Therefore, those whose behavior was conceptualized as unfolding within the worldview which supported the cultural values that African Americans associated with the conjure tradition could be considered "manly."

That African Americans conceptualized badmen as folk heroes whose characteristic behaviors were perceived as justifiable retaliatory actions can be revealed by examining the portrayal of these figures in folklore. Although the folklore of badmen typically revolves around a spectacular act of murder, they are not portrayed primarily as violent individuals or cold-blooded killers. For example, G. Malcolm Laws in his discussion of black badmen ballads notes that "In constrast to the horror frequently expressed in white ballads to the fact of murder, Negro ballads usually describe a shooting briefly and rather casually."[90] The murder, the apparent pivotal event in ballads of the black badman, is actually portrayed most often as secondary to their participation in a lifestyle in which illegal activities are pervasive. In ballads of black badmen, gambling was the illegal activity most frequently identified with these figures. For instance, Railroad Bill, Stackolee, John Hardy, and Harry Duncan are all portrayed as participants in illegal activities, specifically gambling, which, in the folklore, is offered as the motivation for their crime of murder.

The emphasis on gambling rather than murder in badmen ballads, and the implicit imputation of a relationship between badmen and conjurers, could not have been totally accidental. For example, the structure of relationships in gambling games, and the idealized worldview within which gambling functions as a socio-economic system, show marked similarities to those which supported the practice of conjuration in the black community. As in conjuration, participants in gambling games do so willingly and stake the outcome on their ability to buy into a mysterious supernatural power called "luck." Gamblers ideally do not play against each other but rather contest their abilities to control the whims of chance—an indifferent power at best. In the language of black folk heroic creation, gamblers act as conjurer, contesting power over the supernatural, against conjurer. Therefore, as long as gamblers structure their behavior in accordance with the unwritten rules of the game—that is, to allow luck to determine the outcome of the game—gambling poses no threat to the individual or the community. However, if in the course of the game, one gambler has reason to believe that another has abandoned the idealized worldview by manipulating the odds in some way, the nature of the relationship between participants suddenly changes. From the vantage point of black folk heroic traditions, the participants then assume a relationship of trickster to dupe—a relationship in which the dupe's characteristic response is physical aggression. Now, because the dupe and trickster, from the perspective of black folk heroic creation, are both members of the black community, the philosophy of action governing this type of situation must be conceptualized in terms of the conjure tradition. Ideally, in black folk heroic tradition, the tricked or duped indivdual in an act of conjuration looks within himself or to a conjurer for a superior source of power to realign social relationships or bring equilibrium to the situation. However, in the world of gamblers, individuals turn for a superior source of power not to inherent supernatural ability or a conjurer but rather to the gun—that source of power that Laws notes as an endless source of fascination in black badmen ballads.

In the badman folk heroic tradition, those individuals who served as a focus for folk heroic creation were not the professional criminals, but rather their victims who responded to victimization with violence.

For instance, John Hardy's killing another man, most often identified as the "Chinaman," follows a loss, usually in a card game:

> John Hardy drew to a four card straight,
> And the Chinaman drew to a pair.
> John Hardy failed to catch and the Chinaman won,
> And he left him sitting dead in his chair, poor boy.
> And he left him sitting dead in his chair.[91]

Whether John Hardy's actions were precipitated by his belief that he was victimized by the "Chinaman's" cheating is unclear in the ballads chronicling his exploits. However, John Hardy is portrayed as a novice or, at the least, a reluctant participant in the game. In fact, he is most often described as having been lured into the game by a mysterious "yellow gal:'

> John Hardy stood at the gambler's table,
> Didn't have no interest in the game.
> Up stepped a yellow gal and threw a dollar down.
> Said, "Deal John Hardy in the game, poor boy,
> Deal John Hardy in the game."[92]

Even the notorious Stackolee was reacting to the loss of his prized stetson hat in a gambling game when he shot Billy Lyon.

> Stackalee and Billy Lyon was gamblin' one nite late.
> Stackalee fell seven Billy Lyon he fell catch eight.
>
> Slowly, slowly Stack walked from the table,
> He said, "I can't let you go with that—
> You win all my money, now you win my stetson hat."
>
> Stackalee went walkin' down that I. C. track—
> Said "I won't hurt you Bill but bet' not be here when I get back."[93]

Some versions of the ballad of Stackolee strongly suggest that he was the victim of a professional gambler in the person of Billy Lyons, as in the lines

> Stack took out his Elgin, looked directed at de time,
> "I got argument to settle with that gambler, Billy Lyons."[94]

In other versions, Stackolee's adversary is described as simply "Bully." Not uncommonly in the ballads, Stackolee's killing of Billy Lyon is presented in a way which suggests that for him, murder was an extreme response:

Stack-O-lee was a good man
One everybody did love.
Everybody swore by Stack,
Just like the lovin' stars above.
Oh, that Stack-that Stack-O-lee.[95]

Even though black badmen in the late nineteenth century were often portrayed as victims of the secular lifestyle, their crimes were not always connected with illegal activities. For instance, Devil Winston, according to Mary Wheeler, was a well-known resident of the "Nine Hundred" district of Peducah, which she describes as "a questionable Negro section."[96] He becomes the victim of malicious gossips who exploit his violent temper by claiming that Vinnie, his girlfriend, has been unfaithful to him. As a rouster on the Ohio River who spent long periods of time away from home, his case undoubtedly received a more sympathetic hearing from his fellow rousters than from the court which sentenced him to death. Among the rousters where, according to Wheeler the ballad was best known, Devil's actions represented an acceptable, if not justifiable, response to female infidelity. On the other hand, the most consistent image of a victimized badman occurs in the ballad of "Batson" who was accused of killing his employer's family. His image as victim is enhanced by his constant denial of guilt throughout the ballad which chronicles his exploits. The "law's" victimization of Batson is strongly suggested in successive stanzas in which his plea of innocence is ignored by various officers of the court beginning with the sheriff who arrests him:

Batson told Mr. Sheriff,
"Don't you know that's wrong?
You got me charge guilty unfriendly,
And I know I ain't done the crime."[97]

Throughout the ballad of "Batson," the singer implies that he is a victim of the law's need to pin the murder of the Erle family on someone, and he was convenient. The only hint that Batson had any association with the secular lifestyle is contained in a stanza often found in the ballad in which he is arrested upon returning from town on a Saturday evening. Batson, who is tried and convicted of a crime to which he repeatedly pleads innocent, is portrayed in ballads as a man who, in many ways, simply runs out of "luck."

However, the singers of the ballad of "Duncan and Brady" leave little room for doubt that, despite his association with illegal activities, Duncan was a victim of the "law," as personified in the white policeman, Brady:

Said Dunkin to Brady, "You done me wrong;
Come in my house when my game was going on,
Kicked in my windows, yes broke down my door."
Now Brady lays on the barroom floor.[98]

In addition, most of the ballads which treat Duncan's shooting of Brady focus on a Brady who is portrayed as an abusive racist:

Brady went down to the licensed saloon.
He thought he'd arrest him a rowdy coon.[99]

In general, the black conception of the badman as a folk hero in the late nineteenth century was an ambivalent one at best. While badman lore often reflected a sympathetic attitude toward these individuals, it did not skirt the harsher realities of the consequences of participating in the lifestyle with which they were associated. The ambivalence which pervades the legends of black badmen was influenced by several factors. On the one hand, badman folklore was most often transmitted in ballads performed in social contexts such as bars and saloons where the lifestyle and character types portrayed in them would have been well-known. This performance setting undoubtedly influenced the attitude of both the singers and the audiences toward the plight of badmen which Alan Lomax has described as "wholly with the murderer."[100] In the black community, those who frequented these types of establishments were all too familiar with professional criminals and others whose violent eruptions could threaten communal values and bring the power of the "law" down on the entire black community. Of equal importance, they were well aware of the brutality of the "law" in dealing with African Americans in the society. In the folklore of the badman, the favorable attitude toward these figures is characteristically revealed in the reactions of others in the community, especially women, to the fate of the badman and his victim. Frequently, the victim's death is greeted with celebratory displays, especially the donning of red by women. For example, the reaction of women to constable Brady's death is typical:

When King Brady was on de beat,
He 'lowed no ladies to walk de street;

Now King Brady is daid an' gone,
An' de ladies walk de street all night long.

When dey heard King Brady was daid,
Dey all went home an' dressed in red;
Come back dancin' an' singin' a song—
King Brady went to hell wid a stetson on[101]

The women demonstrate a similar celebratory attitude toward the deceased in "The Bully of the Town":

Now the wimmins come to town all dressed in red;
When they heard that bully was dead.[102]

However, the reaction is just the opposite to the announcement that Stackolee has been executed for killing Billy Lyons:

All the men shouted, but de women put on black and mourned
Dat de good man Stackolee had laid down, died and gone.[103]

In some instances, sympathy for the murderer is expressed in tearful visits from family members who, in John Hardy's case, attempt to bail him out, and, in the case of Batson, pray for justice.

At the same time that black badmen evoked empathetic responses to their plights, they were sometimes identified with attitudes and behaviors which reflected the worse aspects of the secular lifestyle. Railroad Bill, for instance, was at times depicted as a ruthless gambler:

Railroad Bill was a mighty sport;
Shot all buttons off high sheriff's coat,
Den hollered, "Right on desperado Bill!"

Lose, lose—I don't keer,
If I win, let me win lak' a man,
If I lose all my money,
I'll be gamblin' for my honey,
Ev'y man ought to know when he lose.

Lose, lose—I don't keer,
If I win, let me win lak' a man.
Lose fohty-one dollars tryin' to win a dime.
Ev'y man plays in tough luck some time.[104]

Stackolee was also portrayed at times as a gambler and womanizer who immersed himself totally in the lifestyle:

> Stackerlee played poker
> And Stackerlee shot dice
> All dem gamblin' niggahs
> They treated Stackerlee nice
> Oh-h-h Stackerlee—Stackerlee.
>
> A dollar worth of coke
> An' a dollar worth o' gin
> Stackerlee's in trouble again
> An' got in jail again
> Oh-h-h Stackerlee—Stackerlee.[105]

In John Hardy's case, his arrest was accomplished with great ease despite his efforts to escape, because he was drunk and confused.

The ambivalent attitude toward black badmen was nowhere more evident than in the fact that, in the folklore celebrating their deeds, they were invariably condemned and punished for their crime. However, as Laws has pointed out in relation to ballads of the badman, "Condemnation of the murderer is usually left to the white judge or perhaps to relatives of the victim."[106] At the same time, even execution does not end their lives; they live on in other forms, in the case of Railroad Bill, or in other realms. In the legend of Stackolee, for instance, he continues his struggles in Hell where he is haunted by his earthly adversary, Billy Lyon, and a new foe in the form of the Devil:

> Jailer, jailer, says Stack, I can't sleep,
> For around my bedside poor Billy Lyon still creeps,
> He comes in the shape of a lion with a blue steel in his hand,
> For he knows I'll stand and fight if he comes in the shape of a man.
> Stackolee went to sleep that night by the city clock bell,
> Dreaming the devil had come all the way from hell.
> Red devil was saying, "you better hunt your hole;
> I've hurried here from hell just to get your soul."[107]

While the moral implication of Stackolee's being forced to fight eternally with his victim and the devil appears ambiguous, the dramatic conversions and baptism of John Hardy and Devil Winston promise them eternal life with a different character. In addition, Batson is portrayed as a completely pious man who is bade farewell by his wife with the promise that "I'll meet you some lonesome day."[108]

In an important sense, what appears to be an ambivalent conception of the badman in the late nineteenth century was, in reality, a function of folk heroic creation in a diverse black community. In the most literal sense, the actions associated with black badmen served as a model of adaptive behavior for African Americans who found in the activities associated with the secular lifestyle a means of enhancing their economic well-being. For those who participated in the activities associated with the secular lifestyle, the brutality of both "bad niggers" and the "law" had the most immediate and profound consequences for individual economic and physical well-being. Therefore, the black badman who challenged the right of both "bad niggers" and the "law" to compromise the ability of their "people" to pursue behaviors perceived as important to their material welfare could serve as a model of emulative behavior. The badman's finding in the gun a power which provided individuals an advantage against both "bad niggers" and the "law" could confer on individuals adaptive behavioral advantages for dealing with their victimization at the hands of these common adversaries. At the same time, reality demanded that, in transmitting a conception of behaviors embodied in badman folklore as heroic, the consequences of these actions be made clear. Therefore, despite a perception of these behaviors as justifiable, from the point of view of the secular black community, African American singers and storytellers had to incorporate a recognition that the badman's brand of justice was not accepted by the society or even the black community as a whole. In the folklore of the badman, however, the alternative to the badman as an avenger of wrongs was not idealized. For example, trials were typically described as kangaroo affairs in which evidence was not heard but rather sentences were passed by judges totally unsympathetic to the plight of the hero or his community.

Suggesting that the black badman tradition served as an emulative model of heroic action for those involved in a secular lifestyle does not mean that diverse segments of the black population could not or did not envision badmen as folk heroes or played no role in shaping the folk traditions embodying their exploits. Regardless of their dominant value orientation, African Americans in the late nineteenth century would have agreed that "bad niggers" and the "law" represented the greatest threats to black communal values and the well being of black people in American society. Nevertheless, African Americans who did not actively participate in the activities with which badmen were associated—activities which tended to involve the most economically depressed strata of the black community—would have envisioned the threat and justified the actions of badmen differently. For instance, the religious community, through its allegiance to the biblically oriented black church, would have viewed the behavior of both "bad niggers" and the "law" as a threat to the moral values of the community. Despite the development of a more diverse black community after emancipation, Christian religious values continued to have a profound influence on the basic value orientation of the entire black community and, therefore, folk heroic creation. Although members of the religious community undoubtedly had a minimal role in directly shaping the oral traditions in which the exploits of badmen were celebrated, the strong influence of Christian religious values was reflected in the folklore of the badman in the concern with the morality of the badman's actions: badmen were ultimately conceptualized as sinners who either paid for their crimes in Hell or atoned for them through dramatic conversions.

Both "bad niggers" and the "law" posed serious problems for African Americans with upper class pretensions. Class conscious African Americans—those individuals who most likely owned land or businesses, had professions or marketable skills and, in some instances, had internalized white social values from intimate association with whites during slavery—often set themselves apart from the masses of black people after emancipation. However, they remained black and, therefore, subject to the same treatment by and under the "law" as any other black person in the society. Although they may have accepted adherence to the law as their social and civic responsibility, they were nevertheless acutely aware of the "law" as a major obstacle to their full participation in the society and the "bad nigger" as threat to the image that they held of themselves. While they may not have openly condoned illegal activities as a means of enhancing economic well-being, they would have been able to identify with those who accepted subversion of the power of the law as an acceptable behavioral strategy for dealing with economic persecution. However, because they tended to emulate and idealize white social and moral values, they viewed the secular lifestyle in general as problematic and "bad niggers" as particularly so. For this segment of the black population, "bad niggers" represented the worst element within the black community and the types of behavior associated with them were accepted as a primary reason for black persecution in the society. The presence of this socially conscious class in the black community influenced black folk heroic creation most directly in the conception of the badman as an individual who, in breaking the law, ultimately paid for the heroic moment.

In the late nineteenth century, the development of patterns of legal persecution, the uncontrolled lawlessness of professional criminals, and the law's apparent indifference to the impact of its own actions and those of professional criminals on the values of the black community created a situation in American society where the badman could become an outlaw hero. As an outlaw heroic tradition, however, the folklore of the black badman reflects the ambiguous situations that African American people faced in the society after emancipation. In acting to protect the values of the black community, black badmen found themselves caught in the double bind all too well known to African Americans who have historically been forced to structure their lives in accordance with two value systems. As actors within the black community, the actions of badmen were evaluated as a reflection of values guiding action traditionally accepted as advantageous in maintaining the harmony and integrity of black communal life. As actors within American society, the actions of badmen also had to be evaluated in terms of American legal values to which African Americans were also subject. Consequently, to African Americans for whom the actions of badmen served as an emulative model of behavior, black badmen became champions, benefactors whose characteristic actions protected their communal identity and values and offered them a model of behavior for securing their rights to the fruits of the society. To white Americans who benefited from black legal oppression, black badmen came to be viewed as criminals whose actions offered a model of behavior which threatened their advantage in the society.

In many ways, however, the types of behaviors associated with black badmen in folklore merely reflected a heightened example of those that African Americans have embraced in dealing with their persecution in the society since the days of slavery. In their own community, enslaved Africans assumed the right to define the behaviors that constituted violations of their values and empowered conjurers to deal with those who violated them. In dealing with their economic and social persecution by slavemasters in the exploitive slave system, enslaved Africans had turned to their African trickster-tale tradition for a model of emulative behavior based on values guiding actions traditionally accepted as advantageous for equalizing social and economic relationships in a hierarchical socio-economic system. In the late nineteenth century, black segregation and economic and legal persecution created in the black community a socio-cultural environment strikingly similar to that experienced by African Americans during slavery. However, the differences in the factors influencing the life-style of African Americans and thereby folk heroic creation after emancipation facilitated African Americans combining their conception of the conjurer and trickster as folk heroes to create the badman. In folklore, the badman emerged as an outlaw folk hero whose characteristic actions offered a model of behavior for dealing with the power of whites under the law that created conditions threatening to the values of the black community from both within and without. That African Americans would envision the badman's adversaries as the "law" and the "bad nigger" is clearly no accident. On the one hand, African Americans since emancipation have had to contend with the power of whites under the law as the greatest threat to their well-being in American society. On various levels and in numerous ways, African Americans have waged an on-going battle against the law in their efforts to achieve social, economic, and political parity for black people in the society. On the other hand, in their own communities, African Americans have had to fight continually against individuals whose actions they have defined as those of a "bad nigger," whether they appeared as professional criminals or simply bullies who sought to take advantage of the law's apparent indifference to the well-being of black people. In addition, in American society, African Americans have had to struggle continually against a more insidious manifestation of the "bad nigger"—the image in the white mind that every black person is a potential "bad nigger." In creating an outlaw folk hero, African Americans conceptualized this figure within a tradition of folk heroic creation based on values traditionally recognized as the most advantageous for protecting their identity and well-being as African people from both external and internal threats.

NOTES

1. This sketch of the life and career of Morris Slater is based on information contained in the following sources: Carl Cramer, *Stars Fell on Alabama* (New York: The Literary Guild, 1934) 122–25; Olive W. Burt, *American Murder Ballads and Their Stories* (New York: Oxford University Press, 1958) 200–202; Paul Oliver, "Railroad Bill," *Jazz and Blues* 1(1971): 12–14; and Norm Cohen, *Long Steel Rail: The Railroad in American Folksong* (Urbana: University of Illinois Press, 1981) 50–56.

2. Howard W. Odum, "Folk-Song and Folk Poetry as Found in the Secular Songs of the Southern Negro," *Journal of American Folklore* 24(1911): 291.

3. Odum 292.

4. Odum 290.

5. John W. Work, *American Negro Songs and Spirituals* (New York: Howell, Soskin, 1940) 240.

6. Odum 292; E. C. Perrow, "Songs and Rhymes from the South," *Journal of American Folklore* 25 (1917): 155.

7. Oliver 14.

8. John David, "Tragedy in Ragtime: Black Folktales from St. Louis," Ph.D. dissertation, St. Louis University, 1976. David offers convincing evidence that the events on which the ballads of "Stackolee" and "Duncan and Brady" are based occured in the city of St. Louis in the 1890s.

9. Lawrence W. Levine, *Black Culture and Black Consciousness: Afro-American Folk Thought from Slavery to Freedom* (New York: Oxford University Press, 1977) 417–18.

10. Roger D. Abrahams, *Deep Down in the Jungle: Negro Narrative Folklore from the Streets of Philadelphia* (Chicago: Aldine, 1970)

11. Bruce Jackson, *Get Your Ass in the Water and Swim Like Me: Narrative Poetry from Black Oral Tradition* (Cambridge, Mass.: Harvard University Press, 1974) 31.

12. G. Malcolm Laws, *Native American Balladry* (Philadelphia: The American Folklore Society, 1950) 93.

13. Abrahams 66.

14. Jackson 33.

15. Levine 415.

16. Levine 420.

17. Eugene Genovese, *Roll, Jordan, Roll: The World the Slaves Made* (New York: Vintage Books, 1976) 625–28.

18. John W. Blassingame, *The Slave Community* (New York: Oxford University Press, 1972) 116–20. Blassingame refers to individuals who behaved in this way as the 'Nat' personality type.

19. H. C. Brearley, "Ba-ad Nigger," in *Mother Wit From the Laughing Barrel: Readings in the Interpretation of Afro-American Folklore*, ed. Alan Dundes (Englewood Cliffs, N. J.: Prentice-Hall, 1976) 581.

20. Leon F. Litwack, *Been in the Storm So Long* (New York: Alfred A. Knopf, 1979) 292–315.

21. Genovese 628.

22. Litwack 275.

23. Litwack 266.

24. Litwack 277.

25. Litwack 278.

26. Litwack 278–79; Nell Painter, *Exodusters* (New York: Alfred A. Knopf, 1977) 27.

27. Benjamin J. Brawley, *A Social History of the American Negro* (New York: The Macmillan Co., 1921) 291–93; Litwack 284–87.

28. Brawley 293.

29. Brawley 216–17; August Meier and Elliot M. Rudwick, *From Plantation to Ghetto* (New York: Hill and Wang, 1966) 160–69; George Brown Tindall, *South Carolina Negroes 1877–1900* (Columbia: University of South Carolina Press, 1952) 251–53.

30. Tindall 245.

31. Michael Wayne, *The Reshaping of Plantation Society* (Baton Rouge: Louisiana State University Press, 1983) 144–46.

32. Charles S. Johnson, *Shadow of the Plantation* (Chicago: University of Chicago Press, 1934) 191.

33. Brearley 580.

34. Litwack 254.

35. Litwack 252–255.

36. Litwack 252.

37. Ken Johnson, "The Vocabulary of Race" in *Rappin' and Stylin' Out*, ed. Thomas Kochman (Urbana: University of Illinois Press, 1972) 150.

38. Levine 415; Eric Hobsbawm, *Bandits* (New York: Dell, 1969) 14.

39. Hobsbawm 13–23.

40. Hobsbawm 21.

41. Hobsbawm 23.

42. Levine 419.

43. Hobsbawm 23.

44. Abrahams 65–66.

45. Jackson 32.

46. Elsie Clews Parson, *Folklore of the Sea Islands, South Carolina* (New York: American Folklore Society, 1923) 5.

47. Eric Foner, *Nothing But Freedom* (Baton Rouge: Louisiana State University Press, 1983) 57.

48. Foner 60.

49. Foner 65–67. Also see, J. Crawford King, Jr., "The Closing of the Southern Range: An Explanatory Study," *Journal of Southern History* 68 (1982): 53–70.

50. Hobsbawm 17.

51. Litwack 307–308.

52. George P. Rawick, ed., *The American Slave: A Composite Autobiography* (Westport, Conn.: Greenwood Press, 1977) vol. IV (*Texas Narratives*) 2, 134.

53. Brawley 298.

54. Litwack 448.

55. Litwack 432.

56. Carter G. Woodson and Lorenzo Greene, *The Negro Wage Earner* (Washington, D. C.: The Association for the Study of Negro Life and History, Inc., 1930) 50.

57. Woodson and Greene 75–99.

58. Johnson 90–99.

59. Tindall 277.

60. E. Franklin Frazier, *The Negro in the United States* (New York: The Macmillan Co., 1957) 229–72.

61. Frazier 568.

62. George M. Frederickson, *The Black Image in the White Mind* (New York: Harper Torchbooks, 1971) 245–52.

63. Frazier 586–99.

64. C. Van Woodward, *The Strange Career of Jim Crow* (New York: Oxford University Press, 1974) 17–21.

65. Robert C. Morris, *Reading, 'Riting, and Reconstruction* (Chicago: University of Chicago Press, 1976) 85–130.

66. Woodward 17–21.

67. Frazier 216–217; Painter 9–10.

68. Painter 10.

69. Painter 10.

70. Painter 11–12

71. Frazier 54–55.

72. Frazier 276; Litwack 503–04.

73. Frazier 281–282; W. E. B. Du Bois, *The Philadelphia Negro* (Philadelphia: University of Pennsylvania Series in Economic and Public Law No. 14, 1899) 310–311.

74. Gunnar Myrdal, *An American Dilemma* (New York: Harper and Row, 1944) 535.

75. Myrdal 536.

76. Myrdal 535.

77. Myrdal 536–37.

78. Lewis G. Clarke, *Narrative of the Sufferings of Lewis G. Clark . . .* (Boston, 1859)

79. Benjamin A. Botkin, *A Treasury of American Folklore* (New York: Crown, 1944) 122.

80. Mary Wheeler, *Steamboatin' Days* (Baton Rouge: Louisiana State University Press, 1944) 103.

81. Wheeler 107.

82. Wheeler 106.

83. Wheeler 107.

84. John Harrington Cox, "John Hardy," *Journal of American Folklore* 32(1919): 517–28.

85. John Harrington Cox, *Folk-Songs of the South* (Cambridge: Harvard University Press, 1925) 179–80.

86. Tindall 263.

87. Tindall 186–88.

88. James Brochert, *Alley Life in Washington: Family, Community, Religion, and Folklife, 1850–1880* (Urbana: University of Illinois Press, 1980) 194.

89. Brochert 186–88.

90. Laws 93.

91. Cox, *Folk-Songs of the South* 179–80.

92. Alan Lomax and John Lomax, *Folksong U. S. A.* (New York: Signet Classic, Mentor, Plume, and Meridian Books, 1947) 85.

93. David 285.

94. David 283.

95. David 282.

96. Wheeler 107.

97. Alan Lomax and John Lomax, *Our Singing Country* (New York: The Macmillan Co., 1941) 335.

98. David 253.

99. Henry M. Belden and Arthur P. Hudson, eds., *Folk Ballads from North Carolina, The Frank C. Brown Collection of North Carolina Folklore*, 7 vols. (Durham: Duke University Press, 1952) 671–72.

100. Lomax and Lomax, *Our Singing Country* 335.

101. David 253.

102. Laws 97.

103. Laws 95.

104. Work 240.

105. David 278.

106. Laws 93.

107. B. A. Botkin, *A Treasury of American Folklore* (New York: Crown, 1940) 129.

108. Lomax and Lomax, *Our Singing Country* 341.

S I X

Conclusion

My aim in the preceding chapters has been to explore black folk heroic creation as a normative cultural activity intimately related to black culture-building in America. From an Afrocentric perspective, I have attempted to demonstrate that an evaluation of the actions of black folk heroes from the point of view of African Americans yields important insights into their approaches to conflict resolution and the values guiding action that they have traditionally accepted as the most advantageous to their well-being. The paradigmatic value of Afrocentricism lies in its ability to both highlight the culture-specific nature of black folk heroic literature and shed light on the process of black folk heroic creation.

My examination of Afro-American folk heroic literature Afrocentrically may be properly labelled reconstructive. However, in the study of Afro-American history and literature, as Houston Baker has convincingly argued, *deconstruction* must almost inevitably precede *reconstruction.*[1] In this regard, my emphasis throughout on previous Afro-American folklore scholarship represents a necessary first step in reevaluating the folklore forms under discussion. In these sections, I have attempted not only to present a bird's eye view of the paths that students of black oral expressive culture have taken in arriving at conclusions about its origins, meanings, and functions, but also to highlight some of the underlying considerations that have informed their choices. In scholarship as in life, the path taken often reveals as much about the traveler's consciousness at a particular moment as the path not taken. By retracing the steps of these scholars, my goal has been to demonstrate that the path most frequently taken in studies of African American folklore in general and folk heroic literature in particular has not been one capable of identifying the basis on which African Americans evaluate the actions of their folk heroes.

In reality, most scholars who have searched the American vernacular landscape for black folk heroes have traveled a Eurocentric path and, therefore, have only glimpsed these figures at the points where they have found them attempting to protect the rights of African Americans to travel the main roads of American life. During these brief moments of visibility for black folk heroes, scholars have seldom asked about the origins of their journeys or their destinations, but rather have looked upon their dark faces and accepted their intent as sinister, their demeanor as threatening, and their goals as subversive. Consequently, they have labeled them as "dissembling tricksters" or destructive "badmen" whose actions, if accepted as emulative models of behavior by African Americans, could only lead to defilement of the ideal vision of American life. In many ways, the terms "trickster" and "badman" as used by folklorists have become as much value judgments as descriptions of character-types accepted as heroic in black culture.

In adopting an Afrocentric perspective, I have attempted to reveal that the path which leads to understanding of the personal attributes and actions of black folk heroes has been one along which survival has been precarious, both individual and collective well-being always in jeopardy, and conflict continuous. Along this path, black folk heroes have traveled as champions of African Americans who have been forced to negotiate the American landscape by being quick of wit and adept at detecting sleight-of-hand. To those who have traditionally looked to black folk heroes for models of behavior, the terms trickster and badman are not value judgments but rather descriptions of folk heroes whose characteristic behaviors have historically and traditionally served as models of and for behavior among people of African descent in America.

In my exploration of black folk heroic creation during the period of black chattel slavery and in the post-emancipation era, my goal has been to examine not merely black folk heroic literature as expression of heroic ideals, but also the interrelationships between these different forms of black oral expressive culture and the ways in which they are connected at the deepest levels of meaning to the African cultural heritage and to each other. In my view, only until we explore fully and Afrocentrically the interrelationships between black oral expressive cultural forms will we be able to offer a satisfying definition of African American folklore. As Lanier Seward points out in her critique of African American folklore scholarship, definitions and studies of African American folklore which envision this oral tradition as merely a collection of disparate genres loosely connected by their association with black people in American "have long been inadequate" in defining the tradition.[2] However, when we accept African culture as the "tradition-rich source" which informs black creativity in America and Afrocentrism as a culture-specific approach to its study, we can begin to examine African American folklore as an expressive tradition deeply rooted in and reflective of the esthetic and cultural values historically embraced by people of African descent in America.

NOTES

1. Houston A. Baker, Jr., *Blues, Ideology, and Afro-American Literature* (Chicago: University of Chicago Press, 1984) 200.

2. Adrienne Lanier Seward, "The Legacy of Early Afro-American Folklore Scholarship," in *Handbook of American Folklore*, ed. Richard M. Dorson (Bloomington: University of Indiana Press,1983) 21–22.

BIBLIOGRAPHY

Books

Abrahams, Roger D. *Deep Down in the Jungle: Negro Narrative Folklore from the Streets of Philadelphia.* Chicago: Aldine, 1970.

Allen, William F., Charles P. Ware, and Lucy McKim Garrison. *Slave Songs of the United States.* New York: Peter Smith, 1951 [1867].

Aptheker, Herbert. *Nat Turner's Slave Rebellion.* New York: Humanities Press, 1966.

Asbury, Herbert. *The French Quarter.* New York: A. A. Knopf, Inc., 1936.

Baker, Houston A., Jr. *Blues, Ideology, and Afro-American Literature.* Chicago: University of Chicago Press, 1984.

Bascom, William R. *Ifa Divination.* Bloomington: Indiana University Press, 1969.

Batume, Elizabeth. *First Days Among the Contraband.* Boston, 1983.

Belden, Henry M. and Arthur P. Hudson, eds. *Folk Ballads from North Carolina. The Frank C. Brown Collection of North Carolina Folklore.* 7 Vols. Durham, N. C.: Duke University Press, 1952.

Biebuyck, Daniel P. *Hero and Chief.* Berkeley: University of California Press, 1978.

Biebuyck, Daniel P. and Kahombo C. Mateene, eds. *The Mwindo Epic.* Berkeley: University of California Press, 1969.

Blassingame, John W. *The Slave Community.* New York: Oxford University Press, 1972.

Botkin, Benjamin A. *A Treasury of American Folklore.* New York: Crown, 1944.

Brawley, Benjamin. *A Social History of the American Negro.* New York: The Macmillan Co., 1921.

Brochert, James. *Alley Life in Washington: Family, Community, Religion, and Folklife, 1850–1880.* Urbana: University of Illinois Press, 1980.

Brown, William Wells. *My Southern Home.* Boston, 1880.

Burt, Olive. *American Murder Ballads and Their Stories.* New York: Oxford University Press, 1958.

Campbell, Israel. *An Autobiography.* Philadelphia, 1861.

Christensen, A. H. M. *Afro-American Folk Lore Told Round Cabin Fires on the Sea Islands of South Carolina.* New York: Negro University Press, 1892.

Clarke, Lewis G. *Narrative of the Sufferings of Lewis G. Clark. . . .* Boston, 1859.

Cohen, Norm. *Long Steel Rail: The Railroad in American Folksong.* Champaign, Ill.: University of Illinois Press, 1981.

Courlander, Harold. *Negro Folk Song U. S. A.* New York: Columbia University Press, 1963.

Courlander, Harold and Olismane Sako. *The Heart of the Ngoni*. New York: Crown Publishing, Inc., 1982.

Cox, John Harrington. *Folk-Songs of the South*. Cambridge: Harvard University Press, 1925.

Cramer, Carl. *Stars Fell on Alabama*. New York: The Literary Guild, 1934.

Crowley, Daniel J. *African Folklore in the New World*. Austin: University of Texas Press, 1977.

Dett, Nathaniel, *Religious Folk-Songs of the Negro as Sung at Hampton Institute*. Hampton, Va.: Hampton Institute, 1927.

Dixon, Christa K. *Negro Spirituals: from Bible to Folksong*. Philadelphia: Fortress Press, 1976.

Dorson, Richard M. *American Negro Folktales*. Greenwich, Conn.: Fawcett Publications, Inc., 1967.

Douglass, Frederick. *My Bondage and My Freedom*. New York: Miller, Orton, and Mulligen, 1855.

———. *Narrative of the Life of Frederick Douglass: An American Slave*. Boston: The Anti-Slavery Office, 1845.

Du Bois, W. E. B. *The Souls of Black Folk*. 1903. New York: Avon Books, 1965.

———. *The Philadelphia Negro*. Philadelphia: University of Pennsylvania Series in Economy and Public Law No. 14, 1899.

Dundes, Alan. *The Study of American Folklore*. Englewood Cliffs, N.J.: Prentice-Hall, 1976.

———, ed. *Mother Wit From the Laughing Barrel: Readings in the Interpretation of Afro-American Folklore* (Englewood Cliffs, N. J.: Prentice-Hall, 1973.

Epstein, Dena. *Sinful Tunes and Spirituals*. Urbana: University of Illinois Press, 1977.

Escott, Paul D. *Slavery Remembered*. Chapel Hill: University of North Carolina Press, 1979.

Feldmann, Susan, *African Myths and Tales*. New York: Dell Publishing Co., 1963.

Fisher, William A. *Seventy Negro Spirituals*. Boston: Oliver Ditson Co., 1926.

Fishwick, Marshall. *American Heroes: Myth and Reality*. Washington, D.C.: Public Affairs Press, 1954.

Fisk University, *Unwritten Record of Slavery: Autobiographical Accounts of Negro Ex-Slaves,* comp. and ed. Ophelia Settle Egypt, J. Musuoka, and Charles S. Johnson. Washington, D. C., 1968 [1945].

Foner, Eric. *Nothing But Freedom*. Baton Rouge: Louisiana State University Press, 1983.

Frazier, E. Franklin. *The Negro Church in America*. New York: Schocken Books, 1964.

———. *The Negro in the United States*. New York: The Macmillan Co., 1957.

Frederickson, George M. *The Black Image in the White Mind*. New York: Harper Torchbooks, 1971.

Genovese, Eugene. *Roll, Jordan, Roll: The World the Slaves Made*. New York: Vintage Books, 1976.

———. *From Rebellion to Revolution*. Baton Rouge: Louisiana University Press, 1979.

Georgia Writers Project. *Drums and Shadows*. Spartanburg, S.C.: The Reprint Company, 1974.

Harding, Vincent. *There Is a River*. New York: Vintage Books, 1983.

Harris, Joel Chandler. *Uncle Remus: His Songs and Sayings*. New York: Penguin Books, 1982.

Harris, Marvin. *Cultural Materialism*. New York: Vintage Books, 1980.

Herskovitz, Melville J. and Frances S. Herskovitz. *Dahomean Narratives*. Evanston, Ill.: Northwestern University Press, 1958.

Hobsbawm, Eric. *Bandits*. New York: Dell, 1969.

Jackson, Bruce. *Get Your Ass in the Water and Swim Like Me: Narrative Poetry from Black Oral Tradition*. Cambridge, Mass.: Harvard University Press, 1974.

Johnson, Charles S. *Shadow of the Plantation*. Chicago: University of Chicago Press, 1934.

Johnson, James Weldon and Rosamond Johnson. *Books of American Negro Spirituals*. New York: Dacapo Press, 1969 [1925, 1926].

Jones, Charles C., Rev. *The Religious Instruction of Negroes in the United States*. Savannah, Ga., 1842.

Katz, Bernard, ed. *The Social Implications of Early Negro Music*. New York: Arno Press, 1969.

Krehbiel, H. E. *Afro-American Folksong*. New York: Schirmer, 1914.

Laws, G. Malcolm. *Native American Balladry*. Philadelphia: The American Folklore Society, 1950.

Levine, Lawrence W. *Black Culture and Black Consciousness: Afro-American Folk Thought from Slavery to Freedom*. New York: Oxford University Press, 1977.

Litwack, Leon. *Been In the Storm So Long*. New York: Alfred A. Knopf, 1979.

Lomax, Alan and John Lomax, *Folksong U. S. A.* New York: Signet Classic, Mentor, Plume, and Meridian Books, 1947.

———. *Our Singing Country*. New York: Macmillan and Company, 1941.

Lovell, John, Jr. *The Forge and The Flame*. New York: Macmillan, 1972.

Magdol, Edward. *A Right to the Land: Essays on the Freedmen's Community*. Westport, Conn.: Greenwood Press, 1977.

Marais, E. J. *African Thought*. Cape Province: Fort Hare University Press, 1972.

Mays, Benjamin E. *The Negro's God as Reflected in His Literature*. Boston: Chapman and Grimes, 1928.

Mbiti, John S. *African Religions and Philosophy*. Garden City, N. Y.: Doubleday & Co., 1970.

Meier, August and Elliot M. Rudwick, *From Plantation to Ghetto*. New York: Hill and Wang, 1969.

Mintz, Sidney W. and Richard Price. *An Anthropological Approach to the Afro-American Past: A Caribbean Perspective*. Philadelphia: Institute for the Study of Human Issues, 1972.

McIlhenny, E. A. *Befo' De War Spirituals*. Boston: Christopher Publishing House, 1933.

Morris, Robert C. *Reading, 'Riting, and Reconstruction*. Chicago: University of Chicago Press, 1976.

Murray, Albert. *The Hero and the Blues*. Columbia: University of Missouri

Press, 1973.

Myrdal, Gunnar. *An American Dilemma*. New York: Harper and Row, 1944.

Nichols, Charles H. *Many Thousand Gone*. Bloomington: Indiana University Press, 1963.

Northup, Solomon. *Twelve Years A Slave*. New York: Dover Publications, 1970.

Odum, Howard W. and Guy B. Johnson. *Negro Workaday Songs*. Chapel Hill: University of North Carolina Press, 1926.

Olmsted, Frederick. *A Journey in the Back Country, 1853–1854*. New York: Mason, 1860; repr. 1970.

Painter, Nell. *Exodusters*. New York: Alfred A. Knopf, 1977.

Parrinder, E. G. *West African Religion*. London: Epworth Press, 1949.

Parsons, Elsie Clews, *Folklore of the Sea Islands, South Carolina*. New York: American Folklore Society, 1923.

Peck, John Mathan. *Forty Years of Pioneer Life. Memoir*. Philadelphia, 1864.

Perdue, Charles L., Thomas E. Burden, and Robert K. Phillips, eds. *Weevils in the Wheat*. Bloomington: Indiana University Press, 1976.

Postell, William D. *The Health of Slaves On Southern Plantations*. Baton Rouge: Louisiana State University Press, 1951.

Puckett, Newbell Niles. *Folk Beliefs of the Southern Negro*. Chapel Hill: University of North Carolina Press, 1926.

Raboteau, Albert J. *Slave Religion*. New York: Oxford University Press, 1978.

Randolph, Peter, *Sketches of Slave Life or, Illustrations of the Peculiar Institution*. Boston, 1855.

Rawick, George P., ed. *The American Slave: A Composite Autobiography*. Westport, Conn.: Greenwood Press, 1977.

Ray, Benjamin C. *African Religion*. Englewood Cliffs, N.J.: Prentice-Hall, 1976.

Roper, Moses. *A Narrative of the Adventures and Escape of Moses Roper from American Slavery*. London, 1840.

Ruch, E. A. and K. C. Anyanwu. *African Philosophy*. Rome: Catholic Book Agency, 1984.

Steward, Austin. *Twenty-Two Years a Slave, and Forty Years a Freeman*. Rochester, N.Y., 1861.

Tindall, George Brown. *South Carolina Negroes 1877–1900*. Columbia: University of South Carolina Press, 1952.

Wayne, Michael. *The Reshaping of Plantation Society*. Baton Rouge: Louisiana University Press, 1983.

Wecter, Dixon. *The Hero in America*. New York: Charles Scribners' Sons, 1972.

Wheeler, Mary. *Steamboatin' Days*. Baton Rouge: Louisiana State University Press, 1944.

White, Newman I. *American Negro Folk-Song*. Cambridge, Mass.: Harvard University Press, 1928; repr. Hatboro, Pa.: Folklore Associates ,1965.

Woodson, Carter G. and Lorenzo Greene. *The Negro Wage Earner*. Washington, D. C.: The Association for the Study of Negro Life and History, Inc., 1930.

Woodward, C. Van. *The Strange Career of Jim Crow.* New York: Oxford University Press,1974.

Work, John W. *American Negro Songs and Spirituals.* New York: Soskin, 1940.

Yetman, Norman R., ed. *Voices of Slavery.* New York: Holt, Rinehart and Winston, 1970.

Zahan, Dominique. *The Religions, Spirituality and Thought of Traditional Africans.* Chicago: University of Chicago Press, 1979.

Articles

Abrahams, Roger D. "Some Varieties of Heroes in America." *Journal of The Folklore Institute* 3(1967): 341–62.

Abrahams, Roger D. and John Szwed. "After the Myth: Studying Afro-American Cultural Patterns in the Plantation Literature." *African Folklore in the New World,* ed. Daniel J. Crowley. Austin: University of Texas Press, 1977. 63–86.

Anderson, John Q. "Old John and the Master." *Southern Folklore Quarterly* 25(1961): 195–97.

Bacon, Alice M. and Leonora Herron. "Conjuring and Conjure-Doctors." *Mother Wit From the Laughing Barrel: Readings in the Interpretation of Afro-American Folklore,* ed. Alan Dundes. Englewood Cliffs, N.J.: Prentice-Hall, 1973. 359–68.

Barton, William E. "Old Plantation Hymns." *New England Magazine* 19(December 1898): 443–65.

Beattie, John. "Divination in Bunyoro, Uganda." *Magic, Witchcraft and Curing,* ed. John Middleton. Garden City, N.Y.: The Natural History Press, 1967. 211–31.

Ben-Amos, Dan. "Toward a Definition of Folklore in Context." *Toward New Perspectives in Folklore,* ed. Americo Paredes and Richard Bauman (Journal of American Folklore 84, no. 331). Austin: University of Texas Press, 1972. 3–15.

Biebuyck, Daniel P. "The Epic as a Genre in Congo Oral Literature." *African Folklore,* ed. Richard M. Dorson. Bloomington: Indiana University Press, 1972. 257–73.

———. "The African Heroic Epic." *Journal of the Folklore Institute* 13(1979): 5–36.

Bird, Charles S. and Martha B. Kendall. "The Mande Hero: Text and Context." *Explorations in African Systems and Thought,* ed. Ivan Karp and Charles S. Bird. Bloomington: Indiana University Press, 1982. 13–27.

Bird, Charles S. "Heroic Song of the Mande Hunters." *African Folklore,* ed. Richard M. Dorson. Bloomington: Indiana University Press, 1972. 275–93.

Brearley, H. C. "Ba-ad Nigger." *Mother Wit From the Laughing Barrel: Readings in the Interpretation of Afro-American Folklore,* ed. Alan Dundes. Englewood Cliffs, N.J.: Prentice-Hall, 1973. 578–85.

Brown, John Mason. "Songs of the Slave." *Lippincott's Magazine* 2(December 1968): 617–23.

Brown, Sterling. "Negro Folk Expression: Spirituals, Seculars, Ballads, and Worksongs." *Phylon* 14(1953): 45–61.

Cox, John Harrington. "John Hardy." *Journal of American Folklore* 32(1919).

Crane, T. F. "Plantation Folklore." *Popular Science Monthly* 18(1880): 824–33.

David, John. "Tragedy in Ragtime: Black Folktales from St. Louis," Ph.D. dissertation, St. Louis University, 1976.

Dickson, Bruce, Jr. "The 'John and Old Master' Stories and the World of Slavery: A Study in Folktales and History." *Phylon* 35(1974):418–29.

Dorson, Richard M. "Davy Crockett and the Heroic Age." *Southern Folklore Quarterly* 6(1942): 95–102.

Ellis, A. E. "Evolution in Folklore: Some West African Prototypes of the Uncle Remus Stories" *Popular Science Monthly* 48(1895): 93–104.

Evans-Pritchard, E. E. "The Morphology and Function of Magic: A Comparative Study of Trobriand and Zande Rituals and Spells." *Magic, Witchcraft and Curing,* ed. John Middleton. Garden City, N.Y.: The Natural History Press, 1967. 1–22.

Genovese, Eugene. "Black Plantation Preachers in the Slave South." *Louisiana Studies* (1972): 188–214.

Gerber, A. "Uncle Remus Traced to the Old World." *Journal of American Folklore* 6(1983): 243–57.

Hall, Julien A. "Negro Conjuring and Tricking." *Journal of American Folklore* 10(1897): 241–43.

Hampton, Bill R. "On Identification and the Trickster." *Southern Folklore Quarterly* 31(1972): 55–63.

Harding, Vincent. "Religion and Resistance Among Antebellum Negro, 1800–1860." *The Making of Black America,* Vol. I, ed. August Meier and Elliot Rudwick. New York: Atheneum, 1969. 179–97.

Haskell, Marion A. "Negro Spirituals." *The Century Magazine* 36(August 1899): 577–81.

Higginson, Thomas Wentworth. "Negro Spirituals." *The Atlantic Monthly* 19(1867): 685–94.

Jackson, George P. "The Genesis of the Negro Spirituals." *The American Mercury* 26(1932): 243–48.

Johnson, John W. "Yes Virginia, There is an Epic in Africa." *Research in African Literature* 11(1980): 309–26.

Johnson, Ken. "The Vocabulary of Race." *Rappin' and Stylin' Out,* ed. Thomas Kochman. Urbana: University of Illinois Press, 1972. 140–51.

Jones, Jerome W. "The Established Virginia Church and the Conversion of Negroes and Indians, 1620–1760." *Journal of Negro History* 46(1961): 12–23.

King, J. Crawford, Jr. "The Closing of the Southern Range: An Explanatory Study." *Journal of Southern History* 68(1982): 53–70.

Kiple, Kenneth F. and Virginia H. "Black Tongue and Black Men: Pellagra and Slavery in the Antebellum South." *Journal of Southern History* XLIII(1977): 404–28.

Lanier Seward, Adrienne. "The Legacy of Early Afro-American Folklore Scholarship." *Handbook of American Folklore,* ed. Richard M. Dorson. Bloomington: Indiana University Press, 1983. 48–56.

Lofton, John W., Jr. "Denmark Vesey's Call to Arms." *Journal of Negro History* 4(1948): 395–417.

Odum, Howard W. "Folk-Song and Folk Poetry as Found in the Secular Songs of the Southern Negro." *Journal of American Folklore* 24(1911):255–294, 351–96.

Oliver, Paul. "Railroad Bill." *Jazz and Blues* 1(1971): 12–14.

Owens, William. "Folklore of the Southern Negroes." *Lippincott's Magazine* 20(1877): 748–55.

McBride, B. "Directions for Cultivating Various Crops Grown at Hickory Hill." *American Agriculturalist* 3(May 1830): 239–42.

Parramore, Thomas C. "Non-Venereal Treponematosis in Colonial North America." *Bulletin of the History of Medicine* XL(1970): 571–81.

Pendleton, Louis. "Negro Folk-Lore and Witchcraft in the South." *Journal of American Folklore* 3(1890): 201–07.

Perrow, E. C. "Songs and Rhymes from the South." *Journal of American Folklore* 25(1917): 137–155.

Ravenel, Henry W. "Recollections of Southern Plantation Life." *Yale Review* 25(1936): 748–77.

Savilt, Todd L. "Smothering and Overlaying of Virginia Slave Children: A Suggested Explanation." *Bulletin of the History of Medicine* XLIX(1975): 400–404.

Semmes, Clovis E. "Foundations of an Afrocentric Social Science." *Journal of Black Studies* 12(1981): 3–16.

Seydou, Christiane. "A Reflection on Narrative Structure of Epic Texts: A Case Example of Bambara and Fulani Epics." *Research in African Literatures* 14(1983): 312–24.

Snead, James A. "Repetition as a Figure in Black Culture." *Black Literature and Literary Theory,* ed. Henry Louis Gates, Jr. New York: Methuen, 1984, 59–80.

Spaulding, Henry. "Negro 'Shouts' and Shout Songs." *Continental Monthly* 4(August 1863): 188–203.

Stuckey, Sterling. "Remembering Denmark Vesey." *Negro Digest* 4(February 1966): 28–41.

Thanet, Octave. "Folklore in Arkansas." *Journal of American Folklore* 5(1892): 121–25.

Weldon, Fred O. "Negro Folktale Heroes." *Publications of the Texas Folklore Society* 29(1959): 170–89.

Wilgus, D. K. "The Negro-White Spirituals." *Mother Wit From the Laughing Barrel: Readings in the Interpretation of Afro-American Folklore,* ed. Alan Dundes. Englewood Cliffs, N.J.: Prentice-Hall, 1973. 67–80.

Wish, Harvey. "American Slave Insurrections Before 1861." *Journal of Negro History* 22(1937): 299–320.

Yankah, Kwesi. "To Praise or Not to Praise the King: The Akan APAE in the Context of Referential Poetry." *Research in African Literatures* 14(1983): 381–400.

INDEX